PLASTICS FOR THE CRAFTSMAN

Designer's Table. Jay and Lee Newman. Polyester resin on acrylic in an extruded aluminum frame *(Top Left)*. *Stained "Glass" Lamp*. Jay and Lee Newman. Fusible thermoplastic tiles and stained glass leading *(Top Right)*.

Stained "Glass" Panel. Jay and Lee Newman. Poly Mosaic tiles and stained glass leading.

A colorful bouquet created with heat-formed fusible thermoplastic tiles. Jay and Lee Newman. Courtesy *Woman's Day* Magazine.

PLASTICS FOR THE CRAFTSMAN

by
Jay Hartley Newman
and
Lee Scott Newman

Crown Publishers, Inc., New York

For the two people who made this possible:
Mom and Dad.

Printed in the United States of America
Published simultaneously in Canada by
General Publishing Company Limited

Design by Nedda Balter

ACKNOWLEDGMENTS

We are most indebted to the many anonymous artists and craftsmen who provided us with inspiration through their work. Our very special thanks to Milo Baughman, Jane Bearman, Phillip Borden, Barbara Darr, Thom Haxo, Carolyn Kriegman, Roslyn Rose, Neal Small, Gary L. Smith, Giorgio Soavi, Curtis Stephens, and Phyllis Stevens for their cooperation in sharing their work and their techniques with us.

The New York Museum of Contemporary Crafts was a valuable research center.

Photographs of the flowers made of fusible thermoplastic tiles are by Ben Calvo, reprinted by permission of *Woman's Day* magazine, copyright © 1969 by Fawcett Publications, Inc.

Thanks also goes to Anna Wiglama at *House Beautiful* for her cooperation, and appreciation to Norm Smith for his dependable work in processing our photographs.

By far, our deepest debt is to our parents. We could never repay our father, Jack Newman, for his tireless legwork and quartermastering. Nor could we ever equal what our mother and mentor, Thelma R. Newman, has given us in time and inspiration.

Jay Hartley Newman
Lee Scott Newman
Westfield, New Jersey

NOTE: All photographs by Thelma, Jay, and Lee Newman unless otherwise credited.

v

This is essentially a project book for craftsmen who want to work with plastics. To familiarize the artisan with the basic processes involved in manipulating this different medium we chose a categorical project approach. This book deals with polyester resins, acrylics, fusible thermoplastics, and plastic foams, and demonstrates the basic techniques involved in working with each material. Step-by-step photographs and detailed instructions were combined to give the craftsman the benefit of our own experiences in the plastics milieu and the experiences of the many other craftsmen whose works are included as well.

Information phrased in technical language is not a prerequisite for a clear understanding of what these fantastically versatile materials can do. We describe plastics in lay terms, but, in order to provide a basis for understanding technical information, many terms of the industry have been defined in the text and included in a glossary.

Of key importance in this book was the recognition that, while plastics may be employed in the pursuit of older craft forms, these materials have qualities and abilities that are distinctly their own. Artists and craftsmen working with plastics, some of whose work has been included, recognize that a material is most validly realized as an art and craft form when it does no more than what its own inherent properties are best suited to do.

PREFACE

TABLE OF CONTENTS

4. WORKING WITH FUSIBLE THERMOPLASTICS   139

5. WORKING WITH PLASTIC FOAMS   178

6. TOWARD A FUTURE   197

LIST OF COLOR PLATES

Fractured Image (16″ x 16″). Jay Newman. Mirrored acrylic reflects from a polystyrene foam base to capture all angles.

MODERN PLASTICS—in only twenty years—have usurped the roles of many ancient materials: wood, glass, metal, and clay. The earliest applications of plastics involved using their chameleonlike ability to copy more precious materials. But plastics have shed this imitative coat to emerge as a dazzling variety of substances that can not only do many old tasks better but fill many new roles too.

Plastics have unique qualities. Many are easy to work with; some can be cast into very large forms without elaborate equipment, and new varieties for different purposes are continually being developed. For the craftsman, this supermaterial of the future holds almost boundless promise today. With a knowledge of basic materials and techniques, a new means of expression is available. The projects that follow provide the craftsman with a guide. Basic plastics and processes that are common and uncommon will give the artisan how-to skills in approaching and solving problems using this marvelous "new" medium.

TWO BASIC CATEGORIES

The fundamental characteristic of the giant man-made molecules we call "plastics" is their moldability. These materials can be shaped using fingers, molds, heat, pressure, or a combination of these forces. Basically, there are two types of plastics: thermoplastics and thermosetting plastics. Thermoplastics are hard and rigid at normal temperatures but become soft and moldable when heated. While it is soft, the plastic can be given the desired shape, and this new shape will be retained when the material cools. This group includes acrylic and styrene. The process of heating and molding, reheating and remolding can be repeated over and over again. The plastic's "memory" returns it to the original shape each time it is heated. Eventually, thermoplastics become exhausted by continual

IN THE BEGINNING

1

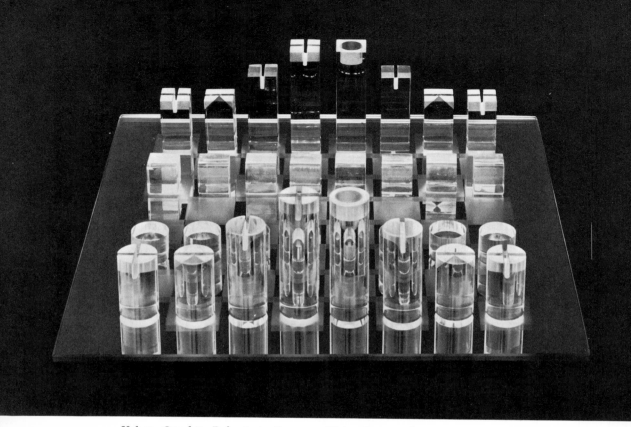

Urban Gambit. Robert A. Propper. This elegant chess set was created from acrylic rods and sheet. Chess Set copyright © Robert A. Propper.

reheatings and reshapings, but, in the meantime, mistakes can easily be corrected. A modern detective story used this "memory" to solve a mysterious murder. The murderer had heated a spoon made out of a thermoplastic and turned it into a knife; after using it, he reheated the knife. It turned into the original spoon and no one could find the weapon.

The other group, thermosetting plastics, have quite different properties. Thermosets can be shaped only once. Initially, these plastics are often liquid for curing at room temperature. During the molding process, when the plastic is heated or catalyzed to make it polymerize (harden), a chemical change occurs in which the molecules are tightly interlinked so that the plastic becomes rigid but will not return to its original state. Clay is a thermosetting material which is moldable before it is heated,

but once heated it never again becomes flexible. In many uses, this property—permanent retension of shape—is an advantage. Plastic glasses, Teflon pans, and synthetic fabric would be impossible without this characteristic. Polyester and epoxy resins and some of the rigid foams are thermosetting materials.

TYPES OF PLASTICS

Within each larger division, there are different plastics that are readily available to the craftsman and easy to work with as well. In the following projects, we deal with all these basic types. But although the materials and processes that follow are described briefly and kept separate for clarity, many of the plastics and processes mentioned can be and are used together on any single project.

Four basic categories of plastics that are applicable for craft activity are:

Acrylic

It comes in 4 x 8 foot sheets, rods, and tubes. These products are manufactured using polymethyl methacrylate resin which is molded under heat and pressure. Because of the complexity and expense involved in this molding operation, few artisans have attempted to cast their own pieces. The basic acrylic sheet is often clear, like glass. In fact, it is used in place of glass because it is stronger and will not shatter as easily. Sheets come in thicknesses from $\frac{1}{16}$″ up to several inches. Colors, including new mirrored acrylic, and crinkle-textured sheets have become increasingly popular. Acrylic is a thermoplastic. Like most thermoplastics, it can be heated and shaped while it is hot; when it cools the new shape will be retained. Any heating should be done carefully, since overheating can result in bubbling and slight shrinkage. This plastic can be machined, using metalworking power tools, and it can be finished to a high gloss.

Fusible Thermoplastics for Craft Use

They come in two basic forms. One is the mosaic tile ¾″ square, and the other is a meltable pellet. Both can fuse to form larger pieces in a household oven or a small broil-oven at 350° F. The mosaics are easily cut with nippers, tile cutters, or even a large pair of nail clippers; the pellets pour like uncooked rice. A wide range of colors is available in both these materials. Since they are thermoplastics as well, once they have been fused, it is still possible to re-shape them into other forms. Machining can be accomplished using a band saw or jigsaw.

Polyester and Epoxy Resins

These are usually syruplike liquids. Thermosetting plastics, they require the addition of a catalyst before they can polymerize (harden into a solid). These resins are available in many different types for different purposes (casting, laminating, impregnating, etc.). Epoxy, which is familiar as an adhesive, is sometimes used because it shrinks less when cast. Polyester, commonly used with fiberglass as the structure of boats, trucks, and car parts, is also used for laminating and casting. Colors —transparent, translucent, and opaque— are available in pastes, powders, or liquid dyes. These are resins which are especially versatile and practical for the craftsman because they polymerize (cure or harden) from their original liquid state at room temperatures. Other resins (like polymethyl methacrylate used in the manufacture of acrylic) require heat and pressure to harden and are impractical for experimentation.

Rigid Polystyrene and Polyurethane Foams

These light, cellular materials are familiar to most everyone. "Styrofoam" (polystyrene foam produced by Dow Chemical Company) and its polyurethane counterpart are both available in large blocks or smaller, precut pieces. These are easily worked with because no machinery—or at most a jigsaw or heated cutting wire—is necessary. Rigid foams can be carved, sanded, painted, and generally treated like balsa wood. But some care should be taken in the selection of paint coatings that might act as solvents and dissolve the material, particularly polystyrene foam. Paints can be tested on a small portion or a scrap piece before covering the entire object. Both foams can be carved using linoleum cutters, X-acto knives, a heated wire, or a handsaw. Neither material, however, should be exposed to heat. Polyurethane foams are long lasting and are enjoying wide use as furniture.

SAFETY FACTORS

Like many chemicals, the plastics mentioned above are safe when they are used properly. Safe usage includes several conditions: adequate ventilation, clean working conditions, and protected skin. For adequate ventilation the use of an exhaust fan is recommended; at the very least windows should be open and there should be an exchange of air. The normal fumes from most of these materials—while often pungent—are nontoxic; otherwise these plastics would not be allowed for home use on such a wide scale. But it would be unwise not to take the basic precautions one would observe when painting a room or cooking for long periods of time.

Working conditions will be easiest if the work area is kept in good order. Especially when the project calls for the mixing of resin with a catalyst, clean work areas will help keep impurities from getting into the mold and showing up in the final product. Working surfaces should be protected from spillage by covering them. Also, when working with a fusible thermoplastic, it is wise to plan where hot oven trays will be placed when they are removed from the oven. Clear planning and an understanding of the steps involved in any project are important; always read the instructions carefully. Finally, since plastics are chemicals, skin contact with resins and catalysts may sometimes result in an allergic reaction. To guard against this, protective gloves or cream coatings may be used. Hands should be washed after contact. And remember that, as chemicals, these plastics should always be kept out of the reach of small children. Common sense, man's best friend, and a growing knowledge of the materials you are working with will help most of all.

PROCESSES

Materials can be grouped by the techniques used in working with them as well as by their physical characteristics. The projects that follow center around five basic processes. These techniques outline the potential available to the craftsman.

Casting

This is the process of forming an object by pouring liquid resin into a mold. This is easily done using polyester or epoxy resins. Basically, the resin is mixed with an appropriate amount of catalyst (determined by the shape and thickness of the form) and then poured into the mold. The resin then hardens and is removed from the mold. (Because it is originally a liquid and flows freely, the resin is able to duplicate intricate designs in a mold.) Types of molds that may be used to cast plastics include: one-piece open molds (like cups or bowls); split molds (two-piece or more); flexible rubber, vinyl, or silicone molds. Mold materials include metal, plastic, rubber, sand, and plaster; both the type of mold and the mold material depend on the type of plastic to be used, the size of the object, and the number of copies desired. Casting offers several advantages: low cost, minimal finishing, and the fact that machinery is often unnecessary. Often, castings may be preferred for aesthetic reasons alone.

Fabrication

This can be defined as any operation involving the machining of a plastic. In general, there are no special difficulties involved in the shaping and machining of plastics. Traditional hand and machine tools and techniques of metalworking are often applicable. But in machining and cutting operations, plastics' special properties should be borne in mind. Thermoplastics, for example, will soften when they are heated. Consequently, care should be taken so that great amounts of heat do not build up during cutting and polishing; excessive heat causes the plastic to gum up. Tools should be kept sharp, the speed slowed down, and the plastic should be given a chance to dissipate the heat that is generated through friction. When the plastic overheats during cutting it begins to cake up. If this

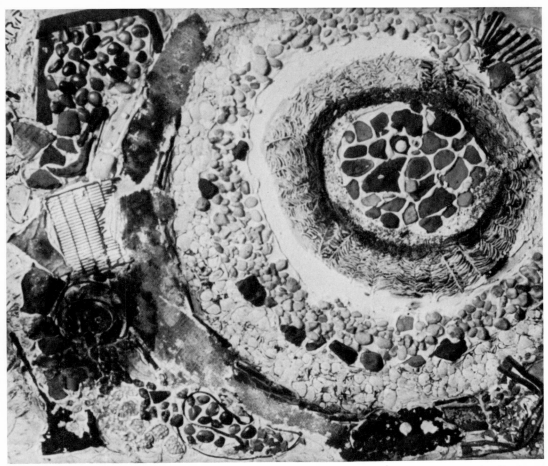

Pulsar (28″ x 24″). Barbara Darr. Vinyl-acrylic modeling paste served as the base for this impasto collage incorporating stones, fir needles, eggshells, masonry nails, pebbles, and even an old spring.

Barbara Darr created these impasto bottles by patterning vinyl-acrylic modeling paste with trivets and wood blocks.

Vase (4½″ x 4½″ x 9″). Neal Small. Clear and opaque acrylic are combined in this design. Courtesy: Neal Small Designs.

This mirrored acrylic box houses a pendant of cast polyester resin.

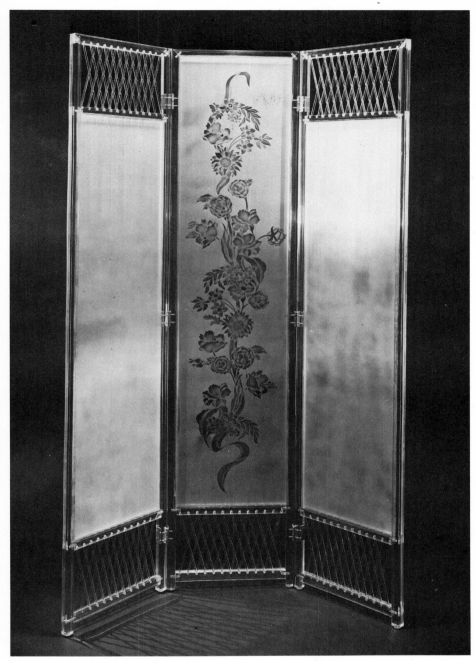

Acrylic and Polyester Screen (6′ high). Gary L. Smith. Polyester resin was used to produce this flowing design on acrylic sheet. Courtesy: Gary L. Smith.

Hanging Ornament (6″ x 10″). Carolyn Kriegman. Poly-Mosaic tiles and a vegetable grater.

gumming occurs, the plastic should be allowed to cool. Then the caked-up material can be broken off or scraped away.

All the plastics discussed above can be machined, finished in various ways, and polished. Acrylic is buffed and polished using a series of buffing wheels; while the fusible plastics are brought to a high gloss easily by using a flame. Special blades for cutting are not necessary since metal-cutting blades work well (carbide-tipped blades are preferable, though). But drill bits made for use with plastics—especially when acrylic is being drilled—are recommended. Detailed step-by-step approaches to basic machining processes are discussed in the projects that follow.

Forming

This process involves the use of heat and sometimes pressure as well to shape plastics. Acrylic, for example, can be bent, sagged, blown, or twisted when it has been heated and becomes a flexible, rubbery sheet. This heating can be done in several ways. There are strip heaters that will heat the plastic only along a straight line that is to be bent. Once cool, the shape will be stabilized. Since we are talking about thermoplastics, it is also possible to correct a mistake by reheating the plastic along a different angle or allowing it to return to its original form by heating it. Fusible plastics can also be treated in this manner after they have been melted and fused into larger pieces. Thermoplastics can be heated in an oven so that the entire piece becomes soft and can then be sagged into a mold (like a bowl) or draped over a form (like a glass that would not be affected by the heat). Some pressure is required here. Again, the shape will be retained upon cooling. In a malleable form, these thermoplastics can be twisted or stretched to reach the desired result, and, in order to cool them quickly, water may be used.

Styrene pellets were heated to form this translucent snowflake mobile.

The decoupage box and candle were created with a vinyl-acrylic glaze. *Teeth and Tongue,* by Carolyn Kriegman, is made of fused Poly-Mosaic tiles.

Fusing

This is probably the easiest process of all since the only tools that are necessary are an oven, an aluminum or Pyrex oven tray, and a spatula. The tiles or pellets can be cut or poured to the desired shape or placed in a mold. Then, by heating the forms in an oven at 350° F. for three to ten minutes, they will melt and fuse into larger pieces. When these forms are cool, it is possible to rework them by using the fabrication or forming techniques that have been described. Although these are thermoplastics as well, they will not return to their original pellet and tile shapes upon reheating because they are very small units. Extra heating will cause them to melt further into flatter and thinner sheets. This property allows the craftsman to decide what texture he will get by controlling the heating process. Texture can also be varied by using both materials together, overlaying, fusing, and re-fusing.

Lamination

It is a process which involves the sandwiching of flat materials between layers of resin. Cloth, photographs, leaves, flowers, can all be suspended in a sheet of clear or colored polyester resin. But while most of these embedments are used as decorations, laminations involving the impregnation of fiberglass with polyester can also provide thin sheets of great strength. These are used in building boats, and car bodies are also being constructed now out of preimpregnated sheets of fiberglass that are molded and formed in large compression molding machines. This technique, using a hand lay-up, is easy to master.

In this plastic realm, after trying these examples, experimenting will produce exciting variations as your knowledge and confidence grow. Possibilities are limited only by the extent of your imagination. Don't be discouraged by failures—they can teach you the limits and potentials of these versatile plastics.

This fiberglass-reinforced polyester (FRP) lamination incorporates pebbles, seeds, wood strips, and burlap.

Sunburst (36″ x 42″). Room divider panel of polyester resin and fiberglass.

Shell and Seaweed Screen (78″ high). Emile Norman. Shells and seaweed give this polyester resin-fiberglass lamination its unique character. Courtesy: Emile Norman.

Group Process. Jay Newman. Cast polyester resin.

A rigid polyurethane foam block (6″ x 3″ x 3″) was hand carved into this intricate configuration.

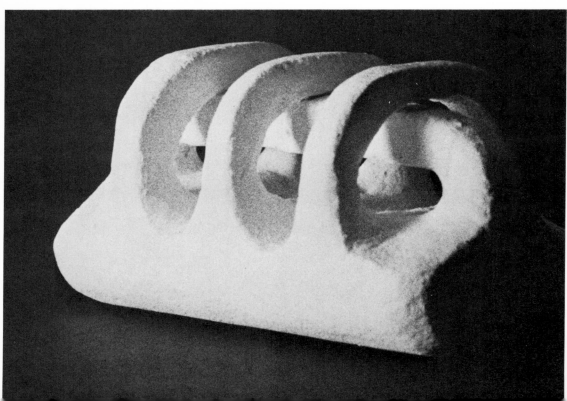

Strips of black Celanese acetate sheet are sewn to fabric of Arnel. Designed by Elisa Stone. Courtesy: Celanese Plastics Co.

Designed by Giorgio Soavi, this pencil holder is an example of commercially injection-molded plastic. Courtesy: Olivetti.

POLYESTER RESINS ARE syruplike plastics. They are available in a variety of formulations for as many different uses. Polyesters can be made rigid, flexible, heat resistant, slow curing, fast curing, transparent, translucent, or opaque. Some are meant specifically for use in laminations; others have been developed for casting thicker pieces.

Polyester resins are thermosetting plastics, and require the addition of a catalyst before they can polymerize (harden into a solid). This is called the "curing" process. Beginning in the liquid state, the resin first "gels." From that jellylike consistency, the plastic soon hardens into a solid piece. Catalysts, which are added to the resins in very small quantities, initiate the curing process by setting off a chemical reaction. This chemical reaction causes the resin to heat up. Depending on the amount of catalyst used, the resin may take from five minutes to several days to cure. If polyesters are left exposed, they will cure, eventually, but without the catalyst the process could take as long as several years.

Methyl ethyl ketone (MEK) peroxide is the most commonly used catalyst for polyester resins. It too is a liquid. A table of proportions of catalyst to resin for a normal room temperature cure follows. Although this table provides a general guide, do not be fooled into thinking that such proportions are fixed and rigid. On the contrary, you will discover that variations will be necessary under certain circumstances. If the work area is cold, for instance, more catalyst will be needed, and the reverse will be true if the workroom is hot. Another variable is the length of *pot-life* desired. Pot-life is the amount of time that the mixture remains workable after the catalyst has been added. Since adding more catalyst will accelerate the cure, your own working requirements will often dictate how much catalyst to add.

Polyesters are available in most hardware, boat, and craft stores, and pigments for coloring them are also easily obtained.

2

WORKING WITH POLYESTER RESINS

Pigments, usually, are prepared especially for polyester resins, coming in pastes, powders, and liquids. Colors may be transparent or opaque—but be certain to make sure you have the kind you want, because there is a big difference between the two. Colors are usually added to the resin before the catalyst. In that way the proper color can be mixed without worrying whether the resin will cure while you are deciding on the proper shade.

Because color is mixed into the resin, it becomes an integral part of the cured piece. Sanding, machining, drilling, and polishing will not remove this color. But, if desired, the resin can also be allowed to cure in its natural state and colored resin can be brushed on afterwards.

To alter their properties for specific applications, a variety of fillers may be added to polyester resins. Usually, fillers serve to make the resin more thixotropic (pastelike). The more filler added, the more thixotropic the resin becomes. These pastes are extremely useful when resins must be applied to steep surfaces or must be used in patching operations where the normal syrup consistency would allow the resin to run off the surface.

A number of organic and inorganic materials are available to make the resins thixotropic. Some common materials—like sand—may be used as fillers. Such fillers contribute a texture and color of their own. An all purpose commercial filler often used with polyester resins is Cab-O-Sil. This material mixes easily and evenly with the resin. When fillers are used, however, it must be remembered that they will make the resins more translucent or opaque.

For cleaning up, acetone or a good grade of lacquer thinner should be used. In both cases, skin contact and vapors should be avoided. Neither acetone or thinner should ever be used for cleaning skin. Several kerosene-based paint and resin removers are made specifically for this purpose.

Along with this admonition go a few more safety precautions. When working with polyesters it is essential to remember that the resins and catalysts are chemicals. They should both be stored carefully in a cool place away from children. Prolonged exposure to them—and this includes working with them for long stretches of time—should be avoided unless a mask is used that will exclude organic vapors. Never smoke or eat while using these materials.

Catalysts are toxic and flammable. They should be stored in polyethylene containers that can be sealed tightly. If possible, they should be refrigerated when not in use.

Working surfaces should be covered with disposable paper; newsprint or waxed paper works fine. Hands should be protected with disposable plastic gloves, and all mixing containers, papers, and gloves covered with resin should be discarded immediately after you finish working.

Uncured and curing polyester emits a gaslike odor, so adequate ventilation should be provided. In its cured state, though, polyester is odorless and nontoxic.

POLYESTER RESIN PROCESSES

Selecting a Resin

Resins are made for different purposes. There are resins specifically for laminations and others for castings. There are other distinctions as well. For castings, there is a choice of using a flexible or a rigid polyester resin. Since polyester shrinks when it hardens, a more flexible resin should be used in cases where there will be embedments in the casting; that way there will be less chance of the polyester cracking when it hardens around the embedment. A rigid resin will not accommodate embedments without some cracking. One final criterion is color; for a crystal-clear casting, a water-white resin will be preferred. One such resin is Diamond Alkali's 6912, another is Reichold Chemical's Polylite 32-032. For

Polyethylene containers and food cans without inside coatings make good mixing containers. Tongue depressors are excellent for mixing.

Color should be added to the polyester resin before the catalyst. That way there is no pressure to decide on a shade before the resin begins to cure.

The catalyst should be measured out with a glass eyedropper or stainless steel or polyethylene measuring spoons. Aluminum spoons should not be used. Wipe the spoons out afterward, but never mix water with either the catalyst or the polyester resin.

The resin, color, and catalyst should be stirred *thoroughly* before use. Polyester should be stored away from the light or in dark glass jars. The catalyst should be stored in a cool or refrigerated place in either a glass or polyethylene container.

other purposes, where the resin will be colored anyway, resins that are tinted may be used with excellent results. Although the above two resins look tinted, they cure to a crystal-clear result.

Coloring

It is best to use colors that have been developed specifically for polyester resins. Colors are available in paste, powder, and liquid forms. The use of random dyes and pigments may prove to be wasteful since their colors may change when the resin heats up during the curing process. In any case, it is wise to test the colors first. By mixing a small amount first and checking the color after the resin has cured you will develop better control of what the final product will look like.

You will find that some colors will be significantly more potent than others; be wary! When you add color, just use a little bit at a time and make certain that it is mixed thoroughly before adding more. If the color is not evenly dispersed you may end up with streaks of color when you pour.

If a project is to be completed in parts, make sure that you take note of how much color was used so that a good color match will be possible in later batches.

Once the color has been mixed into the resin it becomes an integral part of the plastic. There is no way to "erase" the color.

Filling

Many materials may be used a fillers for polyester resins. Chopped glass fibers, flock, asbestos fibers, silica, china, clay, talc, chalk, pumice, sand, whiting, gypsum, wood or shell flour, and sawdust are some commonly available materials that may be used. In commercial polyester thixotropic pastes, Cab-O-Sil is often used as the filler; this product is also available to the craftsman.

Fillers made specifically for use with polyester will usually carry the manufac-

turer's instructions for use. Generally, fillers can be added until they are 50 percent of the final mix without affecting the strength of the resin appreciably. But polyesters should not be made more thixotropic than is necessary for any given application.

Catalyzing

Methyl ethyl ketone (MEK) peroxide is the principal catalyst used with polyester resins. The following table provides general guidelines for catalyzing resin in laminating and casting operations. Laminations usually involve thin layers of resin, and castings require thicker sections. Since the catalyst causes the resin to heat up during the cure, the amount of catalyst added for castings must be less—otherwise the piece will crack from excessive exotherm. By the same token, in laminations more catalyst must be used so that enough exotherm will be generated so that the resin will cure. With experience you will gain the skill needed to regulate the amount of catalyst to your own needs. Experience will also allow you to control the length of the resin's pot-life, or the length of time that the resin remains workable after the addition of the catalyst. In the meantime, this table should prove helpful.

PROPORTIONS OF CATALYST TO RESIN

Thickness of Casting	MEK Peroxide Catalyst Per Ounce of Resin
⅛" or less	15 drops
⅛" to ¼"	12 drops
¼" to ½"	8 drops
½" to 1"	6 drops
1" or more	4 drops

NOTE: If less catalyst is used, the resin will not bleach out to crystal clear.

Courtesy: Thelma R. Newman

Simple, attractive panels can be created by impregnating tissue paper with polyester resin. Be certain to clean the brush in acetone immediately afterward. If resin hardens in your brush, consider it ruined.

Casting

Castings using clear resin, colored polyester, and embedments can be made with molds. The craftsman has many options here: molds can be made from wax, aluminum foil, plaster, rubber, silicone rubber, glass, vinyl, and other plastic materials, or they can be purchased. In any case, a silicone mold release should be sprayed or painted into the mold, according to the instructions on the can or jar, before the catalyzed polyester resin is poured into the cavity. Once the resin has been poured, all that remains to be done is to wait until it cures; then the finished casting may be removed. Sometimes the part of the molded piece that was exposed to the air during the curing process will remain tacky; this can be remedied by painting the surface with highly catalyzed resin (seven parts resin to one part catalyst). This will cure quickly, but in order to obtain a hard, unblemished finish it should be allowed to remain undisturbed at least overnight. Make sure that you wash out your brush in acetone immediately; otherwise it will become stiff and useless. The highly catalyzed coat may also be applied with cotton swabs, which are disposable. Another method is to cover the surface with Mylar to exclude the air. This should be done immediately after pouring the resin and care should be taken not to trap air bubbles between the resin and Mylar, or upon curing the surface will be pitted.

Impregnating

The impregnation of materials like burlap, cloth, canvas, paper, net, dried flowers, and even leather, can result in some interesting effects. Transparent collages can be created in this manner. When the polyester cures, your object will be rigidly preserved and can be mounted or otherwise displayed.

A similar process is used with fiberglass in the making of large panels and forms that involve the use of hand lay-up. Both are discussed in detail later in this chapter.

Sawing

Cured polyester can be easily cut, like most plastics, using a saw made for metal- or woodworking. When using any power-saw equipment, though, precautions should be taken (like using a spray-paint filter-mask and protective glasses) to avoid exposure to excessive polyester fumes, chips, and dust. The plastic should be fed through the saw fairly slowly to avoid "pushing" the plastic faster than the saw will cut, resulting in cracks or fractures. Jig- or saber saws are best for cutting more intricate shapes, circular saws for straight cuts, and band saws for wider curves.

Metal-cutting blades will deliver the cleanest, sharpest results. As with cutting any plastic, the blade preferably should be carbide tipped with uniform teeth.

Drilling and Tapping

Metalworking drill bits may be used to drill into totally cured polyester forms, and a normal tapping set will work in the plastic, too. When doing either procedure, oil coolants or mild soapy water may be used to reduce friction and lubricate the area.

Colored tissue paper can be impregnated with polyester resin to produce attractive translucent panels applied over clear acrylic sheet.

Sanding

Wet sanding is recommended over dry sanding because the dust created by polyester is extremely unhealthful. But, belt sanders can be used if precautions like a filter-mask and adequate ventilation are employed. When sanding, a progression of coarse to fine grits is most effective (i.e., 150, 220, then 400 grit).

Polishing and Buffing

A two-wheel electric buffer with a fairly loose 10″-diameter wheel at 2,000 surface feet per minute will give good results when polishing polyester. However, the polyester must be completely cured, or else the plastic will gum up the wheel. Light pressure on a wheel coated with white tripoli compound, followed by a light buff on a clean wheel, will give the polyester a clear finish where machining or scratching had marred the transparency.

To "polish" polyester without using a buffing wheel, highly catalyzed polyester may be painted over the scratches or machined edges and will fill in most of the marks, giving the piece an almost unflawed, nearly transparent surface. It is not advisable to use the same buffing wheels for both polyester and acrylic because polyester wheels can become gummed and transfer polyester to the acrylic.

19

FILLING RATTAN BUTTERFLIES

Materials and Equipment

> polyester resin
> catalyst
> color
> rattan forms
> waxed paper, cellophane, or Mylar
> several weights
> chips of cured polyester resin
> a knife

Procedures

Rattan forms are made in many delightful patterns. The only requirement for filling their spaces with polyester resin is that they be as flat as possible. If the rattan is warped, pouring will be difficult.

On a sheet of waxed paper, cellophane, or Mylar several inches larger than your form, pour a thin layer of heavily catalyzed uncolored polyester resin. Then set the rattan form into the resin and apply just enough weight on top of the rattan so that the entire piece is surrounded in resin and lies flat. It is important that the rattan be pressed down firmly while the resin is curing, since this thin bottom layer acts as a backing and seal for the colored layers that will be poured later.

When the resin gels, use a knife to scrape away excess resin from the sides of the form, being careful not to pry under the rattan form. If the gelled resin separates (delaminates) from the reed, a leak may develop. The weights may be removed at this point to facilitate the separation of excess resin from the rattan, but they should then be placed on top once again, leaving them until the resin fully cures.

Once cured, the backing should be peeled away. Colored and catalyzed resin is then poured into the sealed spaces. For added color and textural interest, chips of cured polyester resin may be placed in the colored resin while it is still a liquid. To make these chips, pour a thin sheet of heavily catalyzed resin on a waxed paper, cellophane, or Mylar backing and allow it to harden. When the sheet has cured, remove the backing and break the brittle plastic into little pieces. Chips of different colors are most effective when suspended in resin that is light in color.

When the polyester resin cures, your colorful rattan butterfly is finished. Used individually or in groups for window decorations or mobiles, these polyester-filled rattan forms become eye-catching ornaments.

The basic materials necessary to create polyester-filled rattan forms include resin, color, catalyst, the rattan forms, polyester chips, weights, and waxed paper.

The rattan butterfly is set into a thin sheet of heavily catalyzed polyester resin poured on a sheet of waxed paper, cellophane, or Mylar.

Weights are used to make certain that the polyester bonds with the rattan to form a solid seal.

When the resin gels, scrape away the excess resin from the form, but be careful not to separate the resin from the reed. The weights may be removed to facilitate this step but should be replaced and allowed to remain until the resin fully cures.

Colored, catalyzed resin is poured into the sealed spaces.

For added color and textural interest, chips of cured polyester resin are suspended in liquid resin of light color.

The combination of rattan swirls and colorful polyester resin is a highly decorative one.

Colored polyester resin chips and black thixotropic resin were used in this piece. The base was acrylic covered with colored polyester resin.

FREE-FORM POLYESTER JEWELRY

Materials and Equipment

> polyester resin
> color
> catalyst
> stainless steel or aluminum stripping
> wire cutter or heavy shears
> waxed paper, cellophane, or Mylar
> cotton swab or fine brush
> pin backs
> two-part epoxy glue

Procedures

The first step in creating free-form polyester jewelry is to indulge your own fancy by sketching a design for a pin or pendant. Translate your sketch into stainless steel or aluminum stripping. These materials are flat strips, and they usually come coiled. Both are easily bent into shape. Just be certain that your design is flat and is made up of closed spaces that will hold the resin.

From this point on, the steps are similar to those in filling the rattan form. Pour a thin sheet of polyester resin (heavily catalyzed) on some waxed paper, cellophane, or Mylar; set the forms in this resin. Since it is easy to make these pieces flat by bending them, only light weights are needed to keep them flat while the resin sets. When the resin gels, use a knife to cut excess resin from the outside of the stripping and allow the plastic to cure.

Once it has cured, remove the forms and fill their spaces with colored resin. If you are using transparent colors, make them light or they will look black when placed on a dress or blouse. The forms should be filled up to the top—but not to overflowing.

When the resin cures, you may find that the underside of your jewelry is not shiny; this problem is easily remedied. Paint the area with heavily catalyzed polyester resin. Keep fingers off the resin for several days until the surface truly cures. When it does cure, you will have a hard shiny surface.

Pin backs can be glued on using two-part epoxy, and, if desired for a chain, a small hole may be drilled in the polyester with an ordinary drill.

After sketching your form, translate it into stainless steel or aluminum stripping.

Pour a thin sheet of polyester resin on a piece of waxed paper, cellophane, or Mylar . . .

. . . and set the jewelry forms into it. Light pressure should be applied using weights while the resin sets.

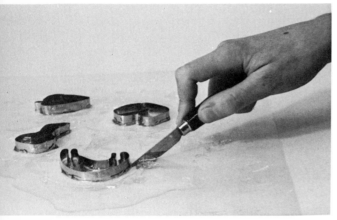

Once the polyester gels, the weights may be removed and the excess resin around the units should be cut away.

The spaces you have created should be filled with colored polyester resin. But if transparent colors are used, be certain that they are light, since dark colors may look black when this jewelry is worn. Dull surfaces may be made glossy by coating them with heavily catalyzed resin.

Pin backs should be adhered with two-part epoxy glue.

The final pins or pendants will embody not only your own tastes in colors but your personal design concept as well.

Press the polyester-sand mixture around the underside of the candle. Courtesy: Thelma R. Newman.

When the polyester cures, the edges may be trimmed on a grinding wheel. The plastic shell may be refilled with wax after the candle burns down. Courtesy: Thelma R. Newman.

A POLYESTER CANDLE

Materials and Equipment

    a candle
    waxed paper
    polyester resin
    catalyst
    sand

Procedures

An attractive, permanent shell for a candle may be made with sand-filled polyester resin.

Mix some resin with catalyst and add 40 percent sand by volume. Beach sand, play sand, or construction sand will all work well. Stir the mixture thoroughly.

Choose a candle that is rounded on the bottom without steep sides. (The legs on this candle proved too difficult to cover so we cut them away). Place the candle upside down on a sheet of waxed paper. With a tongue depressor, press the sand and plastic mixture around the sides of the candle. Allow a rim of polyester and sand to form on the waxed paper. Cover the entire underside of the candle. If the sides of the candle are steep the plastic may slide off.

Allow the polyester to cure. Then remove the waxed paper. The edges of the sand-polyester shell can be trimmed on a grinding wheel.

When the candle burns down, the polyester shell can be reused by filling it with hot wax and a candlewick.

Sand-filled polyester resin and impregnated cord were combined in this composition. The backing is plywood.

DESIGNER'S TABLE

Materials and Equipment

two sheets of acrylic, two feet square,
⅛″ thick
a frame for a piece 24″ x 24″ x 1″
polyester resin
transparent color
catalyst
alcohol and soft flannel cloth
plastic tape
spacers cut from acrylic rod
pizza cutter
cotton swabs

Procedures

The technique used in making this table with acrylic and polyester resin enables the craftsman to create any design or pattern he desires. Colors, textures, and patterns can therefore be custom made to match any setting.

The acrylic sheet comes with paper on both sides. Peel one side off and clean that face with alcohol on a soft flannel cloth. The paper on the other side will protect it while you are working.

Next, stretch plastic tape around the edge of each piece so that at least ½″ extends upward to form a fence, and make certain that it sticks on all four sides. The tape will prevent polyester resin from running off the sheets. Since the tape is not permanent, the color does not matter, but it should be at least an inch wide.

Colored and catalyzed resin should now be poured onto the sheet in the approximate shape you want to achieve. Do not worry if the resin flows more than you want; it is the resin's nature. When the polyester sets, you can correct the pattern. After the resin gels, use a pizza cutter to make the line you want, and then remove the excess plastic with tongue depressors. The acrylic may look sticky and gummy after this operation, but as long as the colored plastic that you want removed is cleared away, this will not matter.

A second layer in another color may then be poured. Once the bottom layer has set, the colors will not mix. They will blend as light passes through the piece, but the colors themselves will not run together.

Additional colors may be added until the desired result has been achieved. Then a final coating of clear resin should be poured on all acrylic surfaces that have not yet been covered with resin. This will erase any blemishes on the surface that may have resulted from cutting or removing the excess plastic.

While this resin is wet, or even earlier while the colored sections are still uncured, small pieces of acrylic that will act as spacers should be placed in the polyester. The size of the spacers will be determined by how large the groove in the frame is. Many commercial do-it-yourself aluminum frames are built to accommodate pieces 1″ thick. If your sheets of acrylic are ⅛″ thick the spacer would then be ¾″ long. It is important that there be some separation between the sheets in order to benefit fully from the interplay of light and reflections between the two surfaces that will be apparent when the table is assembled.

When the resin on both sheets has cured, the table is ready to be assembled. Frames of extruded aluminum work well with this design, and they are readily available and easy to assemble. Your finished table will be especially handsome on an open base that allows the light to highlight the design. It will also be effective if placed on a windowsill where daylight will strike it; as the color and intensity of the light changes so will the texture, color, and mood of your polyester design.

For this project, good transparent color is essential. In the foreground are ¾″ acrylic spacers that will serve to separate the pieces of acrylic when they are framed.

Remove the masking paper from one side of the sheets and clean the surfaces lightly with alcohol and a soft, clean rag.

Using plastic tape 1″ wide, encircle each piece. Overlap the tape on the bottom and press it on firmly until it sticks solidly to dam in the polyester resin.

Polyester resin is poured on the acrylic in the approximate shape that is desired. With the poured polyester serving to adhere them, place spacers cut from acrylic to act as supports for the two acrylic sheets when they are framed. These spacers also let the light play between the pieces, dramatizing the texture and color of polyester resin.

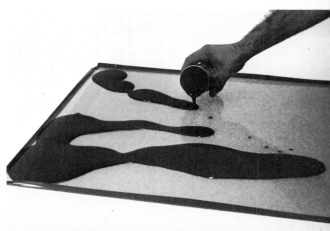

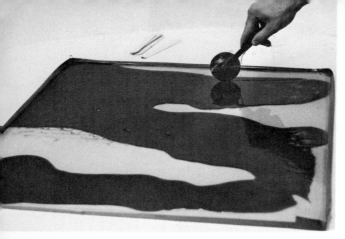

When the resin sets it can be trimmed to the exact shape that you want using a pizza cutter or a knife. The excess resin is then removed with tongue depressors.

Once the bottom layer has cured a second color may be added. In this case, the bottom layer was cut away, but the hard, distinct lines were muted somewhat by allowing the horizontal pourings of the second layer to flow naturally.

After colored layers have cured and uncoated areas of acrylic have been painted with clear resin, the top and bottom are ready to be assembled. Spacers are visible in the two near corners.

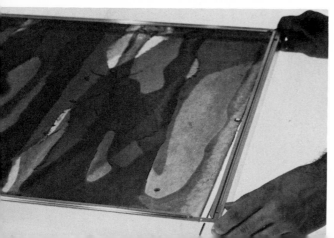

A commercially available frame made of extruded aluminum can be assembled in a few minutes.

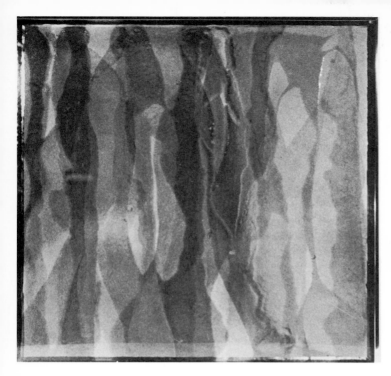

The finished piece shows the over-lapping and blending of several distinct colors.

Custom colors, textures, and designs make this table a handsome addition to any room, any decor.

POLYESTER RESIN AND PARTICLE BOARD TABLE

Materials and Equipment

> polyester resin
> catalyst
> white opaque color
> filler
> ¾"-thick sheet of particle board, 18"
>   x 48"
> router with different-sized bits, ⅛"
>   and ¼"
> squeeze container
> cotton swabs
> spray can of polyurethane semigloss
>   finish
> alcohol-base stain
> legs or base for the table

Procedures

Intricate patterns and linear designs can be permanently inscribed in a table of particle board using polyester resin.

After planning your design, transfer it to your sheet of particle board. Cabinetmakers will usually cut the board to your exact specifications, but lumberyards generally sell it in 4' x 8' sheets. By using a felt-tipped marking pen, different thicknesses of line which will correspond to different router bits may be indicated.

With a router, rout out your design ⅛" deep. For straight lines, clamp guideboards to your tabletop to define the tool's path.

The use of different bit thicknesses could lend added interest to your finished piece.

Once all your lines have been routed, paint the top surface with your choice of paint or stain. Do not paint the routed areas—especially if an alcohol-based stain is used—because the stain may bleed into your resin and cause discoloration. Stains work very well with particle board because the board is extremely absorbent. Allow the paint or stain to dry.

Mix the polyester resin and opaque white color with about 20 percent calcium carbonate. This filler will help to prevent resin shrinkage and give greater impact resistance. Catalyze the mixture and pour it into a squeeze container.

Placing the nozzle partway into each groove, squeeze the resin into the appropriate spaces with a continuous movement. This way you can fill your routed lines with this opaque mixture until the resin levels, filled to almost brimming without spilling over the edges.

When all parts of the design have been filled, allow the polyester to cure overnight.

Once cured, the table should be sprayed with three or four coats of clear polyurethane semigloss. This material is available in hardware stores and gives the board a tough finish that should protect the resin from scratches.

The tabletop may be set on a base or may be mounted with legs.

Your table will be a welcome addition to any room, and the freedom of design that this technique offers should provide a ready outlet for your creative spirit. You will find that this process of polyester inlay can be used in dozens of other craft functions—room dividers, bases for lamps, wall reliefs, doors, wood frames for mirrors. The list is as limitless as the craftsman's innovative capacity.

After sketching your design for the tabletop, transfer it to the surface of the particle board. The board should be ¾" thick. Different thicknesses of line may be used to indicate different thicknesses in the router bits. Particle board is cut to size by most cabinetmakers.

Rout out the design. For long straight lines a brace and guide should be clamped on to direct the router's path.

Paint the surface, but be careful not to paint the routed areas. Stains work especially well with particle board because the board absorbs them so readily.

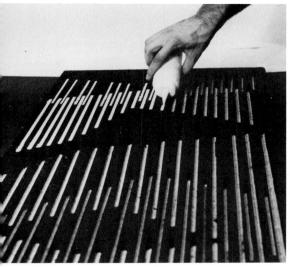

Fill the spaces with a mixture of polyester resin, opaque white color, 20 percent calcium carbonate, and catalyst. The calcium carbonate, a filler, will help to reduce shrinkage which might otherwise result in a separation of the resin from the board.

When the resin cures, spray on three or four coatings of polyurethane semigloss. This will protect the surface of the board and resin from spills and scratches.

The finished table can be designed to suit any decor.

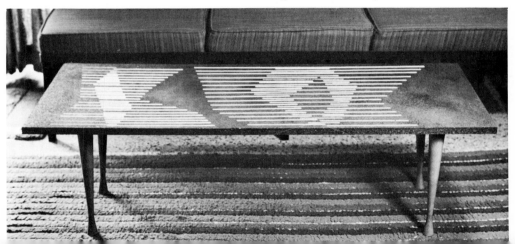

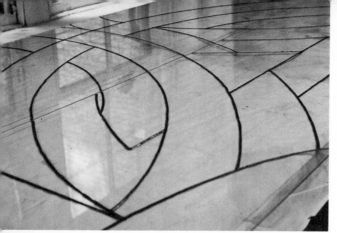

Gary Smith first sketches and then lays the clear acrylic over the full-size original cartoon. He transfers the design to the acrylic with steel-filled epoxy squeezed from a ketchup container.

Gary Smith mixes his polyester resin and catalyst by weight. His formula: 1 percent catalyst by weight.

When the epoxy cures, paint colored polyester resin directly onto the acrylic. The polyester should not be allowed to overflow the epoxy lines.

POLYESTER AND ACRYLIC PANELS

Materials and Equipment

> acrylic sheet
> polyester resin
> color
> catalyst
> aluminum- or steel-filled epoxy
> a squeeze container
> a brush

Procedures

Large panels of acrylic may be decorated with polyester resin. Sketch your design full size, and lay the acrylic sheet over the sketch.

Gary Smith uses steel-filled epoxy to outline the basic design on the acrylic sheet. Aluminum- or steel-filled epoxy can be purchased in a commercial mixture or you can make your own. Aluminum powder may be used in combination with either epoxy resin or a two-part epoxy adhesive.

The metal-filled epoxy is squeezed out of a spouted container onto the sheet. Because the resin is made thixotropic by the filler, it will not run. The result is that the lines you squeeze from your container accurately trace your original sketch.

Allow the epoxy to cure overnight.

Polyester resin is then brushed onto the surface of the acrylic. Since the metal-filled epoxy effectively cordons off sections of the acrylic, different colors may be employed.

Brush the resin on thinly. It should not be applied so thickly that it will overflow your guidelines. Surface tension should prevent the liquid plastic from running off the edge if you do not overfill.

Flower Table in the Art Nouveau Style (24" x 24" x 24"). Gary L. Smith. Finished panels may be combined. Five pieces were cemented together to create this table.

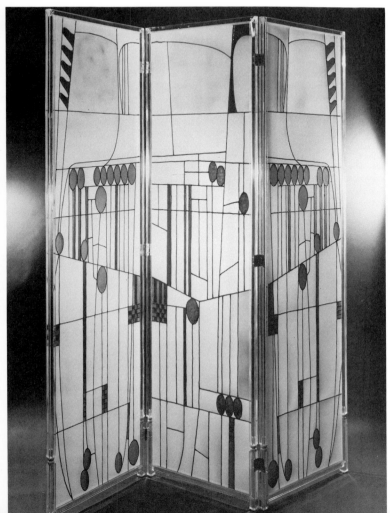

Room Divider (6' high). Gary L. Smith. Steel-filled epoxy and polyester resin on acrylic. Courtesy: Gary L. Smith.

SPARKLING ORNAMENTS

Materials and Equipment

> polyester resin
> catalyst
> color (optional)
> aluminum foil
> piano wire (or similar gauge)

Procedures

The process for making these ornaments utilizes a simple mold made from aluminum foil. Press the foil into shape, but first rumple it so that you will get the full benefit of the crinkly texture when your castings are removed from the makeshift molds.

You can also press the foil around your finger or any other form and make your shape that way. The advantages of using aluminum foil are several: it is inexpensive; it is easy to find; it is easy to shape; and it separates from the polyester without a mold release.

After you have shaped the foil, arrange it so that it will sit without overturning, and pour polyester resin which is catalyzed into the cavities. Wires for suspending the finished objects should be set into the resin while it is uncured, and the resin will harden around them.

But the trick to this technique comes when the resin has gelled. The aluminum foil must be removed *while the polyester is in the gel state*. If you have too many undercuts or intricate convolutions this process may be difficult, but with most basic shapes the foil will peel away easily. The next step is to set your forms down on a piece of cellophane to cure fully. Don't touch them or they will dry with fingermarks.

Polyester resin is then poured into the cavity.

Piano wire or florist's wire and aluminum foil are necessary for these ornaments. The color is optional.

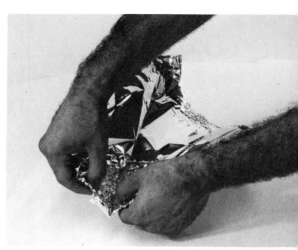

A simple mold is made by crumpling aluminum foil and forming a cavity with your fingers or by pressing the foil around another object.

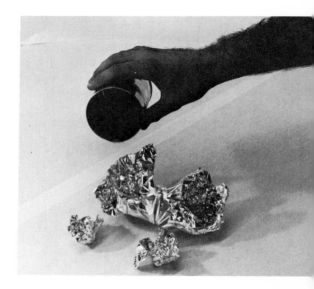

Piano wire has been suspended in the uncured resin. When the polyester cures, the wires will act as stems. The foil must be removed while the resin is in the gel state.

The stems of these light-catching castings have been anchored in a small block of acrylic to finish this sparkling ornament.

A TESSERAE (MOSAIC) PANEL

Materials and Equipment

> polyester resin
> color
> catalyst
> a variety of ice cube trays
> a piece of acrylic
> Mortite or clay
> alcohol and soft flannel cloth
> squeeze dispenser with a small nozzle
> cotton swabs

Procedures

The art of creating tesserae panels dates back to ancient times, and this modern adaptation employs the same technique of using small "tiles" of different colors and shapes to complete a larger piece.

The use of polyester resin, however, adds a new dimension to this art: light. Because polyester resin "tiles" may be cast in any number of different, translucent colors, the old associations of flat mosaics are given a lift with a greater variety of color and texture.

Using polyethylene ice cube trays of different shapes—squares, circles, rectangles—the craftsman can cast his own tiles. You will want units with different intensity of color, too. Pieces that are nearly transparent and clear will be necessary and so will tiles that are black. Of course, your own design will determine what color scheme will predominate.

The polyester resin should be poured into the ice cube trays and allowed to cure completely in these molds. Usually no mold release will be required, but if you find pieces sticking in the trays pull them out with tweezers and spray the tray with some silicone mold release before the next casting. Normally, the tiles will spring out when the tray is flexed.

Once you have an adequate selection of tiles with which to design your tesserae

panel, the acrylic sheet must be prepared. Remove the masking paper from just the top side of the sheet and clean it lightly with alcohol on flannel cloth.

Next, press Mortite or clay strips around the edges to hold the liquid polyester resin. When this edging is removed later it will leave a thin ledge which may be used in mounting your finished mosaic. Make your stripping just wide enough to help in framing.

You are now ready to begin designing. If desired, you may remove the masking from the bottom of the sheet and place a full-sized sketch underneath. It would then be easy to transfer your pattern from paper to polyester tiles on top of the clear acrylic. But you may also begin creating with your polyester forms directly on the acrylic. Since they are not meant to stick to the backing at this point, you may arrange and rearrange them as many times as you wish. Be careful to leave a space between each unit, though, since they will be grouted with black resin later.

Once you have decided on the proper arrangement, polyester resin is used to attach the tiles to the sheet of acrylic. Mix a small amount of uncolored resin and pour it into a squeeze bottle. Lift your mosaic tiles one by one and squeeze the resin onto the acrylic. Then set the tile firmly into the liquid resin. Larger pieces can be picked up easily with the fingers, but tweezers might be better for smaller tiles. Be certain that all your pieces are firmly placed so that they will remain attached and so that the black outlining resin will not seep underneath later on.

For areas that have no specific pattern or for areas that you can arrange quickly, just spread some polyester on the acrylic and begin placing your tiles.

As mentioned earlier, make certain that you leave a narrow space between each tile on all sides. Once the clear polyester resin cures these tiles will need to be grouted (surrounded with black resin) so that their colors will be accented and intensified as the light passes through them. This is optional. You may prefer to eliminate this step or to use another color of resin between the mosaics.

When the polyester cures, fill your clean squeeze container with opaque catalyzed black polyester resin. Using a thin nozzle, fill all the spaces between the polyester tiles. This masking of the light will accent the colors handsomely by allowing the light to pass only through the tiles. Do not worry if you err and get black resin on the tops of some pieces; simply use cotton swabs to clean them off. If you allow this resin to remain until it cures, however, it will be nearly impossible to remove.

Once the black resin cures, the stripping around the edges should be removed. It should pull away easily, but stubborn areas can be scraped away with a knife. (Kerosene is the solvent for putty.)

The finished mosaic panel will look best where light will strike it from behind, revealing your colors and patterns. It may be placed on a windowsill or mounted in a box with light behind it. Either way you will have a striking panel.

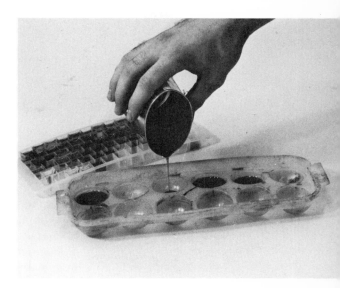

Mosaic tiles are cast in polyethylene ice cube trays of different sizes and shapes.

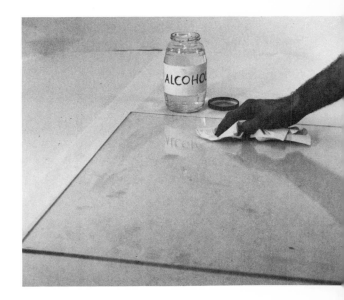

A sheet of acrylic forms the base for your panel. A sketch may be placed underneath this transparent plastic for reference. Clean the working surface lightly with alcohol on a clean flannel cloth before beginning.

Mortite or modeling clay is pressed along all four sides so that no resin drips off. This stripping creates a thin ledge that may be used later in framing.

Assemble all your tiles, and begin planning your mosaic.

Once your planning is complete, squeeze polyester resin under each tile and set the piece down again. Always make certain that the bottom of each piece is fully immersed in clear polyester.

While larger pieces may be lifted by hand, tweezers should prove helpful with the smaller ones.

Once the clear polyester resin that bonds your tiles to the acrylic has cured, black opaque resin should be squeezed into the spaces between tiles. By allowing light to pass through only your cast pieces, their colors and shapes are intensified.

If black resin gets on any tiles, remove it with cotton swabs. Do not let it cure or it will become permanent.

After your black grouting cures, remove the stripping from the edges. It should pull away cleanly. Scrape stubborn areas with a knife.

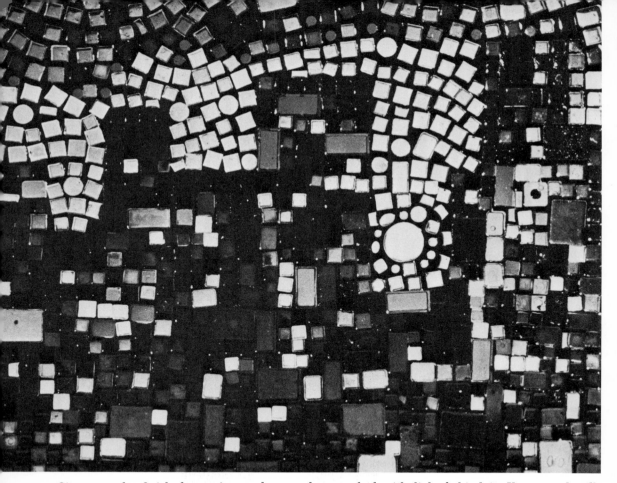

Cityscape, the finished mosaic panel, was photographed with light behind it. Your panel will look best on a window sill where light passes through it, or mounted in a box containing electric lights that will show the full beauty of the different colors, shapes, and patterns.

This translucent "painting" was created on an acrylic base with cast polyester tiles and poured polyester resin. Spaces were defined with metal channels much like the enameling techniques of cloisonné or plique-à-jour.

CASTING POLYESTER IN A WAX MOLD

Materials and Equipment

> a slab of wax
> polyester resin
> color (optional)
> catalyst
> carving tools
> an awl or pointed object

Procedures

Casting polyester resin in hand-carved wax molds has a symbiotic relationship. The polyester resin gels before it begins to heat and melt the wax. At that time the resin already has its permanent shape. When it cools down, the wax cools too and reassumes its original shape against the cured plastic.

Begin with a piece of construction paper. Draw your design, and keep in mind that since your casting will be a relief, you should try to exploit the use of different levels. Place the paper pattern over a slab of wax at least ¾" wider than the projected carving. With the point of a compass, an awl, or other pointed object create a dotted-line image of the pattern on the wax, poking right through the paper.

Remove the paper sketch, and connect the dotted lines to give you a clear picture of your original design. Use chisels, X-acto knives, and even screwdriver blades or other utensils to carve into the wax. By creating different levels you will get the full benefit of this technique.

Remember that the panel should be at least ¼" thick at the thinnest level. It is advisable to first carve one level ¼" below the top surface of the wax even before transferring the design and carving the rest of your relief.

The wax mold may be textured. Smooth, scalloped, curved, and polka-dotted surfaces are all possible because of the ease of carving wax. If you make any mistakes in the carving, you may put some excess wax in a tin can, place it on an oven burner until it melts, and pour the hot wax back over the mistake. When this cools, you may

recarve the area. Beware of one thing: undercuts. If the mold is severely undercut, the cured polyester will leave the mold only by breaking apart the wax.

When you are satisfied with the mold, catalyze some polyester resin, color it if you like, and pour it into the form. The deepest levels should be poured first and allowed to gel before pouring the rest. To accentuate the relief, you may want to do the pouring in several steps, such as one color for the deepest reliefs, another for shallower grooves, and even another hue for the remaining relief areas to be poured. Another method of adding a unique quality of texture and color to the wax-cast panel is to lay in pieces of fabric in different parts of the relief. Pebbles, shells, or other heavy materials may be embedded if you use flexible polyester resin. Polyester resin shrinks as it cures. If you use a rigid resin, the resin will tend to crack. Flexible resin has more latitude.

When the piece has had time to cure fully, remove it from the mold by prying it up. There should be no trouble in removing the casting if there are no undercuts, for wax is itself a natural release.

This relief will certainly stand out.

Before beginning carve an even level ¼" below the top of the block of wax. This will create a "dam" of wax to hold in the polyester resin.

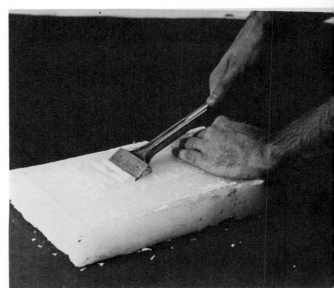

After drawing a design, transfer this pattern to the wax by poking through the paper into the wax with a pointed object like a compass point or an awl.

With wax-carving, foam-carving, chisel, or other tools remove excess wax to form your design in relief.

When you are satisfied with the carved design, pour catalyzed polyester resin into the wax mold. Before pouring be certain that the carved pattern has no undercuts which will lock the cured polyester into the mold and make it difficult to remove.

When the resin cures thoroughly, pry it out of the mold.

The polyester resin casting will have assumed all the marks made in the carved wax.

The resultant panel can be made over and over again in the inexhaustible wax mold. You may even want to experiment with different color mixtures, embedding cloth, adding new hues and textures to the wax-molded polyester relief.

Textures were created in this panel (8″ x 24″) by using fine gravel, pebbles, sand, woven fabrics, bits of chopped glass, and by carving patterns in parts of the wax mold. Cracking resulted because heavy materials were embedded in resin which was not of the flexible type.

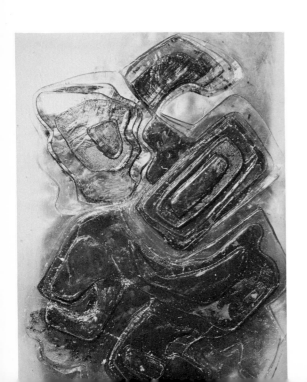

This polyester relief (4′ x 5′) was made from a wax mold.

MAKING AN RTV RUBBER MOLD OF SEASHELLS

Materials and Equipment

>   RTV silicone mold making rubber and
>   catalyst
>   clean cans
>   a scale for weighing the silicone rubber
>   seashells
>   clay
>   a cardboard box large enough for the
>   shells
>   silicone mold release
>   tongue depressors or a spatula for
>   mixing the silicone rubber

Procedures

So far, we have made castings in molds made out of aluminum foil, polyethylene ice cube trays, and wax, but it is also possible to make your own permanent molds of your own objects.

Room Temperature Vulcanizing (RTV) mold-making silicone "rubber" is a flexible mold-making material that is quite simple to use. Coming in liquid form, it is usually mixed by weight and it hardens or cures at room temperature.

Since no heat is generated while the mold material hardens, a mold may be made of almost any object or material, including wax. The only exceptions are pieces that have deep undercuts (unless you brush the silicone on in a thin covering that will need the support of a multipiece plaster jacket). Although the mold may be flexed to help remove finished castings with some undercutting, this material is not flexible enough when thick to allow the removal of pieces that are too large to get out without destroying the mold.

RTV silicone rubbers offer many advantages. Not only will they capture the detail of your forms exactly, but they will also yield hundreds of castings before they wear out if proper care is taken of the mold.

After choosing your subject, it must be prepared. In the case of seashells, the open bottom of the shell must be plugged with modeling clay and be flattened out so they sit squarely. The flat bottom will become the bottom of the finished casting.

In a cardboard box or milk carton big

Room Temperature Vulcanizing (RTV) mold-making silicone rubber is mixed by weight. Molds can be made of many objects with this flexible material.

The openings in the shells first must be plugged with modeling clay and flattened.

enough for all your pieces, press the shells onto the bottom. The clay should help them to stick to the cardboard. With regular boxes the corners should be taped, but with milk containers that is not necessary.

When the shells are secure, spray the entire inside of the box, including the shells, with a silicone mold release agent. This will keep the rubber from sticking when you peel the cardboard away later. Again, milk cartons will not need to be sprayed, but the shells should be. The mold release will not harm anything if it is applied properly (as per manufacturer's instruction).

Allow the silicone to dry. Weigh out the proper amounts of silicone rubber and catalyst. These two components *must* be mixed thoroughly, and at the same time you must be careful not to mix in too much air. If excess amounts of air are entrapped, bubbles may cling to your shells and the castings will end up with bumps on them.

When well mixed (several minutes), pour the RTV silicone rubber into the coated box. Hold your mixing can high so that a very thin strand of rubber strikes the bottom of the box. This will help to exclude air by stretching it out of the rubber as it falls. Continue to allow this thin strand to build up in one spot; that way the shells will be coated from the bottom and the slow filling will gradually but surely force the air out of the box and up to the top. Once your subjects have been covered—an eighth-inch covering will suffice—place the box somewhere level where it will not be disturbed. The rubber should be allowed to cure overnight.

When cured, peel away the paper and remove the clay from the bottoms of the shells. The mold may be flexed to help remove the shells and any thin flaps of rubber at the openings on the face of the mold should be trimmed off.

The finished mold is ready. Castings are easy to make. After spraying the mold cavities with silicone mold release agent (to extend the life of your mold), fill with polyester resin that has been catalyzed for castings.

When this resin cures, remove your finished pieces the same way you extracted the original shells.

Then press your subjects into the bottom of a cardboard box just large enough to accommodate them. The edges should be taped to avoid leaks.

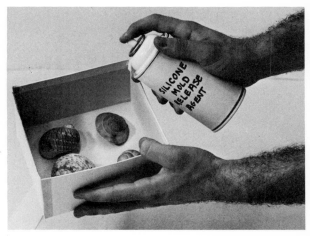

Spray the inside of the box and spray the shells with a silicone mold release agent. Be certain that the undersides of the shells are coated. Allow this mold release to dry.

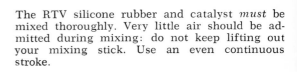

The RTV silicone rubber and catalyst *must* be mixed thoroughly. Very little air should be admitted during mixing: do not keep lifting out your mixing stick. Use an even continuous stroke.

To fill the mold, pour from high up and allow only a thin strand of silicone rubber to trickle down. This will stretch out most of the air bubbles and the slowly rising rubber will seep more evenly into all the facets of your forms. The process is a slow one, but it is the best way to insure that no air bubbles will be entrapped to mar your final castings.

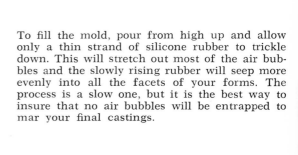

The rubber should remain undisturbed overnight, and then the paper may be peeled away and the shells removed. Flex the mold to help remove your shells—flexibility is one of the RTV silicone rubber's assets.

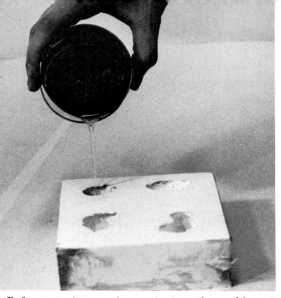 

Before pouring casting resin into the mold cavities, spray the mold with the silicone mold release agent. It will make removing the cured pieces much easier and will increase the lifetime of your mold.

Remove final castings the same way you did the originals.

Castings made from silicone rubber molds are a wonderful way to capture the beauty of both natural and man-made forms.

CASTING IN A STRETCHY RUBBER MOLD

Materials and Equipment

> Adrub Room Temperature Vulcanizing
> (RTV) S-T-R-E-T-C-H-Y Molding Rub-
> ber
> a scale
> paste wax
> aluminum foil
> epoxy putty
> a brush
> silicone spray
> polyester resin
> catalyst
> color (optional)

Procedures

Molds can be made by pouring the molding material around a form in a thick layer, but molds may also be constructed so that they are thin and flexible. Flexible molds should be used when your form has deep undercuts and you do not want to make more complicated multipart molds.

One such material, Adrub RTV S-T-R-E-T-C-H-Y Molding Rubber, is available from the Adhesive Products Corporation, Bronx, N.Y. This molding rubber is painted over the object in three or four layers. The final mold may be as thin as ⅛″ to ¼″.

Paste wax acts as a separator for the rubber. Coat a piece of aluminum foil as well as the object thoroughly with the Butcher's wax or a soapy solution. In this case, the form was modeled first from epoxy putty and allowed to harden.

Mix enough mold material to cover your form. The rubber and hardener should be mixed according to the instructions provided. The recommended proportion would be two parts rubber to one part hardener by weight. It will set very quickly, but must first be mixed for three minutes. Apply it immediately after mixing.

Brush the rubber over the wax-coated form taking care not to trap air bubbles. Wait fifteen minutes, and mix more mold material. The second and third layers may be poured over your form.

Allow the rubber to harden overnight, and pull the mold away. It should release easily—even if there are undercuts. Trim the edges with scissors, spray the cavity with a silicone mold release, and pour catalyzed polyester resin into the mold, creating a cast duplicate of the original form.

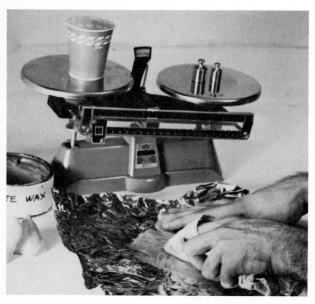

Use a piece of aluminum foil as the base. Coat it with paste wax.

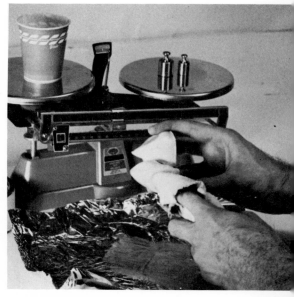

The object, in this case a *Bloop-Bloop* modeled with epoxy putty, should be waxed, too.

Mix the S-T-R-E-T-C-H-Y Molding Rubber according to the manufacturer's instructions. Use different utensils for each component.

The recommended proportion of rubber to hardener is two parts to one part by weight, respectively.

Mix the rubber for three minutes and then apply it by brush immediately. Take care not to trap air bubbles.

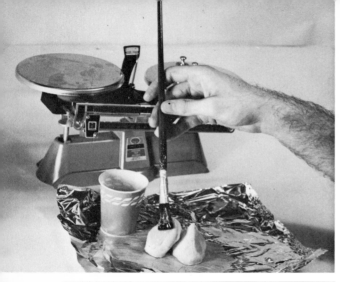

Use a stiff bristled brush to coat the form.

After fifteen minutes, another layer should be applied. The second and third layers may be poured. At least three layers should be applied.

Allow the rubber to harden overnight; then de-mold your form. The mold should pull away easily if your object was adequately coated with wax—even if there are undercuts.

Trim the edges of the rubber mold with scissors.

Spray the cavity with a silicone mold release.

Set the flexible mold in a can or a box to hold it level, and cast with catalyzed polyester resin.

When cured, remove the cast polyester form from the mold.

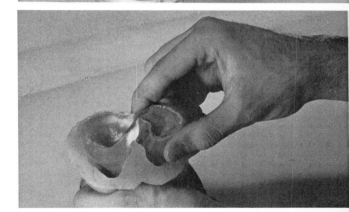

Bloop-Bloops (3″ x 2½″).

FIBERGLASS-REINFORCED POLYESTER BOWL

Materials and Equipment

polyester resin
color
catalyst
fiberglass mat—woven
filler
fiberglass finishing cloth
a bowl
plastic wrap or cellophane
a ridged roller
a stiff bristled brush
band, jig- or saber saw
hand drill with sanding disk
one large C-clamp
wood scraper
buffing wheels and compound

Procedures

Fiberglass-reinforced polyester (FRP) involves the use of woven glass fibers impregnated with polyester resin. This system, used in the construction of car bodies, boat hulls, and weatherproof shelters, creates an amazingly strong—almost indestructible—material.

While auto manufacturers use steel molds for their FRP forms, we have chosen a mixing bowl. In order to protect the bowl from the polyester resin, cover it with plastic wrap or cellophane, taping the edges on the inside of the bowl so that the outer surface is taut.

Next, cut strips of fiberglass cloth. Always wear gloves when handling this material, because nearly invisible glass splinters will get under your skin even if you are careful. Like many other materials, fiberglass is safe if handled properly but can be seriously irritating if cautions are not observed. These strips should be long enough to reach from one edge of the bowl to the other when laid across the diameter; a width of three inches should be adequate for most surfaces. The objective here is to choose a width that will not pop up at the edges when it is laid around a curve. On larger pieces larger strips should be used.

You will need enough strips to cover the surface of the bowl five times.

In a good-sized polyethylene container mix your polyester resin, color, filler (10 percent), and catalyst. Just enough filler is added to make the resin slightly thicker. You will not need a lot of color since there will be six layers of fiberglass on the bowl.

Drop as many of your strips of fiberglass into the container as the resin will saturate. The fiberglass should be completely saturated with resin. You may knead the material to speed this process. Cover your work area well and begin laying the resinated fiberglass over the covered bowl. Start in the center and work down toward the sides always going in the same direction. Smooth the pieces out with your gloved hands but be careful not to squeeze out too much resin so that the fibers of glass are left exposed.

Follow the same process with the next layer of fiberglass, only lay this layer perpendicular to the first.

Before laying on the third set, however, take a minute to get out any air bubbles that might have been trapped between the layers. A ridged roller (that looks corrugated) can be quite helpful for this, but daubing with a stiff brush accomplishes the same thing. Poke at the air bubbles until they are forced through the fiberglass to the surface. Get out as many as possible, but do not spend forever on this since five layers must be applied and your resin will cure if you waste time.

After your last layer of woven mat has been applied, even out the edge by trimming it with an old pair of scissors or a knife. Apply one extra layer of fiberglass around the edge and press it on firmly to be positive that no delamination occurred while you were cutting.

Your final layer should be a single covering of fine fiberglass finishing cloth. This cloth may be applied in one or two pieces; it gives a fine finish.

Daub and roll this layer as well, and then allow the bowl to cure undisturbed.

Once cured, the mixing bowl underneath should be removed. Tongue depressors may be used to help pry it out of its fiberglass and polyester shell. Peel off the plastic wrap or cellophane that was used to protect it.

The edge may be trimmed on a band, saber, or jigsaw. When sawing, however, a filter mask should be worn at all times. Fiberglass and polyester dusts are extremely dangerous. Work areas should be swept or vacuumed immediately after use.

The outside surface may be sanded if desired. It will reveal a delightful moiré pattern similar to a surface map since different layers will be sanded off at different points.

Scratches from sanding may be removed by polishing on a buffing wheel. If you do not desire the moiré effect, the surface may be painted with highly catalyzed resin that will harden to a tough and shiny finish. Polishing with wax will allow you to preserve the moiré on the surface by protecting any exposed areas.

The cut edge should be scraped and painted with highly catalyzed resin in any case.

Your finished bowl will be nearly breakproof but it is not meant for cooking. When the resin is cured it is nontoxic and may be used for fruits or decorative centerpieces. It may be hand washed with mild soap in warm water without damage.

Gather your materials and cut the fiberglass into strips about three inches wide and long enough to fit over the bowl.

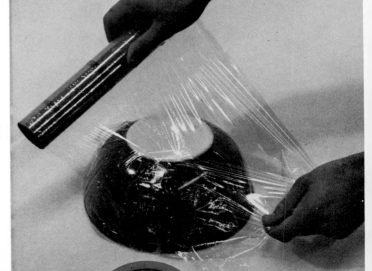

Cover the bowl with plastic wrap or cellophane to protect it from the polyester resin, and protect your working area.

Tape this covering to the inside of the bowl with masking tape. Make certain that the covering is stretched taut.

Saturate the strips of fiberglass with resin that has been mixed with 20 percent calcium carbonate. Do not drain too much resin from the fiberglass; the strips should always have a thick wet coating. Standing the bowl on a large juice can will make work easier but not less messy.

Drape the strips of fiberglass over your form. Start at the top and work down the sides. Continue this process until the first layer is complete. Three or four more layers should be applied, each perpendicular to the strips underneath.

Daub each layer with a stiff brush, or roll it with a ridged roller. This will help to dislodge entrapped air bubbles and force them to the surface.

After applying your final layer, place several pieces of fiberglass around the edge of the bowl for reinforcement.

A final layer of finely woven fiberglass finishing cloth should then be laid over the surface.

Roll the entire surface of the fiberglassed bowl with a ridged roller. This will help free more air bubbles. Daubing with a stiff brush is also effective. Try to get out as many bubbles as you can, otherwise they will cause delamination in the finished product.

Trim the edges with an old pair of scissors or a sharp knife.

Allow the resin to cure. When it has, the original form may be removed. Tongue depressors supply the leverage to force the original bowl out of its fiberglass cocoon.

The edge should be trimmed on a band, saber, or jigsaw. Be exceptionally careful: polyester-fiberglass dust is dangerous. You should wear a filter mask during all cutting and sanding operations.

With your filter mask still on, even out the bottom surface and sides with a sanding disk.

The sanding marks may be polished out on a buffing wheel. This will preserve the moiré pattern revealed during sanding. The surface may also be finished by painting it with a heavily catalyzed layer of polyester resin. This will cure to a hard, tough finish.

The top edge should be painted with heavily catalyzed resin.

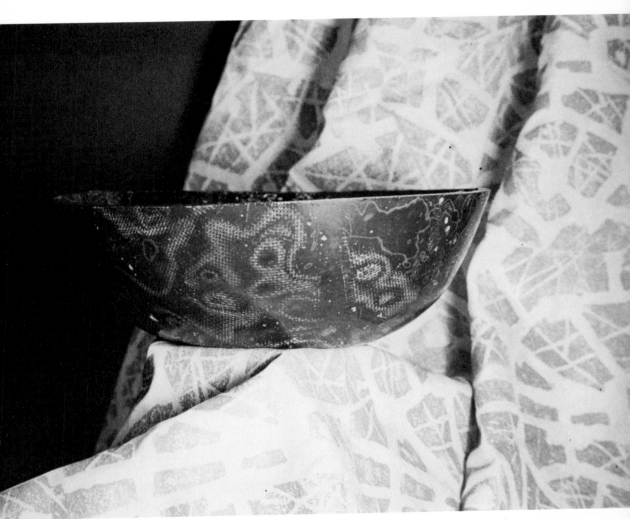

The finished product will be strong and attractive—it may bowl you over!

A ROOM DIVIDER OF FIBERGLASS-REINFORCED POLYESTER

Materials and Equipment

woven fiberglass mat
a sheet of Mylar or cellophane
polyester resin
color
catalyst
a ridged roller
pizza cutter
wood to frame the panels

Procedures

Fiberglass-reinforced polyester resin (FRP) is a combination that cannot be easily matched for lightweight strength. Car bodies and boat hulls are constructed of this combination.

Begin with a sheet of Mylar or cellophane several inches larger than your projected panel. Cut a single piece of fiberglass also a bit larger than the size of the final panel. Then press Mortite or coils of modeling clay around all four edges to prevent polyester resin from running off the sides. Make certain that your working surface is level.

The next step is to impregnate the fiberglass with the plastic. Pour enough

catalyzed, colored polyester resin onto the fiberglass to cover it—but not enough to run over the edging.

Use a tongue depressor or a spatula to distribute the resin evenly. If there are any air bubbles underneath the fiberglass, run over the bubbles with a stiff bristle brush or a ridged metal roller to stipple and push the bubbles out. This should dislodge what could become a delamination or a degraded section of fiberglass.

Allow the resin to cure while you begin the second stage. On a second sheet of Mylar edged with Mortite, pour a layer of heavily catalyzed colored polyester resin. When the sheet gels you are ready to begin decorating the FRP sheet. With a pizza cutter, slice shapes out of the second gelled sheet. Peel the gelled resin off and lay it on the FRP. The pieces will peel away from the Mylar backing easily. As with all polyester projects, wear disposable gloves when working.

The gelled strips will cure on the larger sheet and bond to it securely. A great range of designs is possible with this technique.

The cured panel was cut into three sections with a band saw and mounted in wooden frames attached with two-way hinges. It makes a handsome screen.

On a piece of Mylar several inches larger than your projected panel lay a single piece of woven fiberglass mat.

Press Mortite or modeling clay around the edges and pour on a layer of catalyzed, colored polyester resin.

If you find any air bubbles use a ridged metal roller or a stiff bristle brush to dislodge them.

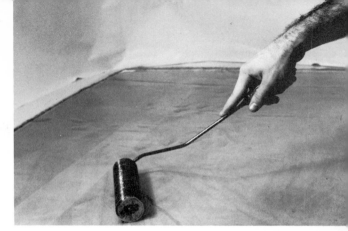

Pour a second sheet of polyester resin and allow it to gel. Once the resin has set, use a pizza cutter to cut shapes. Lift the gelled resin off the sheet and place it in position on the fiberglass-reinforced polyester (FRP) sheet.

Lay the strips of gelled resin down carefully.

As the resin cures the strips and the FRP will bond together.

The cured panel (36″ x 42″) was cut into three sections on a band saw and framed in wood attached with two-way hinges at each section.

Foliage Screen (76″ high). Emile Norman. Many different varieties of plants and butterflies were laminated into this fiberglass-reinforced polyester folding screen. Natural forms may be embedded and laminated in resin, but they must first be "dried" in silica gel to remove all moisture. Courtesy: Emile Norman.

ACRYLIC IS, PROBABLY, the best-known type of plastic. Although invented nearly forty years ago, it has just come into its own as a crafts medium in the past few years.

Recognized most often by the trade-names of Lucite (Du Pont), Plexiglass (Rohm and Haas), Acrylite (American Cyanamid), and Perspex (Imperial Chemical Industries, Ltd.), this thermoplastic is outstanding for crafts use because of its versatility and the ease with which it can be formed and machined.

Acrylic weighs approximately half as much as glass of comparable size and thickness and has optical clarity (about 92 percent light transmission) that rivals that of less flexible, more fragile glass. Shrinkage and decomposition are minimal and, after prolonged exposure to water and moisture, it shows only slight reactions.

The manufacturing process molds polymethyl methacrylate resin under heat and pressure to create acrylic. The result is a plastic which has an indefinite shelf-life. It can be sawed, drilled, tapped, sanded, polished, and otherwise machined, cemented, etched or carved. Standard metalshop and woodworking tools are sufficient to execute most procedures.

As a thermoplastic, it can be heated and shaped while it is hot (softening between 240° and 340° F.). When it cools, the new shape will be retained. If reheated, though, this assumed shape will be lost, since it is a thermoplastic. Thermoplastics have a memory which, under heat, causes them to return to their original flat form. Heating should be done carefully and evenly because, if overheated, shrinkage, scorching, and bubbling may result.

Acrylic resists corrosion by most household chemicals, but turpentine, benzene, lacquer thinner, acetone, ketones, along with some solvents, will attack acrylic causing it to craze or blur.

Acrylic is best known in sheet form which usually is four feet by eight feet and comes in thicknesses ranging from

3

WORKING WITH ACRYLICS AND OTHER SHEET PLASTICS

$\frac{1}{16}''$ up to several inches. Patterned, textured, and even mirrored acrylic sheets are also manufactured, and more varieties are continually being offered.

Acrylic blocks, manufactured the same way as sheets, can be obtained in thicknesses up to one foot and in dimensions of up to three feet by two feet. Extruded and cast rods and tubes can be found in diameters ranging from $\frac{1}{16}''$ to $18''$.

Acrylic gesso and modeling paste are two plastic pastelike materials that can be applied at room temperature with no mixing. Both materials are white but they are easily colored using acrylic colors.

Gesso is often brushed onto a surface to protect materials from resins and other plastics that would normally dissolve or attack the surface. The gesso can also be used to finish carved polystyrene and polyurethane foams.

The paste extender can act as a resin isolator, like the gesso, or it can be used, more appropriately, for deep impastos and

to model. It should be applied in $\frac{1}{8}''$-thick layers, allowed to dry, and then built up with other layers until the desired depth is achieved. Acrylic modeling paste is also extremely moldable when it is wet. These materials usually dry overnight. In its wet state, it is possible to create richly textured surfaces with modeling paste which may later be sanded, carved, or painted.

Both acrylic gesso and acrylic modeling paste are sold widely under several brand names.

LIQUID AND PASTE ACRYLIC PROCESSES

Sealing and Finishing

Acrylic gesso is often used as a sealant for styrene and polyurethane foam surfaces. This thick liquid is brushed on and allowed to dry. Several coats should be applied and, again, allowed to dry fully. After about twenty-four hours—depending upon the hu-

Acrylic sheets, covered with protective paper, can easily be machined using electric or hand tools normally employed in wood- and metalworking. For drilling operations, bits made specifically for plastics are recommended. Courtesy: Rohm and Haas.

midity—the gesso-coated surface will be quite hard and may be sanded smooth. If a sanded surface is not especially desired, the gesso coat can also be left as it is.

Carving and Impasto

Vinyl-acrylic copolymer pastes are adaptable to a number of uses. These pastes may be built up into thick blocks which can then be sawed, carved, drilled, and sanded. To construct a thick unit, however, it is best to work gradually. First smooth out an area no more than 1/8″ thick, and allow this to dry thoroughly. When dry, a second 1/8″-thick layer may be applied. This process should be repeated until the desired thickness is reached. The paste should be allowed to dry thoroughly, however, if full advantage is to be taken of its properties of easy workability and strength.

Impasto, or low relief surfaces, may be created using acrylic pastes, too. The surface to be covered should first be painted with acrylic gesso, and the gesso should be allowed to dry. The paste is then applied over the gesso binder. While the paste is wet it may be sculpted and arranged.

When dry, acrylic gessoes and pastes may be painted using any of the many acrylic or vinyl-acrylic paints that are commercially available.

Collage

A layer of acrylic paste is first spread over a dampened piece of 1/2″-thick exterior plywood. It is often easiest to work in sections so that the paste does not dry out while you are working. If it does begin to get hard, however, simply sprinkle on a little bit of water. Objects like stones, cloth, metal pieces, almost anything available, may be pressed into the wet paste. The paste should be allowed to encircle each embedment so that when it hardens all the pieces pressed into it when wet will be held in place. Once the paste has hardened, sharp protrusions of either embedded objects or hardened

paste may be sanded or scraped down. The entire composition may then be painted or stained as desired.

Decoupage

Decoupage, the art of decorating surfaces with overlapping and intertwining paper cutouts, is easily created with another liquid plastic product: Mod-Podge. This is similar to a polyvinyl acetate/chloride type material. Mod-Podge is first painted on the surface to be decorated; the paper cutout is laid down and painted over with the white liquid. This process is repeated until the whole area is covered. Several coats of Mod-Podge should be applied. It dries to a hard, clear finish in just a few hours. String and cloth may be applied to the surface in the same manner; but all overlays must be completely covered with Mod-Podge if the adhesion is to be complete.

SOLID ACRYLIC PROCESSES

Marking and Sawing

To mark the plastic before sawing, acrylic sheets and blocks come with a protective paper covering which can later be peeled off. Marks can be made in pencil or pen on this paper. If it is necessary to make lines directly on the acrylic, a grease pencil should be used since it can be wiped away with a soft cloth afterward.

Acrylic sheets, rods, and blocks are easily cut using any saw made for wood- or metalworking. When using power equipment in cutting the acrylic sheet, the plastic should be fed through the saw slowly to cut down on excessive friction and heat. For straight cutting, a circular saw is best. Jig or saber types are most effective for cutting small curves or intricate patterns. Band saws are good for cutting larger curves.

Metal-cutting blades are best for acrylic since they deliver the cleanest, sharpest results. If using a circular saw, the blade

Using a sharp scraper, made for woodworking, acrylic edges and surfaces can be made smooth and matte by removing scratches and roughness.

Through wet sanding, the scraped edge can be turned into a uniformly "dressed edge" that has a matte sheen. Begin sanding with a coarse grit paper and then use finer grits as the surface becomes smooth.

should, preferably, be carbide tipped, with teeth of uniform height. As with any power tool, the proper shop precautions should always be taken, including the use of protective glasses.

Drilling and Tapping

In drilling into acrylic, bits normally used in metalwork may be employed although drill bits are now available which are designed specifically for plastics (having a zero rake angle that prevents the bit from catching the plastic). When drilling or tapping, oil coolants are helpful in reducing friction. Mild soapy water also serves as an effective lubricant.

Scraping and Sanding

What is usually known as a "dressed edge" can be obtained on any acrylic surface by using a sharp woodworking scraper and *wet-or-dry* sandpaper. Scraping acts much as a plane does on wood, smoothing a normally coarse machined edge and removing deep scratches from the acrylic. After scraping, wet sanding from coarse to fine (a recommended progression would be using grits 150, then 220, then 400) completes the dressed edge so that it has a matte, translucent surface, unlike the highly glossy transparent finish achieved by polishing.

Solitaire (8″ x 8″). An ancient game interpreted in acrylic. Holes were made by drilling into the acrylic with a special bit made especially for that purpose. The edges were dressed, not polished.

Polishing and Buffing

If using a two-wheel electric buffer, a soft, fairly loose buff 10″ in diameter at 2,000 surface feet per minute will give the best results with acrylic. One buff should be used with white tripoli compound to remove any scratches. Only light pressure is required to clear the surface of shallow marks or to polish a dressed edge to clarity. Very deep scratches should be scraped and sanded first, before polishing. The second buffing wheel should be left clean, to be used in buffing off all remaining compound from the acrylic, delivering an even glossier sheen.

If using a faster, harder buff, use less pressure to avoid marring the surface with unwanted curves and "dents." Sometimes it is possible to slow down the buffing wheel by using different size wheels for the belt.

Etching and Carving

By placing transparent acrylic over a drawing, etching can be done so that it duplicates the original design much like

To turn a dressed edge to a shiny, clear, transparent finish, use a two-wheel buffer. Coat one wheel with white tripoli compound and buff the acrylic for a few seconds.

To remove the excess compound from the plastic, and to add a high gloss to the acrylic, run the piece across the clean buffing wheel.

tracing. Using an etching tool, such as an awl, a flexible shaft drill, or other sharp or pointed devices, scratching on acrylic can turn a sheet into a finished picture (through edge lighting) or it can be printed as an etching.

Using the same tools as when etching into acrylic, carving into plastic disturbs the polished surface, causing it to "leak" light at the carved marks, making the product quite effective as an edge-lighted panel.

Cementing

A strong, almost invisible bond can be made by cementing acrylic to other acrylic depending upon the type of cement used. Some of the best results can be obtained by using a solvent cement like ethylene dichloride or methylene dichloride. To bond, the solvent cement should be applied to both surfaces using a brush, hypodermic-type needle, or eyedropper. Cement can be introduced to the joints of the acrylic pieces to be bonded (with the parts already butted together) through capillary action. When cement is placed at the edge, it will spread over the butted surfaces under light pressure. The solvent will dry in three to ten minutes, be safe to machine in four hours, and will result in a powerful, cohesive bond.

An even stronger bond can be achieved by letting the solvent soak into the acrylic before applying light pressure. To bond acrylic to other materials, two-part (resin and hardener) epoxy is most effective.

Heating and Forming

Acrylic sheets become flexible, rubber-like, and soft between 240° and 340° F., at which time they can be formed into three-dimensional shapes. Once cool, the shape created while the acrylic was hot will retain the form unless reheated.

A regular kitchen oven, for heating large areas of acrylic, or a "strip heater," for bending of acrylic along straight lines

to create joints, is most often used by craftsmen to heat-form acrylics. Using asbestos or other protective gloves, hot pliable acrylic sheets can be handled and held in three-dimensional shapes until they cool.

When heating the acrylic in the oven (preferably on a piece of soft flannel cloth), one should be careful not to exceed the recommended 240°–340° F. temperature range, since this plastic will ignite at around 700° F. If left in the oven or over a strip heater for longer than a few minutes, the acrylic will begin to scorch, bubble, and burn, leaving a textured surface which, depending upon the intentions of the craftsman, may even be desired. At no time, though, should heating acrylic be left unattended.

To heat small areas of acrylic sheet, a propane or other torch may be used, although fear of bubbling and charring is ever present because of the high, uncalibrated temperatures at hand.

Hot acrylic can be made to hold a prescribed shape by using tension or C-clamps, by (gloved) hand-holding it, or by sagging it over other objects until cool. Cooling can be speeded by putting the form in cool water. The acrylic will not crack under the rapid temperature change.

Neck Ornament. Carolyn Kriegman. Clear acrylic. Courtesy: Carolyn Kriegman.

MAKING A STRIP HEATER FOR ACRYLIC

Materials and Equipment

½"-thick plywood, 6" x 42"
two ¼"-thick exterior plywood strips,
  both 2⅝" x 36"
heavy-duty aluminum foil
asbestos paper
stapler
hammer and nails
ground wire and screw
Briskeat RH-36 Heating Element (½"
  wide x 36" long, already wired with a
  2-prong plug). This unit is available
  at hardware stores or directly from
  Briscoe Manufacturing Company,
  Columbus, Ohio 43216

Procedures

By using a strip heater for acrylics, the
plastic can be simply and safely bent with
great ease and control. The strip heater
constructed here, though not a heavy-duty
industrial model, will stand much use, and
the craftsman will discover that it is an
asset for extending the application of acrylic
from two to three dimensions.

After cutting a piece of ½" plywood
6" x 42" and two ¼" plywood strips
2⅝" x 36", place the two wood strips
(number 2 in the accompanying illustration) on top of the ½" plywood base (1).
Arrange the two strips on the base so that
a ¾" channel is left between them. Nail
the strips to the plywood base.

Two pieces of heavy-duty aluminum foil
6" x 36" (3) must be cut and folded to fit
in the ¾" channel, which will house the
heating element. A ground wire should be
attached to the foil with a screw as illustrated (4). This wire must be long enough
to be attached to a common ground such
as a cover plate or outlet screw.

Once this step is completed, take two
pieces of asbestos paper (5) of the same
dimensions as the foil and fit both pieces

over the aluminum foil, maintaining the
¾" groove. The asbestos paper should be
scored before bending. Making certain that
the sheets are smooth, staple the asbestos
paper and aluminum foil to the plywood
strips along the outer edges.

The strip heating element (6) may
then be laid in the channel. This element
must be taut so that it will give straight
and even heating results. To insure this,
drive a centered nail into the base 1½"
from each end. Tie the strings found at the
ends of the heating element to these nails.

After attaching the ground wire to
a common ground and plugging the heater
into an 110-volt outlet, the strip heater
will quickly become hot enough for acrylic
forming.

This heater is especially designed so
that the temperature will never rise so high
that the acrylic will ignite, but when plastic
is placed over the element it should not be
left unattended because of the speed in
which the plastic will be readied for forming (several minutes).

The basic materials for making a strip heater
include asbestos paper (available at most hardware stores), heavy-duty aluminum foil, two
¼"-thick plywood strips 2⅝" x 36", a piece of
½"-thick plywood 6" x 42", and a Briskeat RH-
36 heating element. The element is available in
hardware stores as well.

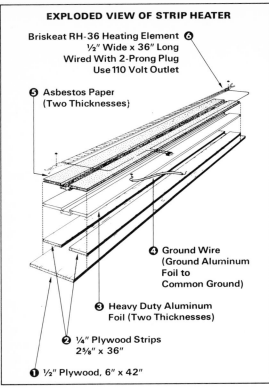

EXPLODED VIEW OF STRIP HEATER

Briskeat RH-36 Heating Element ⑥
½" Wide x 36" Long
Wired With 2-Prong Plug
Use 110 Volt Outlet

⑤ Asbestos Paper
(Two Thicknesses)

④ Ground Wire
(Ground Aluminum
Foil to
Common Ground)

③ Heavy Duty Aluminum
Foil (Two Thicknesses)

② ¼" Plywood Strips
2⅝" x 36"

① ½" Plywood, 6" x 42"

The unit is designed so that the element is recessed below the level on which the acrylic itself should rest because the plastic should at no time touch the element itself. Heat generated by the hot strip which is directed upward by the asbestos paper and aluminum foil rapidly softens the acrylic.

The protective masking paper on the acrylic must always be removed before heat-forming.

This diagram shows the relation of the strip heater's components. Courtesy: Rohm and Haas.

After nailing the plywood strips to the plywood base, leaving a ¾" channel in between, two layers of aluminum foil and a ground wire are placed on the wood, followed by two layers of asbestos paper.

Place the Briskeat RH-36 element in the ¾" channel and pull it taut by tying the strings found at each end of the unit around nails hammered into the plywood base. Your strip heater is now ready for use.

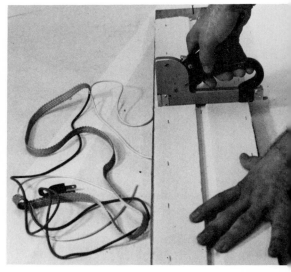

After smoothing out the aluminum foil and asbestos paper, making certain that the center channel is distinct, staple these sheets to the plywood.

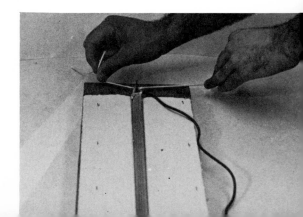

FREESTANDING PICTURE FRAME

Materials and Equipment

> acrylic sheet ⅛" thick. The acrylic should be as wide as your picture and three times as long (e.g. for a 5" x 7" picture, cut a piece of acrylic 7" wide by 15" long)
> strip heater
> ruler
> grease pencil
> buffing wheels and compound
> wood scraper
> sandpapers

Procedures

This freestanding acrylic picture frame, attractive for its simplicity and compatibility with any decor, is one of the easiest craft forms that can be made using a strip heater.

After determining the size of the acrylic sheet and cutting it, scrape, sand, and polish all four edges of this rectangular shape. Then peel off the protective masking paper from both sides of the acrylic and lightly mark the length of plastic in thirds using a ruler and grease pencil. (The marks can be rubbed off with a soft cloth after lining up the acrylic over the strip heater element.)

Lay the acrylic over the heating element with the grease pencil mark centered over the element. Once centered, this mark should be rubbed away before the acrylic heats up. Allow the plastic to heat thoroughly. You will know that it is soft enough to be bent when the acrylic changes its texture slightly or welts in the forming area.

Gently bend the plastic with the heated side out until it meets the longer part of the original acrylic strip. It is essential that the heated side of the acrylic be on the outside of the bend. The piece should be held flush against the other acrylic as snugly as possible to form a 180° angle at the joint. Pictures will be inserted between this acrylic sandwich later on, therefore the bend should be made fairly tight.

Hold the acrylic in this position until it cools. It is important to note that bending the acrylic before it is completely heated will result in internal fractures (crazing) along the bend.

When this acrylic bend has cooled, put the piece across the strip heater again, this time with the other grease pencil mark centered over the element. The shorter end of the acrylic "sandwich" should be facing up, since it is meant to become the back of the frame (*see* photograph).

After sufficiently heating this joint, bend it to an approximate 60° angle to the sandwich part, forming the stand for the picture holder. Hold this joint until it is cool. Use alcohol or a spray wax applied with a soft rag for cleaning.

All that remains now is to slide a photo between the sandwiched acrylic, and the simple, effective, freestanding picture frame is completed.

After cutting the acrylic to the proper dimensions, scrape, sand, and polish the edges. The polishing should be omitted if a dressed edge is desired. Mark the strip in thirds using a ruler and grease pencil.

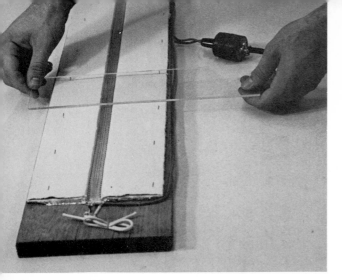

Use the grease pencil mark as a guide. Center this line on the middle of the element. Place the acrylic across the strip heater to soften the area to be bent. If your acrylic is very long it should be supported on the other end so that the part to be softened lies flat on top of the strip heater. After lining up the acrylic, the pencil mark should be carefully removed.

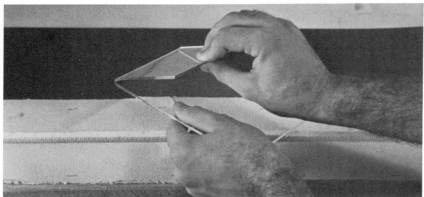

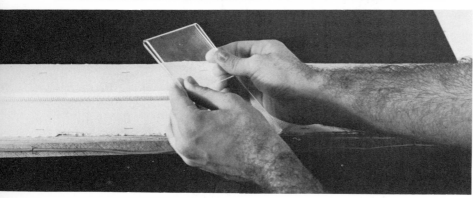

When the heated area begins to welt, it is ready for bending. Making certain that the heated area is on the outside of the bend, fold the plastic back onto itself, and hold it until cool.

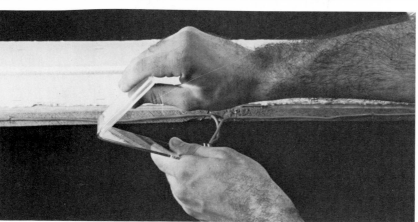

Follow the same procedure for the second bend. When the acrylic is hot enough, gently fold it back to form a 60° angle.

With only two heatings and bendings—one of 180° to form a sandwich of acrylic and the other of 60° to create a stand for the picture holder—a completed frame is ready for *any* picture.

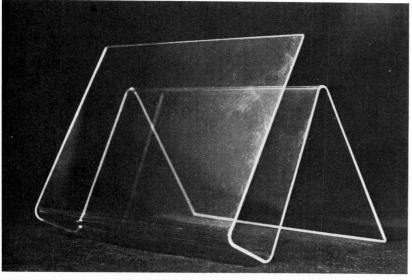

Acrylic with dressed edges was strip-heated and bent to form this book stand.

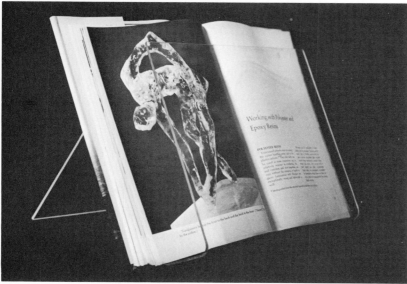

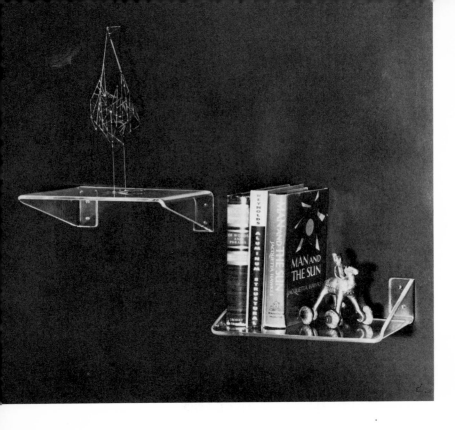

This versatile shelf, 8″ deep and 10″ wide, is designed in acrylic. Only two bends were necessary to form each support for the shelf. Courtesy: Neal Small Designs.

Elegant designs, like this table by Neal Small, may be realized simply by strip-heating and bending acrylic sheet. (30″ x 30″ x 16″.) Courtesy: Neal Small Designs.

ACRYLIC BOOK EASEL

Materials and Equipment

acrylic ⅛″ thick, 7″ x 10″
strip heater
ruler and pencil
band, jig-, saber, or handsaw
buffing wheels and compound
wood scraper
sandpapers

Procedures

A book easel of acrylic, handsome for its simple, functional, linear design, is made from one flat sheet of plastic 7″ x 10″.

Beginning with a piece of acrylic of these dimensions, scrape, sand, and polish the edges so that there will be no need to attempt to finish the edges after the strip heating and bending is completed.

Mark, on the protective masking paper, where the cuts are to be made for bending a back brace and a front lip. The 1″-wide back brace should be centered from the top of the rectangle, 3″ in from each side, extending in little less than halfway down the rectangle.

The 5″-wide lip—which will extend 1″ forward once bent—is made by cutting 1″ up from the bottom of the rectangle, 1″ in from each end.

A circular saw is not recommended for making these cuts since the circular blade leaves a slight portion of an arc in the plastic. A band saw, jigsaw, or saber saw will work best.

After the cuts have been made and the protective paper peeled off, the acrylic rectangle is ready for the transformation into the third dimension. While heating the back brace for bending, protect the rest of the back from being heated by placing double layers of asbestos paper over the parts of the heating element that are not to be used. Only the base of the brace should be heated, otherwise bending will become unnecessarily complicated and difficult. When properly heated, remove the acrylic from the strip heater and bend this back brace strip to the angle desired (about 115° from its original position). Hold it in this shape until it cools.

To bend the front lip, on which the book will rest, again use the two pieces of asbestos paper over the heating element so that only the span to be bent will receive the heat and not the 1″ wide legs. When heated, gently bend the lip perpendicular to the "face" of the book stand.

If desired, the cut edges may be dressed. Polishing is not recommended for these surfaces because these delicate and awkwardly positioned edges cannot be easily reached with a power-driven buffing wheel. Also, if the wheel catches the brace or lip at the wrong angle the easel may easily be broken.

The final product should be cleaned and polished with spray wax.

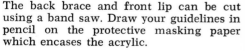

The back brace and front lip can be cut using a band saw. Draw your guidelines in pencil on the protective masking paper which encases the acrylic.

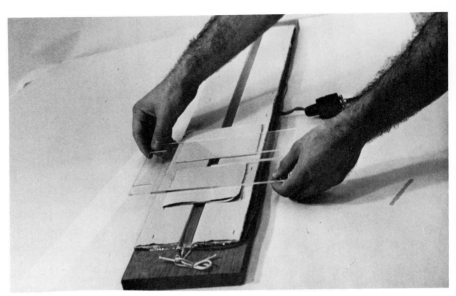

So that only the 1″ span of plastic at the base of the back brace is heated, mask the rest of the acrylic from the heat with doubled pieces of asbestos paper.

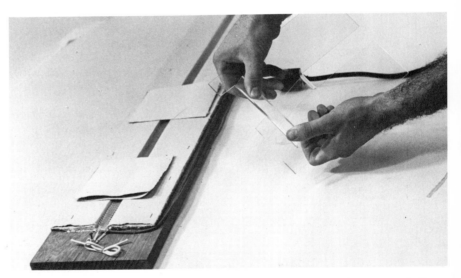

When properly heated, the back brace and front lip can be removed from the heat, bent into position, and held until cool.

The finished book easel may not help you "see through" substandard literature, but it will no doubt help keep it in place.

ACRYLIC COMPOTE DISHES

Materials and Equipment

> ¼"-thick acrylic blow-molded hemispheres (available in crafts stores and plastics outlets, sometimes with a flat lip which must be sawed off on a band saw)
> broil-oven with a metal top, or a stove burner with an aluminum cookie sheet on it
> weights
> flexible-shaft drill with a grinding bit
> masking tape
> water in a flat pan
> wood scraper
> sandpapers
> buffing wheels and compound

Procedures

To make an acrylic compote dish with a translucent design on its outer face, first flatten the bottom of a blow-molded acrylic hemisphere, cool it in water, and then use an electric grinding tool to create a decorative pattern.

Heat the metal oven top or an aluminum cookie sheet on a range to about 400° F. Then take a plastic hemisphere and press it onto the hot metal surface, applying even pressure with weights. In a few minutes, the bottom of the plastic half sphere will be flattened enough so that it will sit without rocking.

Remove it at this point from the metal and immediately dip it into a flat pan of water, quick-cooling it. The basic, unadorned dish is made.

To decorate the dish, stick masking tape onto the outer surface in the pattern of your design. Using a flexible-shaft drill with a grinding bit, lightly run the tool over the surfaces which you want to texture Since the bottom will receive scratches in everyday use, it should be pebbled with the grinding tool.

When grinding, the dish may be braced flat on a table or angled on a piece of foam for support.

Once the grinding is completed, remove the tape. The design may then be further refined using the grinding tool. But be careful not to slip onto the unprotected plastic.

To finish the rough-machined edge of the dish, use the wood scraper, sandpapers, and buffing wheels to polish the edge to a clear sheen.

The completed compote dish is absolutely nontoxic and therefore is safe for edibles. The acrylic dish may be hand washed or else put in the dishwasher with normal dinnerware.

After heating the top of an oven-broiler or an aluminum cookie sheet on top of a range burner to about 400° F., put the half-sphere shape on the metal.

Apply even and constant pressure to the dome, using weights. As the plastic is heated it will soften and the weights will press it down to create a flat, nonrocking bottom.

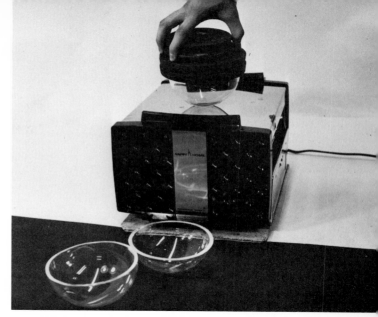

When flattened enough so that it will not be too tipsy to eat from, remove the acrylic from the hot metal.

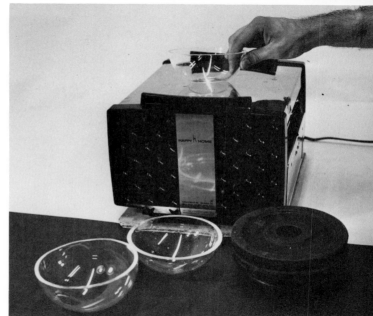

Immediately dip the flat bottom of the bowl into cool water. This will speed up the cooling process considerably.

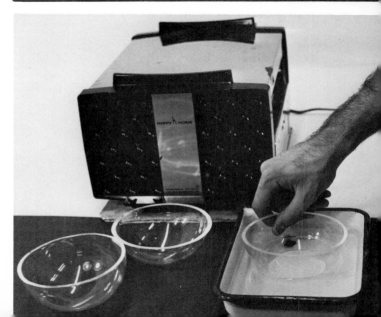

Once the bowls have cooled, designs may be etched into them. First make an outline of the pattern on the outside of each bowl with masking tape. The tape will protect the rest of the dish from being scratched during the etching process.

With a flexible-shaft drill and a grinding bit, lightly run the tool across the surfaces to be etched. This technique will create a translucent and textured surface. Here the bottom is being finished.

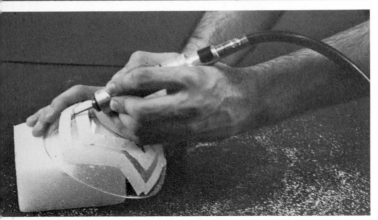

Between the masking-tape lines, grind the design, being careful not to allow the high-speed tool to slip. A foam block can serve as a brace for the form while grinding.

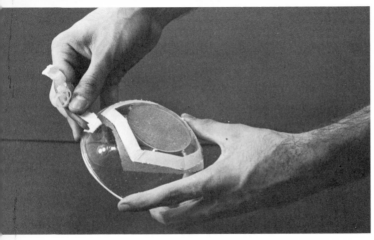

Remove the masking tape after the grinding is done. The grinding tool may now be used freehand to refine the design. To complete the compote dish, scrape, sand, and polish the machined edge.

The final compote dish is a safe, nontoxic form which may even be cleaned in the dishwasher.

HEAT-FORMING AN ACRYLIC CANDY DISH

Materials and Equipment

⅛"-thick acrylic, 8" x 8" square
construction paper (one sheet), 8" x 8"
scissors
ruler and pencil
buffing wheels and compound
wood scraper
sandpapers
band saw, jigsaw, or saber saw
broil-oven or kitchen oven
kitchen (insulated) gloves or mitts
spring clamps (of light tension)

Procedures

Heat-forming an acrylic candy dish from a plastic square demonstrates the flexibility of acrylic when its properties as a thermoplastic are fully utilized.

The actual forming process must be done quickly while the acrylic is sufficiently soft and flexible to be formed. It is wise to plan the final form in a paper model before even touching the plastic.

Taking an 8" x 8" square of construction paper (the bowl may be made in smaller or larger squares to the craftsman's own tastes and design), draw the diagonal lines in pencil. Measure along the diagonals the same distance from each corner. Changing this distance will vary the height of the dish. Cut the proper distance along each diagonal with scissors.

These diagonal slits will allow the square's halved corners to be drawn together so that they will overlap each other. Using a ruler, determine the distance which each corner should be pinched and overlapped. Tape them in this overlapped position.

The result is a completed paper model of the plastic dish. If these proportions are not to your liking, change them—it's never too late if you are still working with paper, but once the plastic has been cut there is really no turning back.

Now, taking an acrylic sheet of the same size, scrape, sand, and polish the edges. Mark the same cutting lines on the protective masking paper, and cut these lines on a band saw.

Remove the masking paper after making the cuts, and place the clear acrylic on a cookie sheet or on soft flannel cloth in an oven preheated to 300° F. Just be certain that it is not too close to any heating elements—contact or close proximity may cause the acrylic to bubble. Heat the form for several minutes until it appears to be flexible enough for bending. Wearing a glove, you may lift a corner of the acrylic while it is still in the oven to determine how flexible it has become before you remove it and start bending. The acrylic should be about as soft as a cooked pancake.

Unlike heating with the strip heater, all of the acrylic is equally hot, and you will need to wear protective gloves for the shaping process.

Take the square from the oven and, using a ruler to line up the amount of overlap (as with the paper form), bend the acrylic into position. To hold the dish in shape at all four corners, use spring clamps of fairly light tension. Quickly dip the dish in tepid water to set the plastic. You may then remove the clamps, since if they are allowed to remain they may mar the surface.

If the plastic cools before you complete the forming, or if the result is not perfect enough to suit you, simply put the form back into the oven. When it reheats, like all thermoplastics, it will flatten out to its original form. When it is hot enough to reattempt the forming process, follow the procedure again.

Clean the finished candy dish with a flannel cloth saturated in alcohol, and polish the form with spray wax. The product is a transparent candy dish which makes a sweet container for any suite.

Construct a scale model of your acrylic candy dish from construction paper. Begin with a piece 8″ square. Mark the diagonals, and cut in the same distance from each corner—in this case three inches.

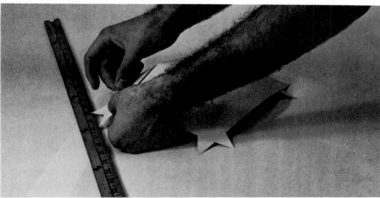

These slits will make it possible to overlap the halved corners. Use a ruler to determine the distance between tips when the paper has been overlapped. Tape or staple the paper in this shape.

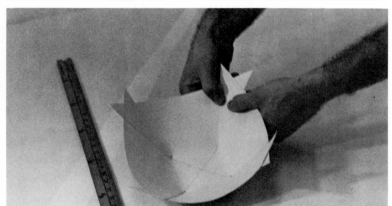

After the proportions have been adjusted to suit the craftsman's taste, the model is complete. Cut a square of acrylic the same size. Scrape, sand, and polish the edges, and cut along the diagonals.

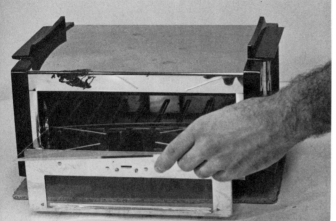

Place the piece of acrylic in an oven preheated to 300°F. It is advisable to rest the plastic on an aluminum cookie sheet or on a piece of flannel.

Use protective gloves to remove the acrylic from the oven when it has softened to the consistency of a cooked pancake. Overlap the corners, and use a ruler to make the distance between points uniform.

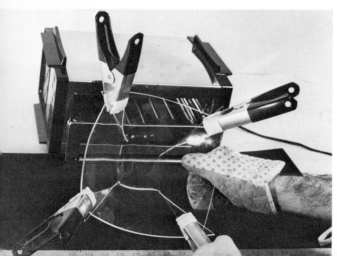

Once aligned so that each corner overlaps the proper distance, use spring clamps with light tension to hold the corners in place.

The product is a candy dish to satisfy any craftsman's sweet tooth.

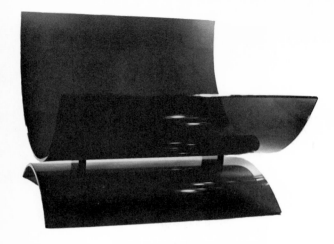

Magazine Rack. Stan Cook, Acrylic was heat-formed and joined with metal bolts to make this magazine rack.

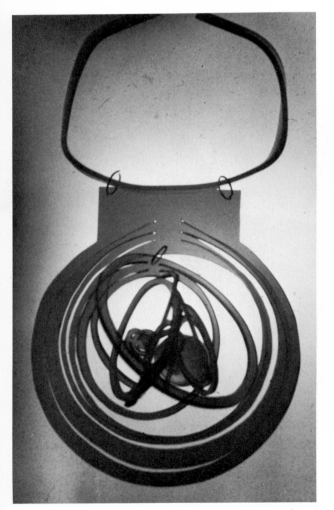

Circle Necklace. Carolyn Kriegman. Colored acrylic was cut and heat-formed to shape. Courtesy: Carolyn Kriegman.

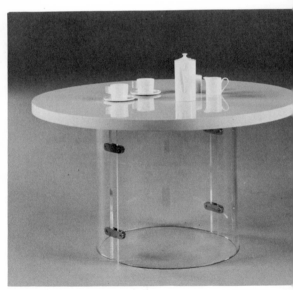

Game Table. Milo Baughman. Heat-formed acrylic with a lacquered top. Courtesy: New Concept.

Circle Necklace. Carolyn Kriegman. Red acrylic. Courtesy Carolyn Kriegman.

Impasto Bottles. Jay and Lee Newman. Vinyl-acrylic modeling paste over glass.

Fractured Image (16″ x 16″). Jay Newman. Mirrored acrylic on Styrofoam.

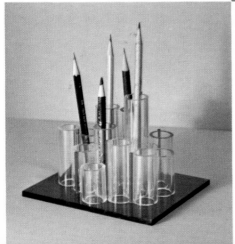

Pencil Holder. Lee Newman. Extruded acrylic rods and tubes on a solid acrylic base.

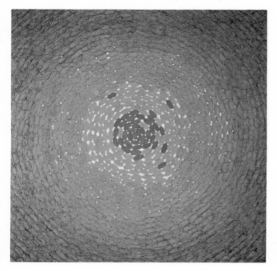

Untitled #2. Phyllis Stevens. Hundreds of individual pieces of colored acrylic adhered to a clear acrylic base.

Cityscape. Jay and Lee Newman. Cast polyester resin tiles on acrylic.

Room Divider. Jay and Lee Newman. Fiberglass-reinforced polyester resin.

PENCIL HOLDER OF EXTRUDED RODS AND TUBES

Materials and Equipment

⅜″-thick acrylic sheet 6″ x 5″
extruded acrylic tubes 1/16″ and ⅛″ thick walls
1/16″ thick extruded acrylic rods in several colors
solvent cement (methylene dichloride or ethylene dichloride)
a fine brush or hypodermic-type needle to apply cement
circular, saber, jig-, band, or handsaw
buffing wheels and compound
wood scraper
sandpapers

Procedures

A unique, utilitarian pencil holder is created through a simple process of gluing different lengths of extruded acrylic tubes and rods to an acrylic sheet base.

Cut lengths of acrylic tubes ranging from 1″ to 4″. Scrape and sand flat one end of each tube, and polish the other end. (The polished end will face upward when glued to the acrylic sheet, and the more porous, sanded surface will be bonded to the acrylic base.)

Arrange the cut tubes (about sixteen of them) in any design so that they will fit on the 5″ x 6″ acrylic slab after the edges of the slab have been polished.

You are now ready to begin gluing. To adhere a tube to the base, simply place it where you want it to be glued and with a brush or hypodermic-type needle, touch a drop or two of solvent cement to the edge of the tube where its base meets the flat acrylic. Though capillary action, the cement will spread (with little or no pressure) over most of the surface to be bonded. To further secure the bond, touch another drop or two of solvent around the joint again. Place each tube on the sheet in this manner.

Since these tubes are clear, you may want to add some accenting color in the form of thin acrylic extruded rods. Cut these rods to desired heights, polish one end of each, and adhere them to the acrylic tubes by holding the rod against the tube and putting one or two drops of cement at the uppermost point of contact. The solvent will run down the length of the joint, effecting complete bonding. Distribute your colored rods at different points.

The solvent cement is quick drying (about three to eight minutes), therefore the pencil holder will be completed almost as soon as the last rod is adhered. Clean the piece with spray wax on a clean flannel cloth.

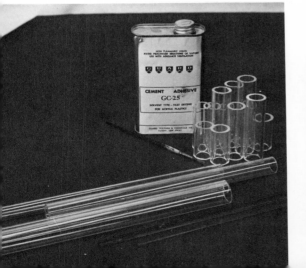

Extruded acrylic tubes and rods, a piece of colored acrylic ⅜″ x 5″ x 6″, solvent cement (methylene or ethylene dichloride), and a brush to apply the cement are the basic materials needed to create this pencil holder.

After laying out your design for the different heights of tube, sand and polish one end of each piece. Glue the unpolished end to the acrylic sheet. Simply touch a drop or two of cement to the edge of the tube that butts against the base.

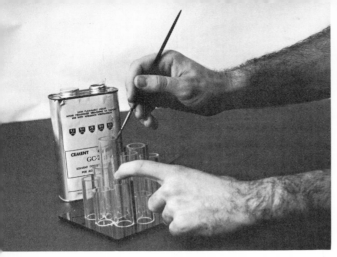

To add bits of color all around the pencil holder, cut lengths of thin extruded colored rods, press them against the tubes and touch the tip of your cement brush to the top of the thin rods. The glue will race down the rod to the base, effecting a complete bond along the entire length of rod and tube.

The result, which has a lavender base, clear tubes with red and lavender rods, is a pencil holder so decorative that . . .

. . . it's almost a pity to use it for pencils.

Sue Irion models jewelry made with commercially manufactured acrylic balls, rings, and blocks.

A MIRROR BOX

Materials and Equipment

mirrored acrylic
solvent cement (methylene dichloride
or ethylene dichloride)
angle clamps
masking tape
a fine brush
rubber cement (liquid and spray)
flocking
alcohol and soft flannel cloth
buffing wheels and compound
wood scraper
sandpapers
spring clamps

Procedures

Acrylic is manufactured in a variety of textures, finishes, and colors. One attractive finish is the mirrored surface. Actually, this acrylic is made the same way as glass mirrors. A clear sheet of acrylic is coated on the back with a special silver paint that reflects through the front of the plastic.

Because the back is covered with this reflective material, the craftsman must be more careful when working with mirrored acrylic. If the backing is scratched, your reflections will be marred—every nick will show. There are special techniques for using the material, however, and there are also easy ways of protecting this backing.

To make a mirrored acrylic box, cut four pieces to make the basic frame. The four pieces will become the sides of your box. Their ends should be beveled at 45° angles so that they will fit together. Since acrylic cannot be glued to the back of the mirror, the mirror coating must be removed or avoided whenever possible.

Polish only one side of each piece that will become the top of the box. When polishing mirrored plastic, be careful not to buff away the mirror coat with your buffing wheels. The coated surface should always face down—away from the buffer. Then, using the angle clamps set for a 90° angle, glue these four sides together with solvent cement. Allow the completed frame to set while you prepare the bottom of your box.

Cut a piece of mirrored acrylic the exact size of the bottom. Mask everything except for an area around each edge as wide as the thickness of your mirrored acrylic. Use masking tape for this process. With the tape as a guide, sand off the gray mirror coating from the edges of the bottom piece.

Use a coarse sandpaper for this operation, and stop sanding as soon as you reach clear acrylic. This way the frame may be glued to the acrylic rather than the mirrored coating (which could possibly delaminate later).

Set the frame in place over the box's bottom piece and run solvent cement on the inside of the box along all four sides. Apply light pressure—no more than a pound—and allow the weight to remain on the box only for a few minutes.

To make a top for your box, cut another piece of mirrored acrylic as large as the piece for the bottom. And cut another piece of clear or mirrored acrylic that will just fit into the frame.

Apply a heavy layer of rubber cement to the coated area of the top piece and the second smaller piece that exactly fits the box's opening. Then clamp the smaller piece of acrylic to the top. Both coated surfaces should be face to face with a layer of rubber cement in between.

Rubber cement will bind these two surfaces. Use spring clamps to hold the two pieces together and use a layer of flannel to keep the clamps from marring the surface of either piece. After the cement has been allowed to dry overnight, rub away any excess that the clamps may have squeezed out, and cover the box. You may want to finish the inside of the box with flocking, a soft powder of synthetic fiber which, when applied with glue, adheres to create a velvet-like matte finish.

Because mirror reflects its surroundings, this box, you will find, enhances any decor in an acrylic tradition of good design.

The side edges of your mirrored acrylic should be beveled to a 45° angle where they are to be joined, so that there will be a good bond between the sides. Acrylic does not bond satisfactorily to the mirror coating.

Use the angle supports to hold the box's sides while you glue the frame together. The corners should fit together perfectly at right angles.

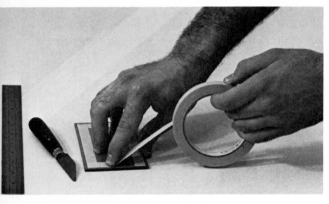

The bottom piece should be masked around the edge with masking tape. An area as wide as the edge thickness of your acrylic should be sanded free of mirror coating. This way acrylic will meet acrylic and a good bond will be possible.

Set the frame on top of the bottom piece and apply the solvent cement along each side of the inside edge.

90

Apply a one-pound weight after gluing. The weight should be allowed to remain on for only a few minutes.

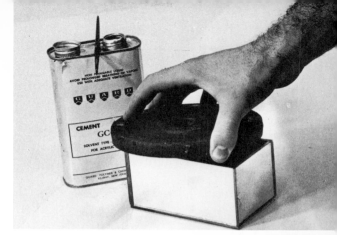

To make a top for the box use rubber cement to bond two pieces of mirrored acrylic. The bottom piece should be smaller so that when the top is placed on the box it will fit into the opening of the box and hold the mirror top in place. Use clamps to hold these pieces together overnight; a piece of flannel will protect the mirror's surfaces from being scratched by the clamps' jaws.

To protect the inside of your box, which is the mirror backing, from being scratched, use flocking. Spray on a coating of rubber cement.

Pour in some flocking over the wet cement. Once the flock has adhered to the rubber cement, pour out the excess and let the rubber cement dry. Repeat this process several times until the desired thickness of flocking is obtained.

The finished box will reflect your excellent craftsmanship.

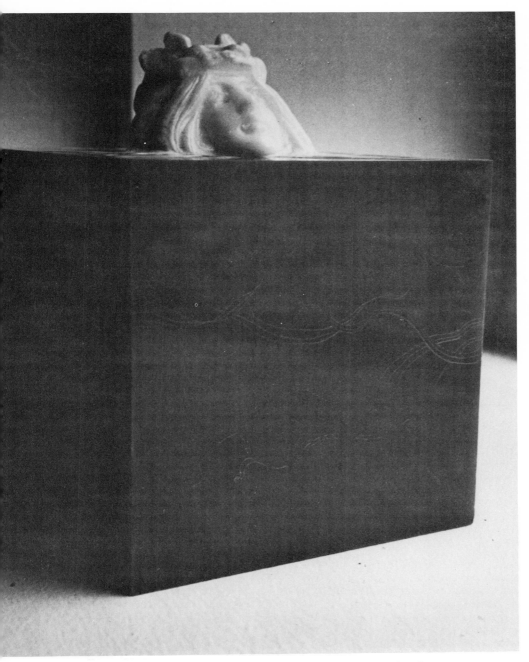

Medusa Box. Phillip Borden. A box of etched acrylic. The Medusa head is cast polyester resin.

HEXAGONAL CANDLE SHADE

Materials and Equipment

Smoked-color acrylic ⅛" thick
clear acrylic ⅜" thick
solvent cement (methylene dichloride
   or ethylene dichloride)
a fine brush or hypodermic-type needle
alcohol and a soft flannel rag
2 angle clamps
circular or handsaw that can miter 30°
   angles
electric router ⅛" bit set to cut ⅛"
   deep (optional)
buffing wheels and compound
scraper
sandpapers

Cut six pieces of ⅛"-thick, smoked acrylic 3¾" x 12" from a larger sheet. Use a circular, radial-arm or saber saw which will cut a 30° angle at the 12" edges. A hand miter box and saw may also be used to miter-cut the 12" edges. Polish the ends of each piece but not the beveled edges.

Procedures

To construct an enclosure for a candle in a hexagonal shape a bit more machining will be necessary.

Using a circular saw which can be adjusted to cut at a 30° angle—or using a miter box and saw—angle-cut six pieces 3¾" x 12" from the smoked-acrylic sheet.

Polish only the shorter edges of the six pieces which will become the top and bottom of the candle holder. The mitered edges which will be glued should remain rough.

Peel back the protective masking paper and butt two of the sheets with their 30° mitered edges against each other in an angle clamp also set for 30°. Glue the plastic along this joint with solvent cement using a fine brush or injection needle. Let the bonded acrylic set for a few minutes.

Continue to cement these pieces of smoked-acrylic together until all six are joined into an hexagon.

To make a clear acrylic base for the candle to rest on, take a ⅜"-thick piece of acrylic and trace the exact outline of the base of the hexagon on the protective paper covering the clear plastic.

Cut out this traced shape on a saw that will deliver a precise, straight cut—if

available, a circular saw is the best bet. Scrape, sand, and then polish the six edges of this clear piece.

So that the smoked-acrylic hexagon will fit onto the clear base without sliding, you may want to use a router which has a ⅛" or ³⁄₁₆" router bit to rout a small channel all around the edges of the clear base.

If this outer edge-channel is made ⅛" deep and ⅛" wide, then it will leave ½" of clear polished acrylic base showing, and will also leave just enough room for the ⅛"-thick smoked-acrylic hexagon walls to fit flush over this base.

An alternative solution that avoids the use of a router is to cut another smaller piece of acrylic for the base and glue it with solvent cement using the same principle as in making the cover for the mirror box project.

Do not cement the finished base to the hexagon walls, because cleaning, dusting, and candle changing will be facilitated if the parts just fit together.

Peel off all of the remaining protective masking paper. Clean the two parts of this holder with alcohol on a soft flannel cloth. All that remains is to place a lighted candle inside the hexagon of acrylic.

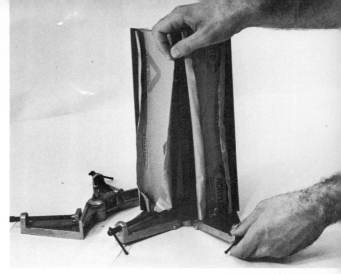

Peel back the protective masking paper from the longer sides of each piece of smoked acrylic. These mitered edges are to be cemented together.

Clamp two of the pieces in one angle clamp so that the edges tightly butt against one another at the proper angle at that end.

Clamp on another angle clamp at the other end so that the entire edge butts exactly.

Apply solvent cement along the braced joint, and allow the cement bond to set for several minutes. Follow the same procedure for bonding every other side to the form. If desired, you may first cement three pairs of sides and then bond the three cemented pairs together to form the hexagon.

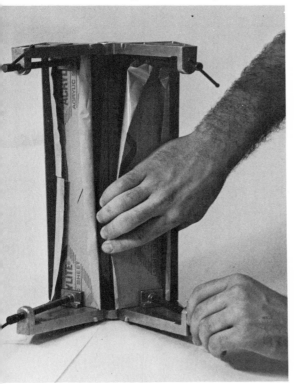

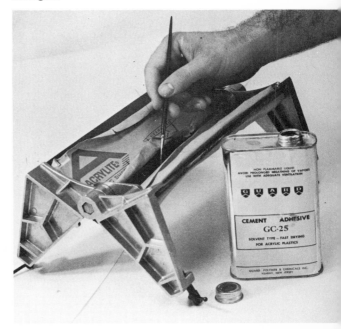

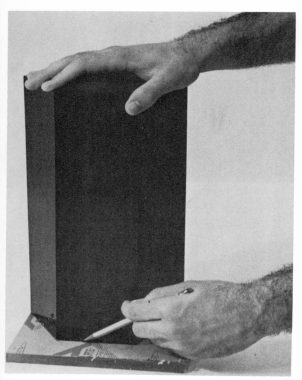

On a piece of ⅜″-thick clear acrylic, trace the outline of the base of the hexagon. Cut out the traced piece for the base and polish all six edges.

After cutting and polishing this shape, rout a ⅛″-deep, ⅛″-wide channel along the outer edges of the clear acrylic base. This will give the smoked-acrylic hexagon sleeve an edge to sit on. To avoid routing the acrylic base, you may take a piece of clear acrylic sheet cut slightly smaller than the base hexagon and cement it to the base as shown in the mirrored box project, using solvent cement.

Clean the project with alcohol on a soft flannel cloth, spray-wax it, strike a light, and let a candle shine on brightly from within.

TRANSLUCENT CANDLE CENTERPIECE

Materials and Equipment

$\frac{1}{8}$"-thick smoked-color acrylic, 16 pieces 5" x 3", 4 pieces 3" x 3"

$\frac{1}{8}$"-thick clear acrylic, 5 pieces 2$\frac{3}{4}$" x 2$\frac{3}{4}$"

Solvent cement (methylene dichloride or ethylene dichloride)

a fine brush or hypodermic-type needle

angle clamps or some other brace and clamps to hold a 90° angle

alcohol and flannel cloth

buffing wheels and compound

wood scraper

sandpapers

Procedures

The smoked-plastic candle centerpiece is constructed from five boxlike units, four of them 5" x 3" x 3" and a fifth box 3" x 3" x 3". A clear "shelf" of $\frac{1}{8}$" thick acrylic, slightly smaller than each side, is glued in each unit two inches from the bottom. A glass candle mount using a votive candle will rest on this support.

To make one of the smoked-acrylic boxes, start with four 5" x 3" pieces of plastic. Scrape, sand, and polish three sides, leaving one 5" edge rough. The unpolished edge will be butted against another piece of acrylic and cemented; it will not show.

Remove the protective masking paper from all four pieces and clean them thoroughly with a piece of flannel saturated with alcohol. To guarantee a 90° angle when cementing, a pair of angle clamps may be used. These are available at most hardware stores. You may also use two surfaces which are already at right angles to each other as an aid in cementing. The acrylic pieces may be held in place with tension clamps while they are being glued.

If using an angle clamp, fit two of the 5" x 3" pieces into the clamps with one of the unpolished edges butting flush against the acrylic. If using some other 90° brace,

clamp the acrylic sheets to the brace using the clamps (again making certain the unpolished edge butts flush against the face of the other piece).

With a brush or a hypodermic-type needle, apply the solvent cement along the crack. Make certain that enough cement has been put between the two surfaces to assure a solid bond by running the brush or needle over the crack several times. Allow the cement to set undisturbed for at least three or four minutes.

Follow this same procedure for forming right angles with the other two pieces of 5" x 3" acrylic. Let this set while you proceed to the next step. Fit one square of clear acrylic into a cemented right angle, and glue it two inches from the bottom of the smoked unit. Hold it in place with one hand and use solvent cement along the two touching edges to adhere it to the smoked plastic. It is essential that this be a strong bond, since it must support the weight of the candle and its container.

Allow this to set for several minutes. Then the other two units of smoked acrylic may be fitted together forming a box. The unpolished edge on each will be butted against an acrylic surface. Cement this unit together. But be certain that the faces are flush before you glue them.

Stand the unit up and glue the two unattached edges of the inside shelf to the frame.

The five completed boxes can function separately, or they may be joined to create a single centerpiece made from five components.

To accomplish this, lay two of the 5" x 3" x 3" boxes flat on their sides (making certain that the clear acrylic piece is placed 2" from the bottom of each). Set the 3" x 3" x 3" box between the other two and cement the three together as illustrated. The smaller box will sit higher in the finished centerpiece and the surrounding boxes lower. Similarly, cement the other two boxes to

the small center box. Allow all joints to set, and stand the finished centerpiece upright.

Put five votive candles in 3″-deep glasses, and set them on the clear acrylic shelves in each box.

Having completed a glowing example of plastics craftsmanship, you will find that your control over the acrylic medium is waxing.

The materials needed to create a candle centerpiece include smoke-colored acrylic, clear acrylic, solvent cement, and alcohol for cleaning. The acrylic should be 1/8″ thick.

After polishing three edges, leaving one 5″ edge rough, peel off the protective masking paper and clean the pieces with alcohol on a soft flannel cloth.

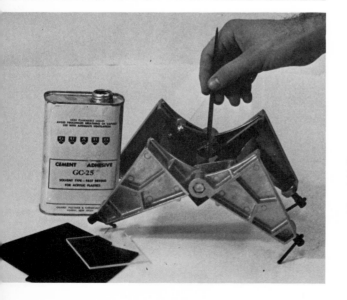

Place two pieces of smoked acrylic, each 5″ x 3″, in miter clamps with one of the unpolished edges flush against the other acrylic face. Run a brush with solvent cement along the joint. Allow the cement to seep into the joint by capillary action. Follow this procedure for two more pieces of acrylic.

If miter clamps are not available, you may use some other 90° angle contrivance as a brace for the two acrylic pieces which must be joined. Attach them temporarily to a brace with tension clamps.

Apply cement along the joint.

Cement a piece of clear acrylic just shy of 3″ square to the newly bonded right angle of smoked acrylic. These pieces should be consistently glued 2″ from one end.

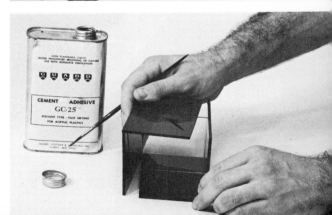

After all the bonds have had time to dry, line up the two right angles of smoked acrylic so that they form a box. No unpolished edges should be showing, since they will be butted against polished surfaces.

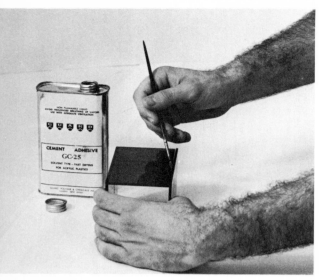

Apply cement at these butted joints. Also glue the clear acrylic, which becomes a shelf inside the box, to the other two sides.

To make the five-component centerpiece, make four more boxes. One of them should be made shorter, 3″ x 3″ x 3″, with the clear acrylic shelf at its base. Connect these forms by temporarily supporting the smaller box between two longer boxes and gluing them as shown. Similarly, cement the remaining two longer boxes to the shorter one.

The result is one candle holder. A votive candle in a small glass should be placed on the clear shelf.

The smaller box will stand above the surrounding 5″ x 3″ x 3″ forms, creating a handsome smoked-acrylic candle centerpiece.

These light fixtures employ smoked and opaque white acrylics. Courtesy: Richard Morgenthau Co., Inc.

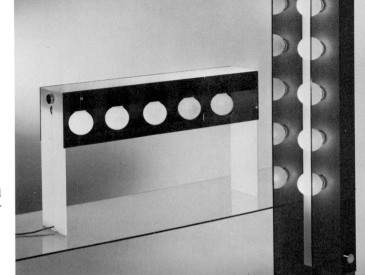

A MIRRORED PANEL

Materials and Equipment

mirrored acrylic
Styrofoam
a sheet of ¼″-thick plywood
rubber cement
a band, jig-, saber, or circular saw

Procedures

Mirrored acrylic can help to create spectacular designs. It has all the advantages of glass mirror with other advantages of its own. Acrylic mirror will not break easily, and it is easily cut into intricate shapes.

To make a base to work on, cement strips of Styrofoam to a plywood board. First apply rubber cement to the plywood and then to the Styrofoam and let them dry until the cement is tacky. Then press on the Styrofoam. The bond should be a permanent one.

Begin cutting your shapes from a sheet of mirrored acrylic. Press the edges of your pieces into the Styrofoam so that they fit securely. You may prop up the pieces of mirror by adding Styrofoam scraps to the Styrofoam base so that the acrylic will project from the surface. When the acrylic has been properly positioned, cement the mirrored pieces to the Styrofoam with rubber cement.

You may create any pattern that you wish because mirrored acrylic may be cut to any shape and size needed.

The final mirror panel will be a reflection of your creativity.

Make a base for your mirrored acrylic panel by cementing strips of Styrofoam to a ¼″-thick plywood board. Press your cut pieces of mirrored acrylic into the Styrofoam to assure a secure fit. A rubber mallet may be used to hammer the acrylic into the foam.

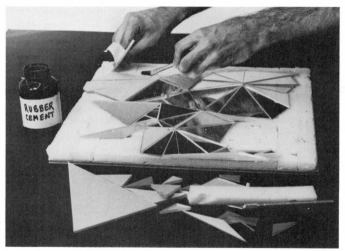

Use rubber cement to glue the acrylic to the plastic foam.
Then peel off the protective paper.

Fractured Image (16″ x 16″). This piece will provide a fractured reflection from any angle.

CANDLESTAND

Materials and Equipment

> several strips of ⅛″-thick acrylic 3″ wide
> construction paper for pattern making
> solvent cement for acrylics (methylene dichloride or ethylene dichloride)
> a fine brush or hypodermic-type needle
> glass votive-size candle holders
> buffing wheels and compound
> wood scraper
> sandpapers
> band, jig-, or saber saw

Procedures

This project relies on acrylic's easy machinability for its success.

First, construct a pattern from construction paper. Cut strips of paper 3″ wide in five different heights from 7″ to 11″. You will need two pieces of each height.

Slit each paper piece halfway down its center and slide the pairs together so that the sides are perpendicular, forming right angles. These five units should stand se-

curely. They are the basic forms for your candle holders.

Once you are satisfied with the proportions of these units, cut your strips of acrylic to the same sizes. Polish the edges of the acrylic pieces.

In addition, you must also cut out an area at the top of each piece of acrylic to accommodate your glass candle holder. Determine the diameter of the glass candle holder form and trace this shape onto the acrylic. Then cut the acrylic so that the holder can later be inserted.

Measuring from the bottom of this cutout, make a ⅛″-wide slit in each strip of acrylic halfway down its center—but watch out! In each pair you must slit one piece from the top and the other from the bottom. That way they will fit together and the perpendicular cutouts at the top will hold your candle mount securely.

To form a base for each candlestand, cut one 3″-square piece of acrylic for each holder. Fit the pairs together and glue them to their bases with a solvent cement.

Arrange the candlestands in any order and with the addition of glass candle mounts this crystal-clear candelabra is ready to glow.

Using 3″-wide strips of construction paper to make your pattern, cut them to different heights and slit the paper halfway down the center of each strip.

The strips will fit together perpendicularly.

Then cut acrylic to the same sizes as your paper models, and polish the edges. Since the acrylic must also accommodate candle mounts, a cross section must be cut out of each piece. Then slit one of each pair halfway down from the top and the other member of the pair halfway up from the bottom. You will need to make each slit ⅛" wide to accommodate its partner.

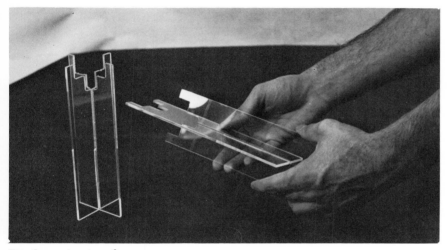

Fit the pairs together.

Glue each set to a 3"-square base.

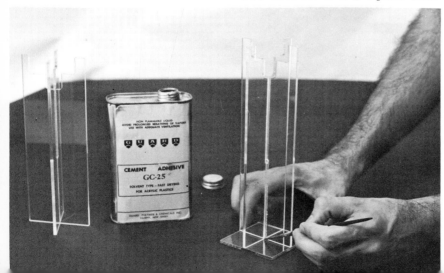

These elegant candle holders will add sparkle to any room.

City Lights. Opaque white-acrylic cylinders and extruded acrylic rods. Courtesy: Milo Baughman.

Bead Screen (7′ high). Gary L. Smith. Acrylic rods and beads. After a frame was constructed of clear-acrylic square rods, acrylic beads were strung and attached to holes that were drilled into the frame. Courtesy: Gary L. Smith.

Jane Bearman has placed her drawing underneath the transparent plastic as a guide. An old dental tool is used to scratch into the acrylic.

After scribing, force the etching ink into all the furrows with your thumb. It is important that the ink is firmly and completely pressed into all the scratches.

ACRYLIC ETCHING

Materials and Equipment

> ¼"-thick acrylic sheet
> etching press or an old clothes wringer press
> oil etching ink
> scribing tools (dental tools, awls, knives, etc.)
> padding (felt, foam rubber, or old newspaper)
> block printing or etching paper
> kitchen oven and aluminum cookie sheet

Procedures

Thin sheets of acrylic are easily scratched and carved with burins, awls, dental tools, knives, and other pointed and sharp objects. This quality makes them exceptionally adaptable to "etching." Etching is the process of scratching shallow furrows in a material. In acrylic, etching acid is not used.

Instead of using copper or zinc plates that are common to traditional etching operations, the acrylic is scratched to create small furrows. These scratches are meant to catch the ink and transfer it to paper in the printing process.

In at least one sense, acrylic has a great advantage over the metal plates. It may be scribed with a variety of sharp tools. Acid, which is used on the metals in etchings, is not used. Secondly, since acrylic is clear, drawings may be taped underneath and used as guides.

After sketching your design—it can be anything human, animal, natural, or abstract—tape it underneath your piece of clear acrylic. Transfer the lines to the acrylic by scratching the surface with your tools using enough pressure to create a distinct line. (Anything with a fine sharp tip will work. Old dental tools make excellent scratches.)

Once the transferral is complete the

plate is ready to be inked. Using oil etching ink, cover the entire scratched area of the acrylic with ink. Use your thumb to force ink into all the furrows. Every scratch must be filled with ink.

Then wipe the plate clean allowing the ink to remain only in the scribed channels. A cardboard squeegee may be used to get most of the ink off, then wipe the acrylic with a clean cloth and, finally, use the heel of your hand to get it cleanest. Do not worry: turpentine will remove the ink from your skin, just be careful not to get it on your clothes.

The plate should now be heated for five minutes on a cookie sheet in an oven preheated to 200° F.

While the plate is heating, ready your printing apparatus. Adjust your press to accept the acrylic plate and prepare the padding. Felt blankets, foam rubber, or old newspaper may be used. The paper to receive the print should be dampened and allowed to dry briefly between sheets of newsprint. Block printing or etching paper will work well.

When the plate is hot, remove it from the oven. Lay the dampened paper over the acrylic and lay several layers of padding over the paper. Quickly place it in the press and draw it through about 1″ and increase the pressure greatly, then roll the plate through the press with a continuous motion.

When the plate, paper, and padding emerge on the other side, the ink will have been transferred to the paper and your print will have a crisp, sharp line. About a hundred prints should be possible with this method, although the more heating the acrylic gets, the shorter the life of the plate.

Clean the acrylic with turpentine after each use. An old toothbush may be used to clean the ink out of the furrows.

The clean plate should not be hidden away while your print is exhibited. When mounted in a light box, the scratched acrylic takes on a beauty all its own.

Remove excess ink from the surface with a cloth. For the final cleaning use the heel of your hand. Care should be taken not to remove any ink from the grooves. Any ink remaining on the surface will show up on your print.

After heating the plate in an oven preheated to 200° F. for five minutes, lay on the dampened paper and several layers of padding. Run the whole sandwich through your press. An etching press will work excellently, but more common devices, such as the old washing machine wringer used here, will also give expert results.

Nude (7″ x 12″). Jane Bearman. An acrylic plate scratched with dental tools produced this print.

Reclining Figure (9″ x 14″). Jane Bearman. This print was made from an acrylic plate. Ink was allowed to remain on the plate to shade the form.

Reclining Figure (9″ x 14″). Jane Bearman. This plate has been cleaned with turpentine and mounted in a light box. When light is piped through the acrylic from one unpolished end all the scratches illuminate as in this line drawing of light.

Zodiac (6″ x 10″). Phillip Borden. Etched acrylic in a light box.

MAKING AN ACRYLIC DOME LAMP

Materials and Equipment

a blow-molded acrylic dome
liquid latex for masking
a grease pencil
acrylic or lacquer spray paint
a circle of ½″ plywood
a light-bulb socket, low-watt bulb, electrical cord, and plug

Procedures

The acrylic dome used here was blow-molded commercially, but clear acrylic domes can be made by blow-molding acrylic if you have the proper setup.

An acrylic sheet is placed in a frame and heated in an oven. When the plastic has been softened, it is removed and the frame is placed between two sheets of wood. The top sheet has a hole cut in the outline of the dome desired and the bottom piece has a small opening through which air pressure is introduced. Air pressure forces the softened plastic to stretch up into a dome shape.

Acrylic domes are available from manufacturers of electrical signs, plastic fabricators, and skylight manufacturers. The craftsman may choose from a number of ready-made sizes or he may specify the dimensions and have a dome custom blow-molded.

Handsome lamps may be created by painting the inside surface of acrylic domes with opaque and translucent paints. In order to paint on a design the use of rubber masking is recommended.

First draw your pattern on the outside of the dome with a grease pencil. The lines may be rubbed away later. Follow these guides, and paint the areas that you will want to mask from the first coat of paint on the inside of the dome. Liquid latex will work very well. It may be painted on with a brush. There are other commercial products available for this purpose as well. Test your masking material first to make certain that it will peel away from the acrylic and not etch into the surface.

When the mask is dry, spray several coats of a dark acrylic or lacquer paint. Two color combinations using a dark and a light color work best with this technique. By holding the dome up to the light and looking at the convex surface you can see whether the inside surface is fully coated. If not, spray a little more paint, each time spraying a very thin coat. It is much better to spray on several thin coats and let each one dry than to spray on a thick coat and have the paint run. Make certain that the area is well ventilated.

After the paint has completely dried, the masking rubber may be pulled away.

The inside surface of the dome should then be sprayed with an opaque white acrylic paint. This will diffuse the light, giving the dome lamp a special gleam.

Mount your dome over a piece of plywood with a 20-watt light bulb in the center. As you admire your lamp with pride, both you and your lamp will appear to glow.

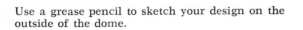
Use a grease pencil to sketch your design on the outside of the dome.

Mask the areas that you do not want painted with liquid latex or any other commercial masking material for acrylic.

When the mask has dried, spray on your first acrylic or lacquer color. Apply thin coats, and allow each coat to dry for a few minutes before applying the next. If the paint is sprayed on too thickly it will run.

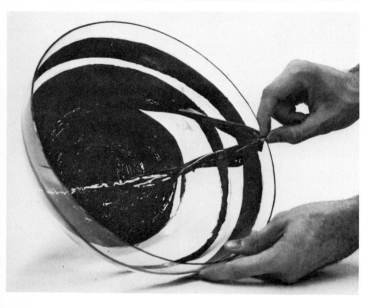

Pull off the masking after the paint has dried, and spray several coats of white opaque acrylic paint on the inside surface. This coating will diffuse the light.

A plywood base will support the dome, and a 20-watt bulb will supply the illumination.

The completed lamp measures 12″ in diameter and 7″ in height.

SILK-SCREENING ON ACRYLIC SHEETS

Materials and Equipment

a silk-screening frame on which to mount the screen hinged to plywood base (available in standard sizes or may be custom built)

silk or polyester fabric (polyester is preferred)

medium-hard rubber squeegee

stapler or thumbtacks

packing tape

cardboard and masking tape

acrylic sheets

litho crayon

shellac

LePage's Original Glue #132, water, vinegar, and optional glycerin

brush

turpentine

waxed paper

extra wood boards to prop up frame

NAZ-DAR Screen Process Color (ink)

NAZ-DAR Screen Process Color Clear Gloss

lacquer thinner

old newspaper

soft cloth rags

Procedures

Serigraphy, a print-making process, can be applied in silk-screening acrylic sheets readily. Basically, the process involves blocking out parts of the silk (or polyester fabric) using a tusche (usually glue or litho crayon). The ink, which is spread over the screen with a squeegee, only passes through the untreated parts of the screen, yielding a print on the acrylic beneath.

Silk-screening requires no elaborate presses to produce high-quality prints, and screens can be reused many times. With special inks it is possible to go beyond traditional prints on paper and cloth and work on acrylic sheet. Because acrylic pipes light, the result is a colorful, transparent-translucent panel.

Begin by stretching the silk or polyester screening fabric onto the frame using thumbtacks or a staple gun. Make the screen very taut.

Use brown packing tape to seal the inside and outside of the frame where the screen is tacked to the wood frame. Apply two or three layers of the tape. This will keep the ink from escaping later on. Make the taped parts wide enough to serve as a type of tray for the ink. Allow twenty-four hours for the tape to dry fully.

Place wads of newspaper beneath the screen, and apply three thin coats of shellac over the tape. Dilute the shellac with 50 percent denatured alcohol. Apply the shellac so that it saturates a ¼" margin of the screen. This will help the silk-tape bond to hold when you wash the screen later.

Once the shellac solution is dry, begin to design. If using a litho crayon, rub the crayon into the screen very well. This seals the holes in the screen and will stop the glue from passing through. For the litho crayon to be effective, be certain that it completely seals the fabric.

Pour glue at one end of the frame and, using stiff cardboard, run the glue across the screen for several thin coats. Make certain that when "carding" you work evenly. Also be sure that there are no pinholes in the carded sections.

Roslyn Rose uses a glue combination of about 50 percent LePage's Original Glue #132, 40 percent water, 8 percent vinegar, and 2 percent glycerin. The last element may be omitted. But, along with the vinegar, glycerin does add flexibility and serves as a preservative. LePage's glue has a raunchy odor, so adequate ventilation must be provided.

After the glue has dried, add more wads of newspaper under the frame. Now rinse the screen with turpentine. The turpentine will dissolve the litho crayon but leave the glue intact. The glued parts will remain sealed. The parts of this design which ink through to the acrylic are the sections on which crayon was first applied.

Another technique for designing a screen is to paint directly on the screen with the glue combination. This is the exact opposite of the previous method. In many ways it is just as effective, and it saves time and materials.

To obtain transparent ink, you will want to combine the standard ink with NAZ-DAR Clear Gloss. Start out with some clear gloss and add color little by little to the gloss. Never add gloss to the color because you will end up making much more of the combination than you need. The color is quite potent.

If the ink gets too thick, add lacquer thinner by the drop. This too will be quite effective in small doses so don't overdo it.

After mixing the ink, you are almost ready to begin printing. Make certain that your baseboard which is underneath the frame is well shellacked.

When printing on acrylic, line up the acrylic on the baseboard so that the screen design will go on the right parts of the plastic. Peel off the protective paper from the acrylic on one side only. With that peeled side facing up, brace it in the lined-up position using cardboard taped to the board.

Set the framed screen on top of the acrylic and baseboard. Stir the paint. Position the squeegee at one end of the frame and pour a stream of paint in front of it on the packing-taped area. Run the squeegee through the paint and across the screen in an even, steady sweep. Two sweeps should be all that you will need.

To remove the printed plastic, lift the frame only a few inches from the base board (otherwise the ink will run), and slide the acrylic out. Let the ink air-dry for about one hour. Use lacquer thinner as the clean-up solvent since you are working with lacquer-based inks. Again, at this stage an exhaust fan is highly advisable. Disposable gloves are also a good idea for cleanup.

To clean the screen, put newspaper under the propped up frame and use lacquer thinner, constantly wiping the screen with fresh clean rags.

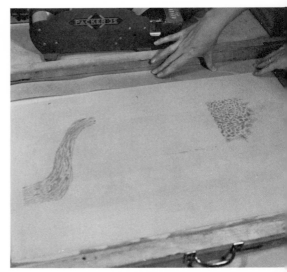

After stretching silk or polyester fabric over your screen, apply two or three layers of brown packing tape around the edges—inside and out—to keep ink from escaping later on.

Shellac the tape after it dries. First dilute the shellac with 50 percent denatured alcohol. The shellac should be painted ¼″ over the screen to insure a good bond between fabric and tape.

One technique of silk-screening involves the use of a litho crayon as a tusche. Seal the areas that you want printed with the crayon.

Then paint the entire screen with the glue mixture. Use a piece of cardboard to sweep the glue across the screen. When the glue has dried, dissolve the litho crayon on the screen with turpentine, and your screen is complete.

Another technique for designing a screen is to paint directly on the screen with the glue. The areas painted with glue will not receive ink when the screen is printed.

When the screen is ready, tape cardboard guides to the base beneath your screen and set the acrylic in place. Remove the protective masking paper from the top of the plastic.

If the acrylic is too thick you may need to elevate the screen by inserting paper underneath the hinges.

To print, pour ink on the packing-tape border on one side and . . .

. . . run the rubber squeegee through the paint and across the screen in one steady sweep.

To remove the printed acrylic, lift up the screen a few inches and slide the plastic out. Let the ink air-dry for one hour.

Flower Table in the Art Nouveau Style (24″ cube). Gary L. Smith. Steel filled epoxy and polyester resin on acrylic.

Modular units of scored vinyl were assembled to form this unusual lamp. Curtis Stephens. Courtesy Curtis Stephens.

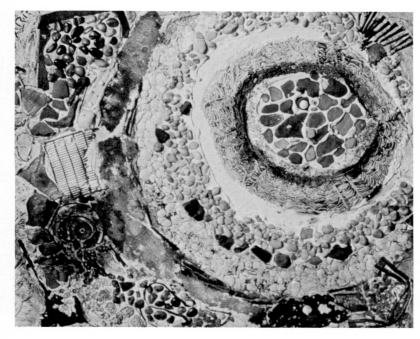

Pulsar. Barbara Darr. An impasto collage of plastic modeling paste and found objects. Courtesy Barbara Darr.

Sheets of vinyl were silk-
screened, scored, and glued
together. Curtis Stephens.
Courtesy Curtis Stephens.

Hanging Ornament. Carolyn
Kriegman. Poly-Mosaic tiles
fused around a vegetable grater.

Nude. Thom Haxo. Polyurethane
foam finished with acrylic gesso.

Wrench Motif. Barbara Darr. Vinyl-acrylic modeling paste and found
objects. Courtesy Barbara Darr.

Lorelei. Roslyn Rose. Three sheets of acrylic were silk-screened and joined together over a diffused light.

A side view of the same piece by Roslyn Rose shows that the pieces are joined together but that there are spaces between them. This separation allows the viewer fully to appreciate the refractions and interactions of pattern and color that occur as light passes through the plastic.

Galaxy. Roslyn Rose. Front view of a composition involving four sheets of silk-screened acrylic.

The back view of the same piece, *Galaxy,* shows tremendous expressive possibility available through this process; a single piece, viewed from different angles, can have very different moods.

A SCORED VINYL LAMP

Materials and Equipment

> matte vinyl sheet .015" thick
> nylon tube, 1/8" outer diameter
> a knife
> a scoring tool
> patterns for cutting and scoring
> lamp findings
> metal grommets
> solvent cement for vinyl
> hypodermic-type needle or brush

Procedures

Exciting lamps can be created with translucent vinyl sheets. By cutting the vinyl to shape and scoring the plastic so that it will fold or bend, delightful forms are possible.

Opaque white matte vinyl sheets are made by many companies. Firestone and Union Carbide are two good sources. Make certain that the plastic is no more than .015" thick, however, otherwise it will be too difficult to work with.

Begin by cutting a pattern from a piece of vinyl. Since this technique lends itself very well to the use of modular units, it is possible to make large pieces with only a single pattern.

Using the pattern, cut several pieces from the vinyl sheets. It is not necessary to actually cut the vinyl. Simply score the line, fold the plastic along the score, and tear the vinyl.

Once you have several pieces cut, you may score them to suit your design. Use a blunt instrument to score the plastic for folding. A dull point—like the tip of a ballpoint pen—works best. Score the plastic on the side that it will be folded on (i.e., if a piece has several curved folds, and the curves will be bent in different directions the plastic should be scored on opposite sides).

Fold the edges of each seam by scoring the line down the edge and folding the plastic up to create a thin lip. Split the nylon tube on one side, butt the sections of vinyl together so that the proper seams meet and use the split tube to mechanically hold the joint in place. Apply a solvent cement along the seam with a hypodermic-type needle.

Assemble the sections of your lamp this way, and add metal grommets at the top to attach your lamp findings.

The basic materials for making a lamp with vinyl sheeting include matte vinyl sheets .015" thick, nylon tube with an outer diameter of 1/8", a knife, a scoring tool with a rounded point, and patterns for cutting and scoring.

Curtis Stephens cuts lamp segments from 21" x 50" sheets with the aid of a pattern made from the same material. Cutting can be achieved by scoring with a knife, folding along the scored line and tearing. Courtesy: Curtis Stephens.

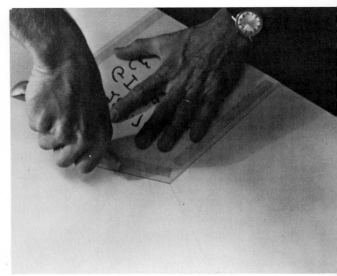

Score the edges of individual units for the seam. Courtesy: Curtis Stephens.

Curved folds should be scored with a pattern. The larger and smaller curves will be folded in opposite directions and are scored alternately on opposite sides of the plastic. Courtesy: Curtis Stephens.

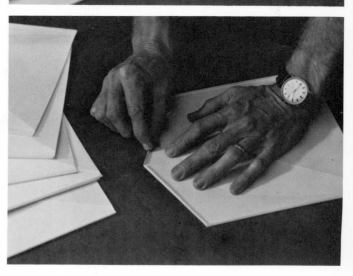

Fold the edge back for the seam. Courtesy: Curtis Stephens.

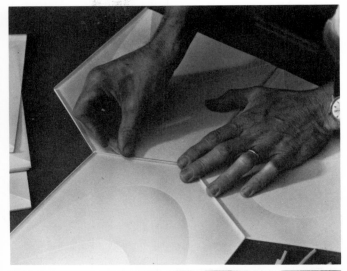

The folded edges are butted together and joined first with nylon tubing that has been slit on one side. Solvent cement should also be applied along the seam to make the joint permanent. Courtesy: Curtis Stephens.

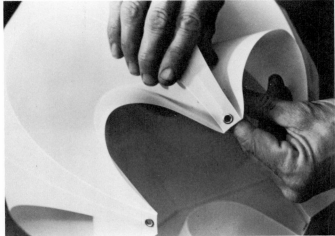

After all the seams have been completed, the curved folds are bent and grommets are added at the ends of the seams for the attachment of lamp hardware. Courtesy: Curtis Stephens.

Translucent Lamp. Curtis Stephens. Large and graceful forms are possible with this material. Courtesy: Curtis Stephens.

Large forms may be con-
structed from single sheets
of vinyl as well as from
modular units. Faceted folds
are also possible, but this material is particularly suited
to curved patterns. Cour-
tesy: Curtis Stephens.

Curtis Stephens gazes through
a construction in clear plastic. Courtesy: Curtis Stephens.

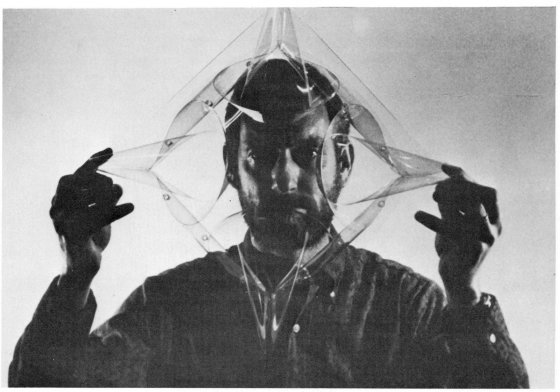

For this form, clear vinyl was silk-screened. When assembled, a delightful moiré pattern is evident. Courtesy: Curtis Stephens.

A DECOUPAGE BOX

Materials and Equipment

> a metal or wooden box
> rubber brayer
> Mod-Podge or PVA (polyvinyl acetate)
>   such as Elmer's Glue
> a brush
> scissors
> old magazines

Procedures

The art of decoupage is an easy one to master and the results are highly decorative. Mod-Podge, which is probably similar to polyvinyl acetate/chloride, makes this technique even easier. Acrylic polymer emulsion will also work almost as effectively.

Begin with a metal or wooden box. Cut pictures, letters, or random shapes from glossy magazines. Arrange your cutouts to cover the box.

In some cases, you may want to cover the surface of your box with a larger sheet of paper. Paint the surface first with Mod-Podge and use a rubber roller to press on the paper. This will help squeeze out air bubbles as well.

Paint the background paper with more Mod-Podge and tuck the edges under. Apply your cutouts the same way. First coat the background paper with the glaze, and then paint the cutout.

After you have laid on all of your cutouts, paint the entire box with Mod-Podge. Allow the plastic glaze to dry and then apply another coat. At least three or four coats should be applied. When the glaze dries, you will have a hard, scuff-resistant, glossy surface.

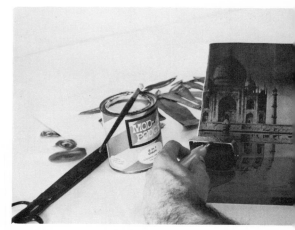

Apply a base sheet by painting the surface of the box with Mod-Podge. Place the sheet of paper on this coated surface and, using a rubber brayer, roll it until smooth. When smooth, coat it with more of the glaze. An acrylic polymer emulsion will do a decoupage job almost as well as Mod-Podge.

Apply the cutouts the same way. Paint the Mod-Podge on the surface, lay down the cutout, and apply another layer of Mod-Podge over the paper.

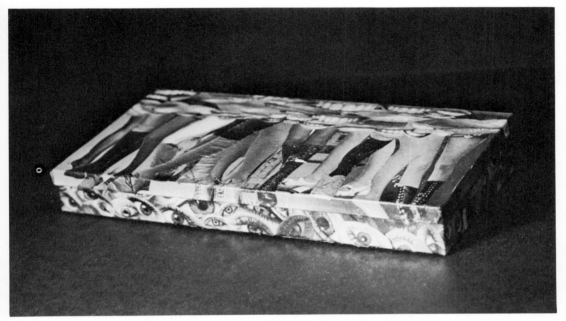

Apply three or four coats of Mod-Podge to the finished box.

Before beginning work, Barbara Darr gathers as many found objects around her as possible. A collage can combine many seemingly diverse objects into an exciting, unified whole. Pebbles, stones, metal scraps, leaves, pieces of glass, nails, and even an old wrench can find a home in a well-designed, well-organized composition. Courtesy: Barbara Darr.

After sprinkling an area of ½" plywood with water to moisten it, spread on a ¼" layer of vinyl-acrylic modeling paste. Courtesy: Barbara Darr.

AN IMPASTO COLLAGE

Materials and Equipment

rocks, stones, nails, metal scraps, and other assorted and sundry odds and ends
vinyl-acrylic modeling paste
½"-thick exterior plywood base
water in a jar
wood stain

Procedures

Acrylic-vinyl modeling paste is another extremely versatile plastic medium for the craftsman. It can be used to sculpture, to make reliefs, and as a medium for holding found objects in an impasto relief it is unsurpassed.

Before beginning, gather as many stones, shells, nails, metal scraps, pieces of glass, buttons, cloth scraps—and even leaves—as you can. Plan roughly the sort of a relief you will be making, including the textures and patterns you wish to create. You may make a sample piece to use as a "vocabulary" showing what each impression will make.

On a piece of exterior plywood ½" thick, sprinkle some water. Do not soak the wood, but apply a few drops to the area you will be working on first. Rub this around. It keeps the acrylic underneath from drying faster than the surface and therefore prevents cracking.

With a spatula or palette knife, spread a layer of modeling paste ¼" thick on the area you will be working first. Unless your

She begins by placing some pieces in the modeling paste, pressing them down firmly. Courtesy: Barbara Darr.

panel is very small, you should work in sections. Otherwise the modeling paste may dry before you have finished. If the paste begins to show signs of hardening, a thin spray of water will help to keep it moist.

Begin placing your forms in the paste. Press them in firmly. The modeling paste should surround them and even overlap them slightly so that, when it dries, your objects will be held firmly in place.

When you have finished one section, sprinkle water on the next area to be decorated and spread on the paste. Press in your objects the same as before. Continue this process until your panel is complete.

Allow the modeling paste to dry. Depending on the humidity, this may take several hours to several days. Remember that ¼″ is a thick layer of modeling paste, and for maximum strength this material should be allowed to remain undisturbed until it is hard and no longer damp.

In some areas, the modeling paste may crack as it dries. Simply fill in cracks with some acrylic gesso and allow this medium to harden.

When the paste hardens, your panel may be finished with wood stain or paint. You may add accents to your textures and patterns by pouring stain on a cloth and darkening appropriate areas. Be careful not to overdo it—too much stain will destroy the beauty of the many contrasting textures by reducing the entire piece to a single, muddied color. Gold, silver, and copper effects can be created with wax-based materials such as Rub'n Buff.

If the paste shows signs of drying, sprinkle on some water from a handy jar to help keep the plastic modeling paste moist and workable. Courtesy: Barbara Darr.

Barbara Darr works in sections. After one area is complete she spreads modeling paste on another section. Otherwise, unless the panel is a small one, the vinyl-acrylic paste will harden before you finish. Courtesy: Barbara Darr.

As the modeling paste hardens, it is still possible to adjust pieces. In this panel it is easy to see how Barbara Darr has incorporated apparently disparate objects in a single piece. Rocks, birdseed, fir needles, eggshells, pebbles, carpenter's cloth, and even a spring are all arranged so that they work together. Courtesy: Barbara Darr.

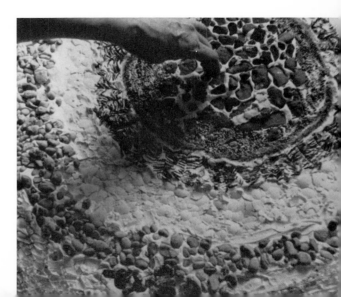

129

Pulsar (28″ x 24″). Barbara Darr. The finished panel has been accented with a dark stain.

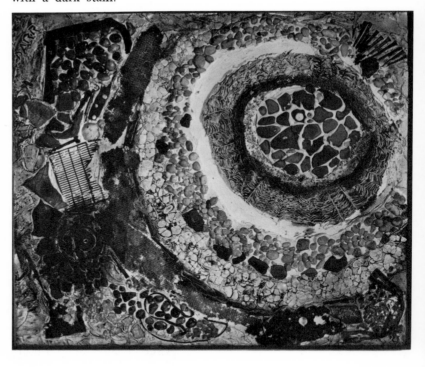

Wrench Motif. Barbara Darr. Wrenches, masonry nails, nuts, and metal buttons are the basis for this composition. Courtesy: Barbara Darr.

This detail shows the use of glass slugs and metal-punch scrap. The modeling paste clearly acts as a bonding agent, but it supplies a rich texture as well. Courtesy: Barbara Darr.

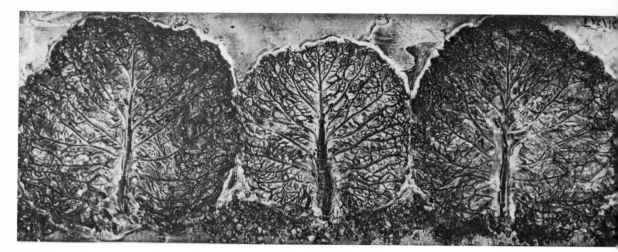

Cabbage Relief. Barbara Darr. Plastic modeling paste has been given the texture of cabbage leaves. After pressing the wet leaves into the paste, the plastic was allowed to harden for a few hours and then the leaves were removed. Courtesy: Barbara Darr.

Nailburst. Barbara Darr. Masonry nails and fingerprints account for the rich texture in this relief. Courtesy: Barbara Darr.

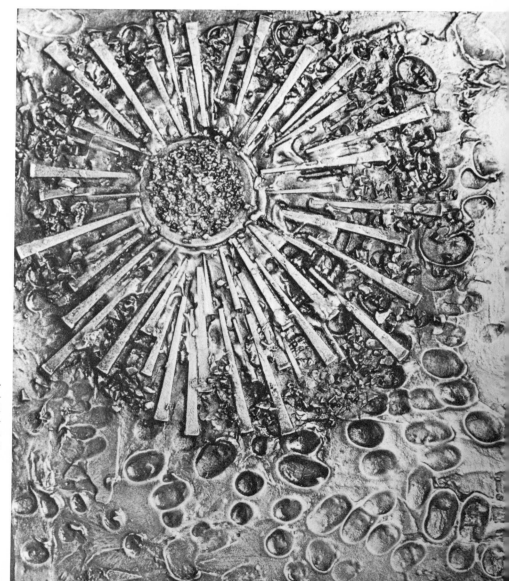

Shells, Sun and Seeds. Barbara Darr. This panel was named after the principal elements in its composition. Courtesy: Barbara Darr.

IMPASTO BOTTLES

Materials and Equipment

> a glass bottle
> acrylic gesso
> vinyl-acrylic modeling paste
> a brush
> patterned plastic doily or a trivet
> acrylic paint

Procedures

With vinyl-acrylic modeling paste you can transform empty bottles into attractive and useful objects.

Paint the outside of the bottle first with acrylic gesso. Cover the entire surface and allow the gesso to dry. Apply a second coat to make certain that the bottle is completely covered. This coating does not have to be thick, but the glass should be coated so that the dry gesso surface will act as a base for the modeling paste.

When the gesso dries, apply a layer of modeling paste to one area of the bottle. This layer should be $\frac{1}{8}$ " thick. The modeling paste should be allowed to dry for about two hours. Then apply a second layer directly over the first; this layer of paste should be $\frac{1}{8}$ " thick as well. You should have nearly $\frac{1}{4}$ " of modeling paste on the surface of the bottle.

Allow the second layer to remain undisturbed for five hours. At the end of that time the modeling paste will be drier, but still workable.

Seven hours after the first layer of modeling paste has been applied you will be ready to create patterns in the paste. Anything—wood, metal or plastic—with a pattern in low relief may be used for this purpose.

Wet your pattern-forming object, in this case a plastic doily. Shake off the excess water. (The doily or trivet must be wet or it will stick to the paste.) Press the pattern into the paste, forcing the paste to push up through the holes in the plastic and immediately lift away the pattern carefully.

The impression left on the surface of the modeling paste may not appear to be very deep, but when the modeling paste hardens the definition will become more apparent.

Repeat this process until the bottle is covered with your designs. To avoid damage to completed parts, however, allow each section to harden for a few hours before beginning the next.

When the entire piece is dry it may be painted with acrylic paints. Before painting, check to see if there are any cracks in the surface. If there are, fill them with acrylic gesso and allow the gesso to dry before painting.

To accentuate your pattern, first paint the entire bottle in one color, and then dry-brush the relief surfaces in a contrasting color to highlight the designs. Metallic finishes are particularly good as accent color.

The finished containers make attractive vases, or they may be used just to keep things bottled up.

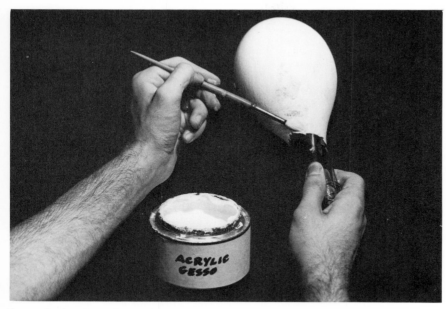

Paint the bottle with acrylic gesso. Allow the gesso to harden and then apply a second coat to make certain that the entire surface is completely covered, and let this dry, too.

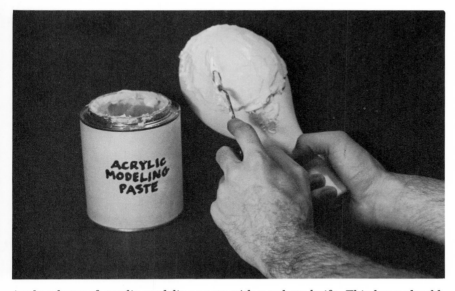

Apply a layer of acrylic modeling paste with a palette knife. This layer should be ⅛" thick. After the first layer has dried for two hours apply a second layer of the same thickness.

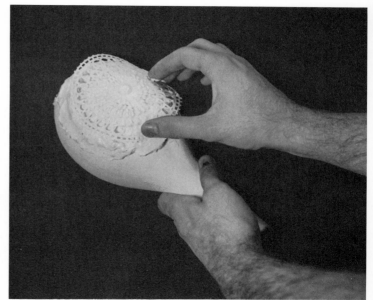

The second layer should be allowed to dry for five hours, then press on your pattern. Force the modeling paste up through the holes in the wet doily or trivet and remove it carefully. Although the relief may not look very deep, the definition will increase as the paste hardens.

Repeat this process until the entire bottle is covered.

When the modeling paste is completely hard, the bottle may be painted with acrylic paints. To accentuate your pattern, first paint the entire bottle in one color. Then dry brush the raised surfaces in a contrasting color.

The completed bottle (left) shows the pattern imparted by a plastic doily. The two on the right have been textured with a palette knife and painted.

These three bottles by Barbara Darr show the design possibilities when metal trivets and old block-printing patterns are used to pattern the moist plastic paste.

ONE OF THE MOST inexpensive yet highly versatile thermoplastics available to the craftsman is polystyrene. Usually called "styrene" for short, it is a very commonly used plastic in industry and has equal potential for the artist-craftsman, because of its ease of forming, availability, and creative potential. Machining of these fusible thermoplastics can be performed with any of the tools used for wood- or metalworking. Pellets of styrene and other styrene-type thermoplastics are fusible at low temperatures (about 350° F.). Manufacturers pigment them in a rainbow of hues and intensities. Fusible thermoplastics have an indefinite shelf-life and may be glued together as well, using Duco or other cements for plastics.

There are two basic types of fusible thermoplastics which are readily available to the craftsman. They can both be easily realized as craft materials just using the equipment found in a kitchen. These two types are polystyrene "cooking" pellets and a thermoplastic mosaic tile, which probably has a base related to polystyrene, called Poly-Mosaics.

Poly-Mosaics, available at crafts stores or directly from the manufacturer, in seventeen transparent to translucent colors and also in opaque white and black, are square plastic units, the size of a standard mosaic tile. They are easily cut with a tile cutter or nippers, and are fusible into rigid forms in a kitchen oven (350° F.) or almost any other heat source. While hot, Poly-Mosaic fused forms may be sagged and bent, much like other thermoplastics such as acrylic. When cool, they are easily machined.

The colored fusible pellets usually are available in small packages at crafts stores. Handsomely crystallike, almost pointillist in form, pellets combine to be any shape, always shimmering with textures that catch the light. The pellets fuse in an ordinary oven, or almost any consistent heat source, yielding (depending upon the length of exposure to heat) a jewellike surface, bubbly texture, or (after half an hour under 350° F.) a nearly smooth finish.

4

WORKING WITH FUSIBLE THERMOPLASTICS

Pellets, since they can be machined, heated, and heat-shaped much the same as the Poly-Mosaics, may be combined with Poly-Mosaic tiles in the same fusing process. Both products are nontoxic, although, particularly with the pellets, adequate ventilation should be provided. Most polystyrene products give off an odor if cooked for extended lengths of time beyond the recommended temperature.

Poly-Mosaics also are odorless unless left in the oven with temperatures over 350° F., or for longer than fusing time. As with all thermoplastics under heat, these materials should at no time be left unattended if in the oven.

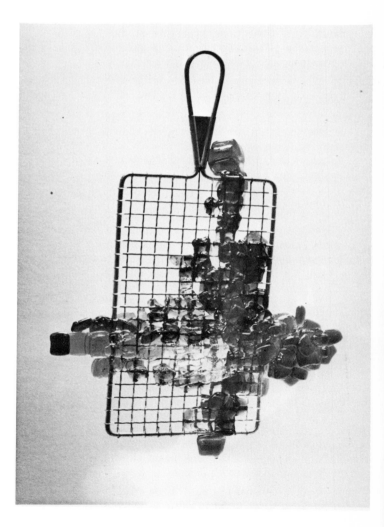

Hanging Ornament. Carolyn Kriegman. This Pop form was created with thermoplastic tiles fused around a vegetable grater.

MOSAIC AND PELLET PROCESSES

Fusing

The mosaic tiles and cooking pellets easily fuse in three to ten minutes in an oven at 350° F. The time varies depending upon the thickness of materials to be fused, the dimensions of the piece, and the desired surface texture. They can be arranged on an aluminum tray (preferably unscarred and shiny) or on a Pyrex dish and placed in the kitchen oven or portable broil-oven, where they melt and fuse together. While hot, they may be shaped using tweezers, spatula, and other utensils. Sometimes air caught between pellets or tiles can cause gaps that need to be coaxed together with your implements.

Texture can be varied by allowing pieces to fuse for different lengths of time: the longer the mosaic and pellet forms remain in the oven the more they will melt and the thinner and smoother the final piece will become. Temperatures above 400° F. will cause the materials to decompose. Avoid this. Once they fuse, the tray should be removed from the heat source and placed with the plastic away from the heat to allow the form to cool (if you do not plan to sag or otherwise manipulate the heated product). Cool pieces can still be cut into other shapes. When cool, other fusible mosaics or pellets may be added to the form by returning the enlarged piece to the oven for more fusing.

Shaping

While still soft and warm, fused Poly-Mosaic and pellet forms may be molded into three-dimensional shapes by sagging, bending, or rolling.

To sag the plastic, pry the warm fused piece from the aluminum tray using a spatula or other flat utensil. Then, lift the plastic off the tray as you would a pancake and drape the piece over a cup, bottleneck, can, or any appropriate form. You may also sag the pieces by holding them in shape and immediately running the fused form through cool water.

Similarly, to bend fused sheets and shapes of either Poly-Mosaics or pellets, pry the form from the tray and prop the piece so that all surfaces are flat except at the desired bent angle.

Mistakes made in either of these heat-forming processes can be corrected by reheating in the oven and then reshaping them. The smallest scraps can also be saved for future use.

Rolling single tiles can create a colorful bead. To roll a tile, place a knitting needle across the middle of a soft, hot single tile. Using a tweezers, lift one end of the Poly-Mosaic and cross the plastic over the needle. Press edge to edge. It will immediately fuse to itself. Now roll the entire tile around the knitting needle on the tray (like a rolling pin) to form a smooth bead. When it cools, the rolled bead will slide off the needle, and will have a neat hole running through it.

Cutting

Fused units of plastic mosaic tiles and/or pellets can be cut using any kind of saw, hand-, jig-, saber-, radial arm, band, or circular saws, though the heavier cutting tools are not really necessary.

To cut individual unfused Poly-Mosaic tiles, place the jaw of end nippers or any other tile-cutting device in the direction of the cut desired, about ¼" over the tile. Shield the tile with one hand to keep pieces from scattering, and squeeze the handles together with the other hand. These tiles may be cut to exact shapes with just a little practice.

Sanding

Pieces may also be sanded by hand or machine. When sanding by machine, however, be careful that the plastic does not get too hot; use slow motor speeds (not above 1,725 rpm). If your work does gum up, let the piece cool and then scrape or sand off the caked plastic.

Polishing

Polishing is easiest using the flame from a propane torch or candle—with caution, however, because charring and smoking are always a possibility. The underside of a piece or the markings from a sanding operation may be shined to a glossy surface by quickly glancing these heat sources over your piece. Always keep the flame moving, because otherwise the plastic will char, depositing carbon in a smoky coating on the piece. A slow hand with the propane torch could cause burning.

Drilling and Embedding

A hand drill or a drill press operating at a slow speed may be used to make holes.

But an awl or a needle (with its blunt end in a cork to act as a handle) may be heated on a stove or in a flame and then be pushed through the plastic, leaving a clean hole. Using this same method, you can embed metal by pushing the metal into the fusible thermoplastic and allowing it to remain in place until the piece cools. (This is the best way to attach wire stems to plastic flowers and leaves.)

Gluing

Unfused Poly-Mosaics may be joined to other plastics and materials using a cement meant for plastics. Glues like Duco plastic cement are excellent for this purpose. This type of glue is not as thin as solvent cements such as methylene dichloride, so to bond the plastic no brushes or needles are needed. Simply daub the glue on the tile or on the spot to be adhered, press on the plastic, and allow it to set for several minutes.

Units of fused tiles may be linked together with jewelry findings to create much larger pieces. The cabochons were pressed into the plastic while it was still hot.

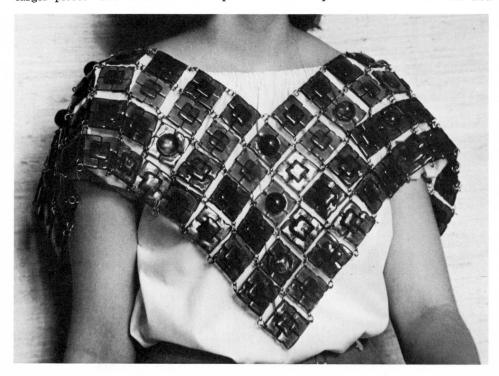

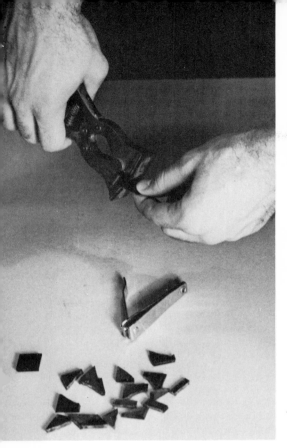

Poly-Mosaic tiles can be cut with tile nippers or ordinary nail clippers.

Using a cement for plastic, like Duco, Poly-Mosaic tiles can be glued to a variety of backings like acrylic and polystyrene backing board. Apply a daub of cement to the board and press on the tile. It will dry in several minutes. Courtesy: DuMont High School.

Handsome murals and panels may be created in this way, using unfused Poly-Mosaics and glue. Use a light-colored or transparent backing so that the transparent colors will be most effective. Courtesy: DuMont High School.

A PELLET "PAINTING"

Materials and Equipment

> a colorful assortment of thermoplastic
> pellets
> aluminum cookie sheet
> kitchen oven or broil-oven
> tweezers
> frame

Procedures

A pointillist-type, impressionistic pellet "painting" can be created using different colors of cooking pellets carefully arranged on an aluminum tray.

Determine how large your picture should be, and rule off the size of the "painting" on the aluminum tray with a fine marking pen before you begin your piece. This way the picture will be pre-tailored to fit your frame. Place pellets exactly where you want them. Using tweezers will ease frustration in removing unwanted units. When you are satisfied with the colors and design, carefully slide the tray into an oven preheated to 350° F. Let the piece fuse for several minutes until the pellets have formed a solid unit. Then remove the tray from the oven. You may find that there are some holes in the painting or that there are places where the color, thickness, or texture is weak. Remedy this, and physically strengthen the entire "painting" by sprinkling more of the unfused pellets onto the fused design. Replace the tray in the oven. When fused, again remove it from the heat source and allow the panel to cool.

With a white background or a light box and a handsome frame, this "painting" with fusible thermoplastics will brighten any wall.

Using an assortment of pellet colors, plan your design on an aluminum cookie sheet. Try to keep your picture within the boundaries of your picture frame. Carefully slide the "painting" into the oven. Melt it at 350° F. When fused, remove the piece. Add more color if you like. You can build up the texture to at least ¼″ thickness if you wish. It will make the panel stronger and will also fill in any gaps in the design if you sprinkle clear pellets over the piece.

When the re-fused panel has melted and cooled, attach it to a frame.

Working with Fusible Thermoplastics

After designing fusible pellet snowflakes on an aluminum tray, heating them, and forming holes from which to suspend them, attach swivel joints which will allow the pieces to rotate independently when combined in the mobile.

A SNOWFLAKE MOBILE

Materials and Equipment

> fusible thermoplastic pellets
> kitchen oven or broil-oven
> aluminum cookie sheet
> propane torch or candle flame
> nylon cord
> extruded acrylic rods or wooden dowels
> swivels (available at hardware stores)

Procedures

A glittering, decorative snowflake mobile of the crystallike pellets is made by arranging the fusible plastic pellets on an aluminum tray in the pattern of a snowflake and fusing the pellets.

Create the snowflake on a tray or Pyrex dish, place it in the oven at 350° F. and allow the pellets to fuse. When the plastic has melted, remove the tray from the heat source and allow the snowflake to cool. If the piece is too thin, add more pellets and reheat.

Allow the completed snowflake to cool while flat. When cool, make a hole in one tip with a hand drill, drill press, or with the heated tip of an awl or other pointed object. If you use an awl, push the hot point through the plastic with a twisting motion.

To give the pellet snowflake a glossy surface on the side that faced the aluminum tray, quickly and lightly run the flame of a propane torch or candle across the face, taking care not to char or deposit smoke on the forms.

After you have designed several snowflakes, you may decide to simply string them individually for a window ornament, or to assemble a mobile of these forms using nylon cord to attach the snowflakes to clear, extruded acrylic rods. Fishing line swivels used as connectors will stimulate more movement.

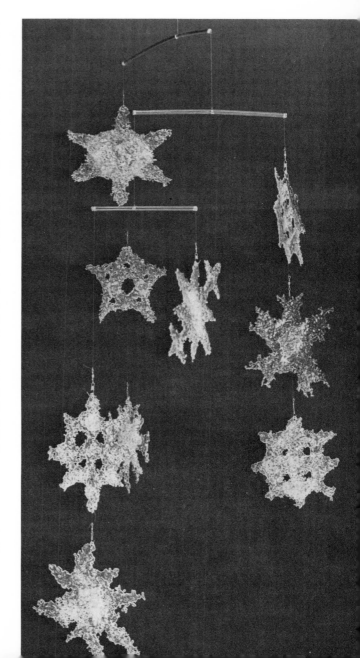

This lively mobile, moving more swiftly with the use of swivel joints and nylon cord attached with balanced precision to acrylic rods, blows gently in the breezes.

As with Poly-Mosaics, fusible thermoplastic pellets may be melted, shaped, and sagged to create imaginative flowers such as these three bouquets.

A MOBILE FISH OF FUSIBLE PELLETS

Materials and Equipment

fusible thermoplastic pellets
Poly-Mosaic tiles and nippers
kitchen oven or broil-oven
aluminum cookie sheet or a flat Pyrex
    dish
stainless-steel stripping
an awl; propane torch or candle flame
    for heating the tip (or a hand drill
    press)
florist's wire or other similar-gauge
    flexible wire

Procedures

By pouring fusible pellets into a frame of stainless-steel stripping, this material can be formed to exact shapes.

Bend the stripping to the desired shape. A different frame should be made for each section of the fish body. But this stripping may be used several times.

Be certain that the stainless-steel frame lies flat against the aluminum tray, forming channels in which to pour the pellets. Then pour the colorful plastic pellets into each frame. Carefully slide the tray in an oven preheated to 350° F.

In a few minutes, the pellets will fuse. In the meantime, cut some Poly-Mosaic tiles in half diagonally so that you have two triangles. Remove the pellet forms from the oven. Carefully place the triangular Poly-Mosaic pieces over the pellet shape. If you lay the tile pieces in rows, the triangles of fusible thermoplastic will assume the appearance of scales on the fish mobile.

Now replace the form in the oven still keeping the stainless-steel frame around each unit. The two thermoplastics will melt and fuse. Once fused, remove these forms and allow them to cool. Pull away the stainless-steel frames.

You may want to "polish" the back side of each piece with a propane torch if the piece has been dulled by the alumi-num tray. Keep the propane flame moving quickly. You do not want the pellet forms to heat to the point of charring.

Form the other sections of the fish in the same manner by constructing a frame; fusing the plastic; adding more plastic pieces and re-fusing them. Then refine the form by flame polishing.

When you have constructed all the pieces necessary, holes must be pierced in the top center of each piece. Holes may be formed using a hand or electric drill. You may also utilize an awl or other pointed object which has been heated in a flame. Push the hot tip through the plastic, leaving a hole adequate enough to accommodate a wire.

Attach the pieces together with wire as shown in the final mobile. Florist's wire or similar-gauge wire is best, since it has qualities of being both flexible and strong. Hook the fish anywhere. In an easy breeze, you will think you've got a live one.

Shape the stainless steel stripping into a frame for the plastic pellets to fuse in. Lay the form flat on the aluminum cookie sheet.

Pour colored pellets into the metal frame.

Carefully place the framed pellets in an oven preheated to 350° F., taking care not to dislodge the pellets from the boundary of their metal frame. Allow the plastic to fuse into a solid piece.

You may want to add another texture to the surface of the fish using Poly-Mosaic tiles. While the pellets are still fusing in the oven, cut some tiles into triangular halves.

Remove the partially fused pellets from the oven and place the half tiles over the hot pellets. When fused, the tiles will give the impression of being scales on the fish.

Let the two thermoplastic materials melt together, and then remove each unit from the heat and allow it to cool. When cooled, the metal stripping may be peeled away.

Form a head, a tail and several body segments for the fish in the same manner. Connect these pieces with florist's wire or a similar type of wire so that the pieces will rotate freely, yet retain their place in space.

A TWINKLE CHIME

Materials and Equipment

> Poly-Mosaic tiles
> kitchen oven or broil-oven
> aluminum cookie sheet or Pyrex dish
> nylon cord
> an awl with propane torch or candle
>   flame or a hand drill or drill press

Procedures

On an aluminum cookie sheet, fuse 49 Poly-Mosaic tiles together to form a solid square 7 tiles x 7 tiles. The finished piece should be solid with the lines between tiles becoming all but invisible.

Form holes in the center of the tiles indicated by the diagram. Holes may be drilled with a hand drill or a drill press. You may also heat the tip of an awl in a flame and then press it through the tile.

The twinkling strands are made of single tiles strung on nylon cord. To string the tiles, first make holes in their centers —the same as with the larger square—then pass the string through and tie knots or loop a bead beneath each tile.

Pass the end of the nylon through the holes in the larger square of plastic and tie them there. True to its name, this wind chime will twinkle in the breeze.

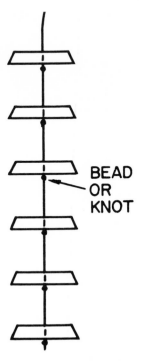

Make the strands of single tiles by stringing tiles on thin nylon cord. Tie a knot or loop a bead beneath each tile to keep the tile from slipping down on the string.

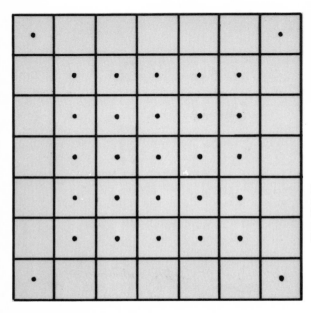

Fuse 49 Poly-Mosaic tiles together to form a larger square 7 tiles x 7 tiles. Make holes in this piece as indicated. Strands of single tiles will be strung through these holes later.

Attach all the strands from the fused piece to finish this
twinkling chime.

Poly-Mosaic tiles were fused to create these two variations on a wind chime theme. Each has a distinctive sound.

Lengths of single Poly-Mosaic tiles were threaded together to form this necklace.

BRIGHT BEADS

Materials and Equipment

Poly-Mosaic tiles
tile cutters or end nippers (optional)
kitchen oven or broil-oven
aluminum cookie sheet or Pyrex dish
knitting needle
tweezers
spatula

Procedures

Use a simple rolling procedure to create colorful, bright beads with Poly-Mosaic tiles.

One type of bead is made with a single uncut tile. Place a tile on an aluminum cookie sheet and slide the tray into an oven preheated to 350° F.

When the corners of the tile have rounded and the plastic appears to have softened, remove the tray from the oven. Loosen the soft tile from the tray by sliding a spatula under it. Press a knitting needle diagonally across the melted tile. With tweezers, lift one corner of the Poly-Mosaic and pull the plastic over the needle, pressing it down on the other side. It will immediately fuse to itself. Roll the entire tile around the knitting needle on the tray to form a smooth colorful bead.

Allow the bead to cool on the needle. When cool, the rolled bead will slide off the needle, and you will have a neat hole piercing the bead.

A number of variations are possible. Try using different shapes and thicknesses of tile to vary your result.

Heat a single tile and press a metal knitting needle diagonally across it.

With tweezers, lift one corner of the heated Poly-Mosaic and pull the plastic over the needle, pressing it down on the other side. The plastic will immediately fuse to itself. When the tile cools it will slide off the needle easily, and a clean hole will pierce your bead.

Sue Irion holds a string of beads formed from whole tiles. Beads can also be made from half tiles or tiles cut to special shapes.

A CRYSTAL WIND CHIME

Materials and Equipment

>   crystal-clear Poly-Mosaic tiles
>   kitchen oven or broil-oven
>   aluminum cookie sheet
>   aluminum spatula
>   thin nylon cord

Procedures

The crystal wind chime is comprised of many separate tile units strung together with thin nylon string on a Poly-Mosaic crossbar.

To make a unit, place four tiles together on an aluminum cookie sheet so that they form a square.

Heat this square until the tiles have fused together—but be careful not to overheat it so that it begins to bubble. If you notice spaces between the tiles, press them together with a spatula and replace under heat until they join completely.

Remove the joined pieces from the oven. Slide your spatula underneath to loosen the unit, raise and then lift and press the four corners together with your gloved fingers. Since the plastic will still be hot at that point, the corners will stick together forming a small pillow shape, as illustrated. Dip the pinched form into some cool water to set the plastic.

You will need about thirty of these units for this wind chime. To construct the crossbar, heat four individual tiles on a cookie sheet. They should not be touching while they melt. When they have melted somewhat, stack them on top of each other to form a column and press them together. Continue to heat more single tiles and press them together until your crossbar is the required length (about forty tiles). Once the bar is long enough, place the entire piece in your oven and heat it briefly to make certain that the tiles are firmly fused.

String your pinched "pillow" forms on nylon string and tie the strands around the crossbar. Your light-catching wind chime will have a delightful tinkle as it hangs from a tree, doorjamb, window, or ceiling.

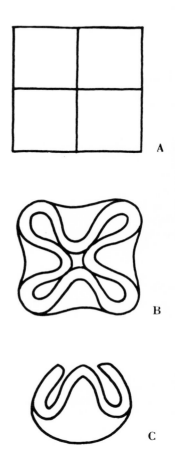

A. The basic four-tile square. B. A top view of a finished unit. C. A side view of one unit.

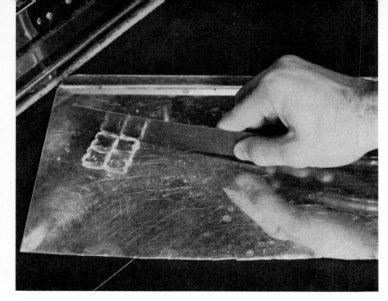

Heat a four-tile square. Remove it from the oven briefly and straighten the sides with a metal spatula. Then return the Poly-Mosaic tile square to the oven.

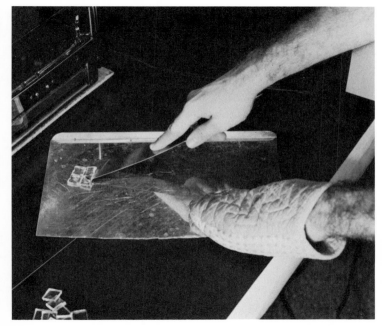

Allow the tiles to heat for a few seconds, remove the tray, and slide your spatula under the plastic to loosen it.

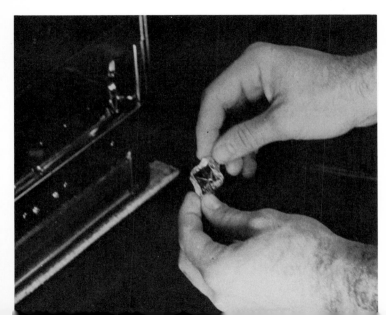

With your hands—use gloves if the plastic is too hot—pinch the tiles together . . .

. . . and press the sides together. The hot tiles should fuse together immediately.

A single finished unit. Photo by Allen Amdur.

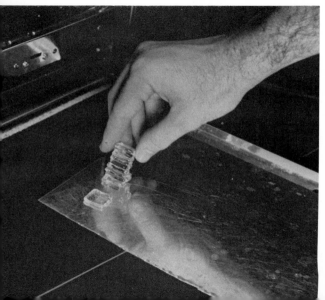

Construct a crosspiece by heating single tiles and pressing them together while the plastic is hot. When your piece is the desired length, lay it down on the tray and place it in your oven for a few minutes, then remove it and flatten the sides with the metal spatula.

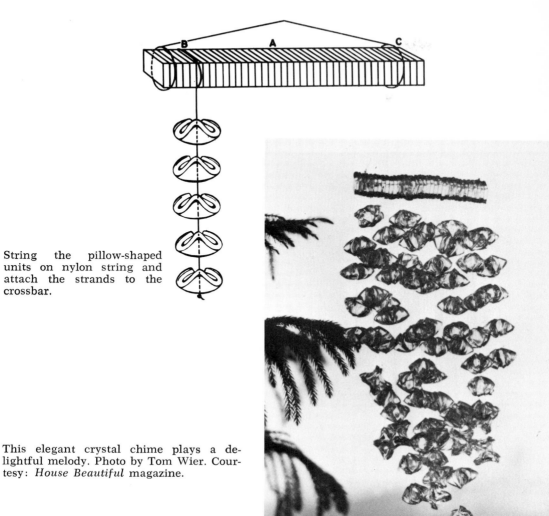

String the pillow-shaped units on nylon string and attach the strands to the crossbar.

This elegant crystal chime plays a delightful melody. Photo by Tom Wier. Courtesy: *House Beautiful* magazine.

The individual units can be strung differently, too. Here they were used to create this light-catching—and eye-catching—necklace.

Cut several tiles in thirds with tile nippers or nail clippers.

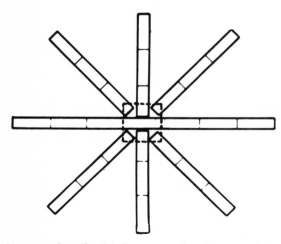

Arrange the tile thirds on an aluminum cookie sheet as shown in the diagram. Place a whole tile over the intersection to make certain that the bond is a solid one.

PLUMA

Materials and Equipment

> Poly-Mosaic tiles
> tile cutter or end nippers
> florist's wire (or similar gauge)
> kitchen oven or broil-oven
> aluminum cookie sheet
> Pyrex custard cup for shaping the plastic
> spatula

Procedures

These flowers consist of three cup-shaped layers nested in graduated sizes. For the largest outside layer, cut several tiles in thirds and arrange them on the aluminum tray as shown in the diagram. Place a whole tile over the intersection to make certain that the bond is a solid one.

Heat the thermoplastic tiles in your oven until they fuse thoroughly. Remove the tray from the oven and allow the plastic to cool slightly. Then prod the heated plastic loose with a metal spatula and immediately sag the hot form over a Pyrex custard cup. Allow the plastic to cool in this draped position so that it will assume this shape.

For the two inner layers, subtract one tile from each projection and follow the same procedure for heating and forming.

To assemble all three cup-shaped forms into a flower, heat the tip of a piece of florist's wire and press it through the center of the largest cup. Allow several inches to protrude. Heat the wire again and press it through the second and third layers. The excess wire in the center of the flower may be cut off with wire nippers.

Additional flowers should be constructed in the same manner. Leaves may be made as well. Simply cut the tiles to shape, arrange them on the aluminum tray and heat the plastic. Leaves may be sagged to shape and given wire stems, too.

Heat the Poly-Mosaic tiles until they fuse thoroughly. Then slide a metal spatula under the plastic to free it from the aluminum tray.

Sag the hot form over a Pyrex custard cup. Allow the plastic to cool in this draped position.

Make the other layers in the same manner. The smallest layer—for the center—consists of a single tile with single thirds that are pinched toward the center.

Sag the middle layer—which is one-third tile smaller on each extremity—into the custard cup rather than over it.

Assemble the three forms into a flower by heating the tip of a piece of florist's wire and pressing it through the center of each layer of petals.

Leaves may be fused the same way . . .

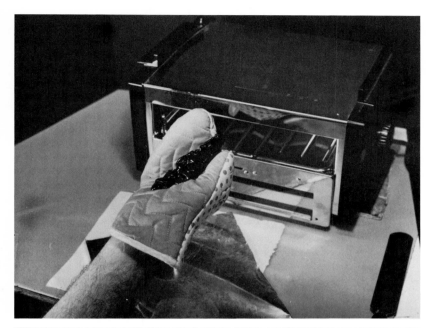

. . . and then shaped by holding the soft plastic in an oven mitt until it cools. The leaf may be given a stem the same as the flower.

A closeup of the flowers and leaves shows their layered construction. Courtesy: *Woman's Day* magazine.

The finished bouquets are displayed in acrylic vases. Courtesy: *Woman's Day* magazine.

Eucalyptuslike leaves are made by pressing whole Poly-Mosaics onto a heated wire. The tiles were rounded first by heating them briefly in the bowl of a metal spoon. Courtesy: *Woman's Day* magazine.

These four bouquets were all created with fusible Poly-Mosaic tiles. Flower photos courtesy *Woman's Day* magazine.*

* See Acknowledgments.

STAINED "GLASS" PANEL

Materials and Equipment

Poly-Mosaic tiles
kitchen oven or broil-oven
aluminum cookie sheet
spatula
plywood a few inches larger than
   projected panel size
large sheet of paper and scissors to
   make a full-scale pattern
U and H channeled leading
solder and soldering iron
two-part epoxy putty (steel-filled putty
   looks best)
nails and hammer

Procedures

The art of creating a stained-glass panel with precisely cut glass pieces held together by leading (cames) is an ancient one. And our modern adaptation follows the same basic process. Instead of glass, however, we substitute lightweight fusible thermoplastic mosaic tiles. This medium offers many advantages over glass. Like glass, there are many nonfading colors to choose from, but, unlike glass, the plastic tiles are easily fused at low temperatures in a home oven. There are not the dangers of working with glass, nor the extended time factors. Stained-glass windows take at least twice as much time to make.

After a sketch of the design is made, it is scaled to the desired size on a larger piece of paper. The individual units are cut from the paper and then trimmed so that when they are arranged together there will be a small space between each unit —corresponding to the leading space.

The individual units are formed by cutting tiles of the proper color to the approximate shape, according to the pattern piece, and fusing them in an oven at 350° F. Different colors and varying intensities of color can be obtained by overlapping different shades. Textures can be created by regulating the amount of time

a piece is heated. Shorter lengths of time will result in raised and bumpy surfaces.

When the unit has fused, remove the tray from the oven and allow it to cool. Cooled pieces may then be cut to their exact size with a saw. If the underside has been dulled by transferring the texture of a dull tray, the plastic can be given a high gloss by lightly sweeping the surface with the flame from a propane torch.

When each element of your window has been completed in this way, assemble them on a table as they will fit together. They are ready to be leaded. On a piece of plywood several inches larger than the proposed panel, draw a straight line along one side (this will be used as a guide for the edge). Lightly drive in nails 1½″ apart along this guideline.

Two types of leading (cames)—both readily available in hobby and crafts stores—will be necessary. These are the U and the H channel leads. The U channel is used around the perimeter and the H channel is placed between pieces. A small soldering iron is also necessary.

A strip of U channel should be laid against the nails. Starting at one side, fit the first piece into the first channel. Next, cut a strip of H channel and lay it next to this piece on the side where another unit will fit. Solder this piece to the outside U channel that is acting as the frame. In the meantime, the plastic units should be held in place by thin nails. The nail technique —originated by the stained-glass makers— makes the operations much easier; in fact, the nails almost give you a third hand. Now take the next unit and repeat the process. The nailing and soldering, nailing and soldering is continued until the panel is completed. Try to use continuous H channel strips wherever possible. It makes for a stronger panel. Occasionally, you may find a piece that does not fit perfectly or butts unevenly. It can often be trimmed to shape, but some units may need to be made again. When all the joints have been soldered on the top, turn the panel over and solder the joints on the reverse side as well. Wash away the solder acid on both sides with water.

When the leading is completed, steel-filled epoxy putty should be rubbed into the channels. This putty is a two-part compound; the parts—resin and catalyst—usually come in stick form and must be mixed together in equal parts before use.

In this case, the putty seals the channels and keeps the plastic units locked in tightly.

The cames are reasonably strong and will amply support most panels. Very large pieces, however, can be further supported by a thin sheet of acrylic held to the stained "glass" panel by a ready-made aluminum frame. Room dividers can be made this way if pieces are supported in the channels of the room divider frame.

The initial sketch (*upper left-hand corner*) is scaled into the desired size. Coloring identifies each shape.

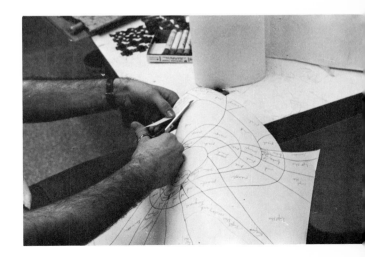

This scale model is cut into individual units. The color of each shape is written on the face.

These pieces are trimmed so that they will fit together with a small space in between to accommodate the leading (cames) to be added later.

Tiles are arranged on an aluminum tray according to the basic shape. The tiles are then cut more precisely using tile cutters, nippers, or even a large pair of nail clippers.

The tray is then placed in the oven (350° F.) until the tiles melt and fuse together, three to ten minutes.

When fused, the tiles are removed from the oven and allowed to cool.

When cool, the pattern is checked once more. Edges are trimmed using a handsaw, band saw, saber saw, or jigsaw with the pattern taped on as a guide.

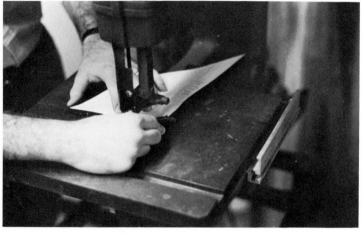

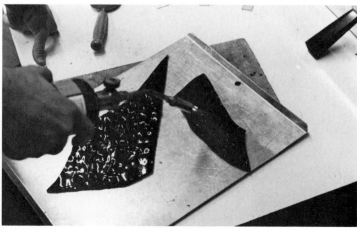

The underside of trimmed pieces can be brought to a high gloss using a propane torch or a candle flame.

Finished pieces are fitted into the overall design.

When all the smaller units have been completed and are ready to be leaded, a straight line is drawn on a piece of plywood a few inches larger than the finished panel.

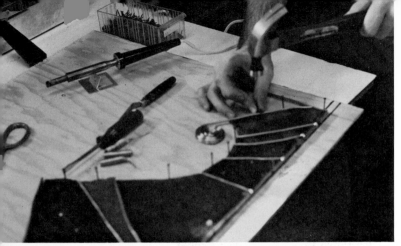

Nails are driven into the wood along that line, and U-channeled stained-glass leading is laid against that edge. Units are fitted into the channel, and nails are used to hold these pieces in place. H-channeled leading is cut and placed between pieces and soldered to the border channel.

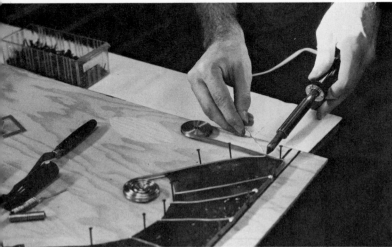

This process of using nails for support, soldering, fitting in new pieces, nailing, and soldering is continued until the panel is completed.

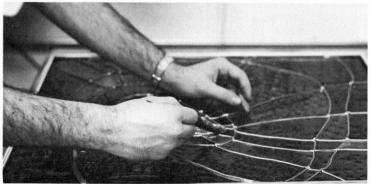

When all the leading has been soldered, epoxy putty is pressed around the cames for additional support.

The final panel is 18″ x 26″.

STAINED "GLASS" LAMP

Materials and Equipment

> Poly-Mosaic tiles
> kitchen oven or broil-oven
> aluminum cookie sheet
> spatula
> plywood a few inches larger than the projected circumference and height of the lamp
> nails and hammer
> U and H channeled leading
> solder and soldering iron
> two-part epoxy putty (steel-filled looks best)

Procedures

The techniques used in making this Spanish-style stained "glass" lamp are basically the same as those applied in making the stained "glass" panel. Here, though, after the geometric design is completed as a flat panel, the sheet is carefully bent at the joints to form a cylindrical shape.

Individual units are formed by fitting six tiles together in a three-tile by two-tile rectangle. Fuse these forms in the oven at 350° F. Heat the units long enough so that they join solidly. While the units are still hot, a spatula should be used to press the sides in, making the edges straight. Or, they can be trimmed, when cool, on a jig-, saber, or band saw. Tiles should not be overlapped since the lead cames have channels just wide enough to accommodate the thickness of one tile.

When the units have fused, remove the tray from the oven and allow them to cool. If the undersides of the pieces have been dulled by the tray, the plastic may be given a high gloss by lightly sweeping the surface with a flame from a propane torch.

When all the pieces have been completed in this way, organize them on a table as they should be fitted together. In the lamp illustrated, the light blue, sapphire blue, and turquoise tile pieces are arranged in a more or less random pattern so that the cylindrical final product shows no beginning or ending point, but instead maintains the same continuity all around.

Once the pattern is established, the pieces are ready to be leaded. The leading procedure is identical to that used in the stained "glass" panel, except that all the cames used in the lamp will be H channel except for the lamp's bottom and top, which are the last pieces to be soldered on. To begin leading, a strip of H channel should be placed against the row of nails.

You will find that since all the pieces are of the same dimensions and will come at regular intervals, one direction of cames can easily be made a continuous H channel. Make the vertical pieces continuous, since when the lamp is ready to be bent into a cylinder, the rows of rectangles will form stronger, straighter, more evenly stressed sides.

When the H channel leading for the flat panel is completed, solder strips of U channel to the top and bottom. Next, bend the panel into a cylinder. To do this, bend each row individually a little bit at a time, putting as little stress on the soldered joints as possible. After doing this several times, always being careful not to force too many joints, the cylinder should be completed. Then, the opposite ends which now meet should be soldered together.

You may find that some soldering spots have come apart and that some of the tile pieces are slightly out of their channels. These two slight deformities may be repaired by gently pressing the jutting pieces back into their proper channels and re-soldering the faulty joints.

Make sure that all the solder acid left on the lamp has been washed off, using mild soapy water. Then you may use steel-filled epoxy, as in the previous project, to strengthen the lamp and seal the spaces between channel and pieces through which light may escape. This procedure also assures that, if jolted, tile units will remain firmly in place. The light that filters through the finished lamp can help to create a subdued and romantic atmosphere.

After nails are driven into the wood along a starting line, H-channel stained-glass leading is laid against the edge. Units can then be fitted into the channel and be temporarily braced in place by nails.

More strips of H-channel leading are then cut, placed between pieces, and soldered around the units to complete the grid.

Having completed the flat panel, the form should be carefully bent into a cylindrical shape. Breaks in the cames created by stress can be mended by resoldering. Any gaps between the plastic and the leading should be filled with steel-filled epoxy putty.

The completed lamp is 14″ tall with a 5″ diameter.

A TRANSLUCENT MOSAIC BOWL

Materials and Equipment

Poly-Mosaic tiles
kitchen oven or broil-oven
Pyrex bowl or other heatable form (to
be used for sagging in the oven)
aluminum cookie sheet
spatula
tile nippers

Procedures

A sturdy bowl of fusible mosaic tiles is made by first forming and melting Poly-Mosaics into a flat plastic sheet. (The bowl shown here is made with two layers of Poly-Mosaic tiles, one built over the other.) This fused flat unit is then placed over a bowl and is sagged in an oven until the plastic assumes the curved shape.

Cut and arrange Poly-Mosaic tiles in a circular shape on a cookie sheet large enough to overlap and later sag over your mold form. Arrange clear tiles as an overlapping layer of plastic on the base layer.

This will fill in any gaps that may form between the tiles of the first layer and will also strengthen the form.

Gingerly place the double-level piece in your oven heated to 350° F. Melt the form until it fuses. Remove this fused plastic from the oven and allow it to cool for just a moment. While still hot and pliable, pry it from the tray with a spatula.

Place your ovenware or Pyrex bowl (which will serve as the mold for sagging the plastic) face down on the cookie sheet. Be certain that your mold has no undercuts, otherwise the sagged form when cool will lock into place. Lay the fused plastic unit on top of the bowl.

Both the bowl and plastic are placed in the oven. Under heat, the Poly-Mosaic sheet will quickly sag over the bowl. When sufficiently curved, remove the bowl and its plastic counterpart from the oven. Allow both to cool.

The Poly-Mosaic bowl will release easily from its mold. Any dull surfaces may be "polished" with a propane torch or candle flame.

After cutting and arranging the design layer of Poly-Mosaic tiles on the cookie sheet, place an entire level of clear tiles over the first level. This will strengthen the unit by invisibly filling in any gaps in the first layer.

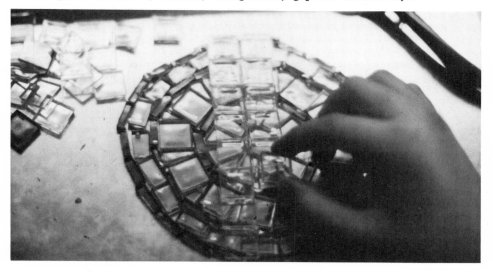

Put the double-layer form in the oven at 350° F.

Allow it to melt until both layers of tiles fuse together completely. Then remove the piece from the oven.

While still hot, use a metal spatula to lift the plastic sheet from the tray. Place an ovenware or Pyrex bowl top down on the aluminum tray and lay the still hot circle of fused plastic over the rounded bottom of the bowl. Return the tray to the oven and allow the plastic to sag over the bowl.

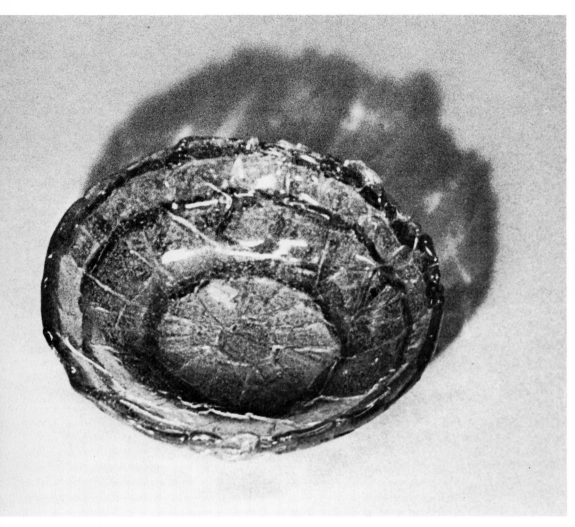

The bowl may be brought to a high gloss by sweeping its surface lightly with a flame.

PLASTIC FOAMS, also called cellular or expanded plastics, are used extensively as packing materials and for insulation but also can be utilized by the craftsman in many ways.

The two solid foams we work with, polystyrene and polyurethane foams, are both readily available through hardware stores, lumberyards, and craft suppliers. Styrofoam (Dow Chemical Company's trade name for polystyrene foam) is so familiar to most of us that it has become a household word.

Both plastic foams are available in blocks of different sizes. They are fire resistant (although they will melt when heated), and more importantly, they are lightweight and easy to work with. No elaborate equipment is required for gluing, cutting, sanding or the other working procedures.

Most rigid polystyrene foams are white in color. Polyurethane foams may be white, yellow, or even light blue.

Both foams are considered nontoxic. The only exception here are the gases given off when polyurethane is heated. But since there is no reason for the craftsman ever to expose this material to heat, this should not pose any problem.

POLYSTYRENE AND POLYURETHANE FOAM PROCESSES

Choosing a Foam

Polystyrene and polyurethane foams have different properties. The former usually comes in just one density or hardness, while polyurethane is available in many different densities for different uses. Where strength is a requirement, polyurethane foams of greater densities are specified. Polyurethane foams are also resistant to corrosion by many chemicals. Polyester resins, lacquer, and other coatings may be applied directly to the polyurethane foam surface. Polystyrene, on the other hand, is dissolved by polyesters, lacquers, and other solvents and thinners. But this quality is not the universal disadvantage that you might think. As you will see later in this chapter, the dissolvability of polystyrene foam can be an asset.

Cutting

Both foams may be sawed using handsaws, band, saber, circular, or jigsaws. Blade speeds of 2,000' to 5,000' per minute are recommended for polyurethane foams, and polystyrene can also be scored and broken relatively evenly if the piece is thin enough.

Intricate shapes may be cut in polystyrene foam with the use of a hot-wire cutter. Plans for construction of your own may be obtained by writing directly to Dow Chemical Company, Plastics Department, Midland, Michigan. Commercially designed hot-wire cutters are manufactured by the Dura-Tech Corporation, 1555 N.W. First Avenue, Boca Raton, Florida. Do not use hot-wire cutters on polyurethane foams since the fumes are extremely toxic, and even when cutting polystyrene foam, adequate ventilation should be provided. Electric carving knives also make excellent tools for cutting these materials.

Polystyrene foams are available in blocks several feet long and up to a foot square. Rigid polyurethane foams can be obtained in a wide variety of thicknesses and dimensions.

Sanding

Both rigid foams may be sanded by hand or with sanding disks or belts. You will find that scrap pieces of foam may be used as sanding instruments as well. Simply use these scraps as you would sandpaper.

Coatings

Since polystyrene foams are attacked by many coatings, it is best to seal the pores with acrylic gesso or a thin coating of plaster of Paris before painting. Usually this will work. Water-based paints like vinyls, latex paints, or acrylics may be applied directly, and epoxy resin pastes will not affect this material. If you think a paint will work but you are not certain, test it out on a small section first. You can tell right away because the polystyrene will shrink and become soft and sticky as it dissolves.

Polyurethane foams may be coated with any number of materials, although here too a test is worth the time. Polyesters, lacquers, and most commercially available paints will not injure this foam.

Adhesives

Polystyrene foam is just as choosy about its adhesives as it is about surface coatings. There are several adhesives that will bond pieces of this foam together or to other surfaces. Epoxy resin adhesives, acrylic or polyvinyl acetate pastes, and rubber cement will all perform admirably. There are also some liquid and rubber-based cements made especially for polystyrene foams.

Epoxy and urea or resorcinol-based resin adhesives are recommended for adhering polyurethane foams. Rubber glues will also provide a firm bond.

Carving

Polystyrene and polyurethane foams may be carved with knives or linoleum cutters, and they can be scraped with pointed instruments.

In this line, polystyrene foams have the added advantage of being readily cut

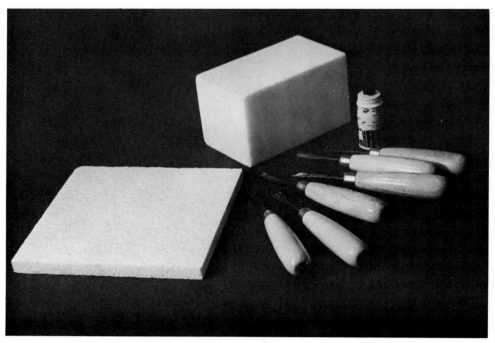

Polystyrene and polyurethane foams are often used for packing, but both materials are easily purchased commercially. Use linoleum cutting tools, X-acto knives, or other sharp instruments to carve these foams. Polystyrene foams may be heat-carved with a soldering pen.

by soldering pens. Intricate designs may be created by melting the surface with the point of an electric pen or needle or blade heated in a flame.

Solvents may also be used to "carve" into polystyrene foams. Turpentine and lacquer—which will dissolve this material on contact—may be used in controlled amounts to create intriguing patterns, surfaces, and textures. For many artisans, the fact that polystyrene is so easily affected by these solvents has become its chief asset.

CARVING IN A POLYURETHANE BLOCK

Materials and Equipment

    rigid polyurethane block
    a pencil
    carving knife
    acrylic gesso and fine brush
    sandpaper and files (both optional)

Procedures

Rigid polyurethane is a cellular plastic, and several grades are readily available through arts and crafts suppliers. Intricate shapes can be created by carving this plastic form with X-acto knives or other sharp tools. It has great strength for its weight, and it is possible to carve very thin sections.

Begin with a block. Pencil sketch your plan on the sides and ends. Begin carving by removing the largest areas first, such as corners. For example, the form shown has an evenly curved top; the top's corners were first cut away and the lines redrawn.

This process of cutting away the undesired polyurethane is then a simple one. Mistakes are easily corrected. If you cut away too much plastic in one area, use some two-part epoxy adhesive to glue on some scraps. Then cut away the excess again.

When your form is almost complete you may want to sand the surface. Sandpaper, files, or even a piece of the foam itself will serve quite well.

For an even matte finish, paint the rigid polyurethane foam with several coats of acrylic gesso. If you want a perfectly smooth surface, apply about five coats of acrylic gesso and sand until smooth with medium-fine, dry sandpaper.

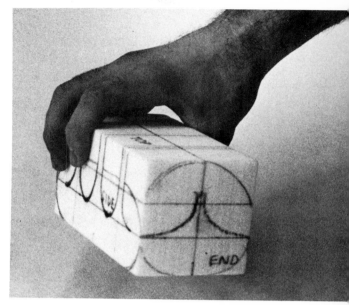

Sketch your projected shape on the rigid polyurethane block in pencil.

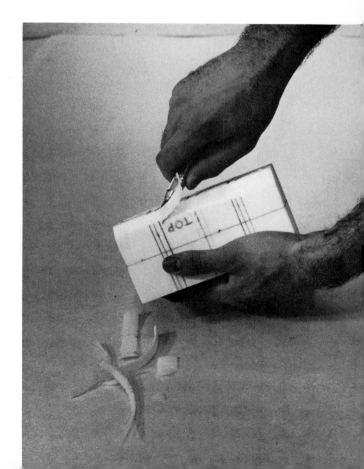

Begin cutting away with a carving knife.

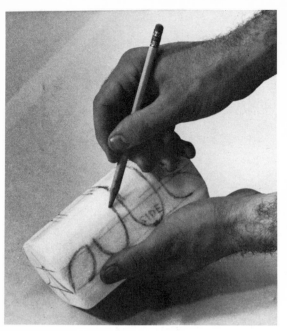

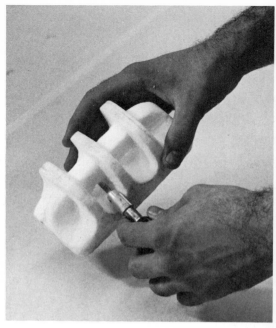

Lines may be redrawn when necessary as a guide to your progress.

Curves and undercuts are easily carved in this material. If you cut away too much, glue on some scraps with two-part epoxy glue, then cut away the excess.

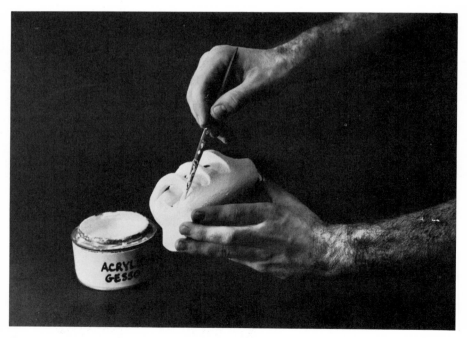

Paint the polyurethane with acrylic gesso. Apply several coats. The gesso may be sanded smooth when dry.

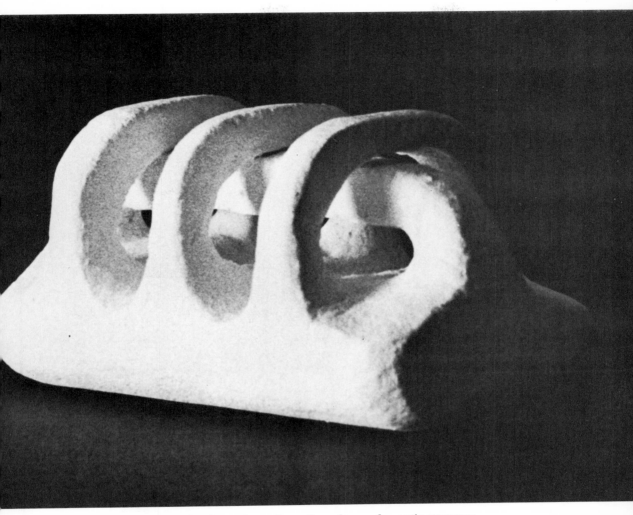

This hand-carved polyurethane foam form has a dramatic presence.

Nude. Thom Haxo. Beginning with a clay model, Thom Haxo carved this sculpture from blocks of polyurethane foam that were joined with two-part epoxy glue. The foam was finished with several coats of acrylic gesso that were sanded smooth.

HEAT-CARVED POLYSTYRENE PANELS

Materials and Equipment

> rigid polystyrene foam blocks
> soldering pencil
> Masonite base
> acrylic paints

Procedures

A controlled heat source may be used to heat-carve patterns into rigid polystyrene foam blocks. Here, a soldering pencil is employed as the tool for heat-carving.

With the hot soldering pencil, simply draw the lines and designs you wish to inscribe into the foam. The heat will melt the polystyrene foam leaving a carved channel in its wake. Different widths and depths may be carved by using different widths in the soldering pencil.

After carving the designs in the foam, arrange the units as you like on a piece of Masonite. This board may be painted first with acrylic paint. After the paint has dried, adhere carved polystyrene in an arrangement on the Masonite with rubber cement.

To accent the relief of the carved polystyrene, roll acrylic paint on the face of the foam pieces.

The result, depending upon the design, may become anything from a delicate, realistic animal form to an abstract, rhythmic expression.

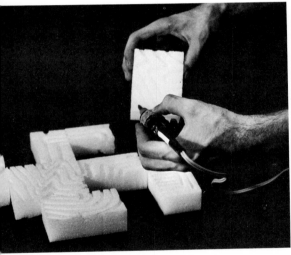

Carve into rigid polystyrene foam with a soldering pen. Use rubber cement to glue your design to a piece of Masonite which has been painted with acrylic paint.

This abstract *Indian Bird* was hatched from heat-carved polystyrene blocks. The top surface was painted with acrylic paint.

PRINTING WITH RIGID POLYURETHANE FOAM

Materials and Equipment

> rigid polyurethane foam
> two-part epoxy glue
> block cutting tools
> an inking plate
> block-printing ink
> soft rubber brayer
> block-printing paper
> metal spoon

Procedures

Pieces of rigid polyurethane foam may be cemented together to make larger printing blocks. Two-part epoxy glue works best. Apply the glue and use pressure to hold the foam pieces together. When the epoxy hardens, the surface may be sanded by rubbing with another piece of polyurethane foam.

Pieces of rigid polyurethane foam may be cemented together with a two-part epoxy cement.

Polyurethane foam may be carved with almost any tool. Block-carving knives and even kitchen knives will give you accurate results.

When the epoxy hardens the surface may be evened by rubbing with another piece of foam.

Once your block is completely carved and flattened, it should be inked with block-printing ink. Water-soluble inks are recommended, since they are much easier to clean from your inking plate and brayer. Oil inks give a professional result, but the clean-up process is more difficult.

Give your block a complete coating with ink. Then lay a sheet of dampened block-printing paper over the inked foam. Paper may be dampened by wetting it and then laying it between sheets of newspaper to remove excess water. Smooth out the paper with your hands, and burnish the surface with the back of a metal spoon. You will be able to see clearly which areas of the block need more burnishing in order to transfer the ink to the paper.

Remove the paper by lifting it quickly and carefully from one corner straight up. Allow the print to dry fully before framing. To make more prints just repeat the process.

The ink was first rolled out on a glass plate and then transferred to the block with a soft rubber brayer.

Thom Haxo used linoleum-cutting tools to carve this block. He began with the ink sketch shown in the foreground.

Lay the dampened paper over the inked block carefully. Begin in the center and then lower the ends.

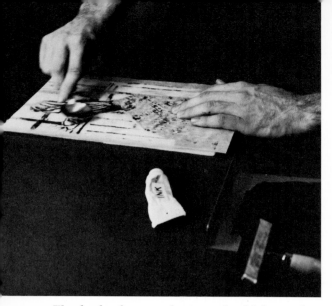

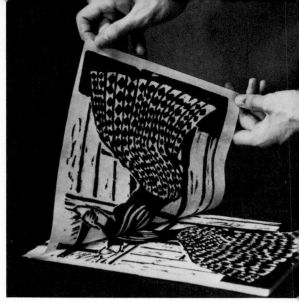

The back of a metal spoon should be used to burnish the paper until the ink is transferred from the block.

To remove the print lift it carefully from one end.

Wistful Gaze (8″ x 10″). Thom Haxo. The print is on the left and the block is on the right.

Rigid polyurethane foam blocks can be printed in many combinations. These three prints show· how a single block, cut in concentric circles, can be used to create three very different results. With proper care rigid polyurethane foam blocks will survive at least a hundred printings.

Rigid polyurethane foam may be "carved" by pressing in as well as carving.

Thom Haxo shows the use of a beaded chain to texture the queen's tresses.

Another printing method is to press the block onto dampened paper that is laid over a sandwich of newspaper and foam rubber.

PRINTING WITH A RIGID POLYURETHANE FOAM BLOCK

Materials and Equipment

rigid polyurethane foam
two-part epoxy glue
block-cutting tools
an inking plate
block-printing ink
soft rubber brayer
block-printing paper
metal spoon
newspapers and a layer of foam rubber

Procedures

The materials and equipment necessary for this printing with a polyurethane block are the same as in the preceding project. Thom Haxo has added an interesting variation to printing with foam by carving two sides of a single block of polyurethane.

This block was "carved" by pressing an object into the foam rather than carving it out. Chains and other common household forms may be pressed into the foam and then removed to give it pattern.

In this case, instead of laying the dampened paper over the block, the block is pressed onto the paper.

Sandwich a sheet of foam rubber between several sections of newspaper. Place the dampened paper over the newspaper and press down your block.

Maintain firm pressure for a few seconds to make certain that the ink will be transferred to the paper.

190

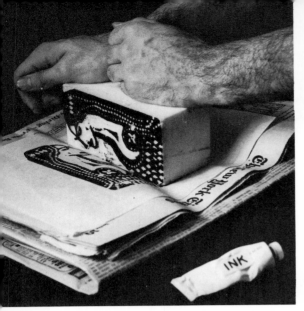

Press the block down firmly and maintain pressure for a few seconds to make certain that the ink will be transferred.

Remove the block carefully and allow the ink and paper to dry.

Face to Face (6″ x 6″). Thom Haxo.

191

PRINTING ON CLOTH WITH ACRYLIC PAINT AND A RIGID POLYSTYRENE FOAM BLOCK

Materials and Equipment

    rigid polystyrene foam block
    acrylic paint
    metal spoon
    hand barren
    inking plate
    soft rubber brayer
    piece of cloth

Procedures

Cloth may be printed with either polystyrene or polyurethane blocks. But polystyrene has the added advantage of being easily heat-carved with a soldering pen.

After washing and ironing the textile —in this case a fine silk—apply ink to your block. You may brush the acrylic paint directly onto the block or you may apply it with a soft rubber brayer.

In this case the inked block was pressed firmly onto the cloth, and then the whole thing turned over so that the cloth was on top of the block. Burnish the surface with the barren and with the back of a spoon to make certain that the paint is being transferred. With thin fabrics, the acrylic paint will penetrate. It is not a mistake if this happens—in fact it makes it easier to see which areas need more pressure to transfer the paint to the textile. Just be careful that you do not rub the surface *too* vigorously. If you do, the soft plastic foam will become crushed and lose its definition.

Continue the printing process until the entire cloth is covered. Variations may be obtained by printing over the first color with another acrylic pigment, or printing on the reverse side.

Allow the acrylic paint to dry thoroughly. When it is dry, the acrylic paint will be permanent, and the fabric may be washed by hand with mild soap and water.

Paint the block with a brush or spread the acrylic paint with a soft rubber brayer. Press the painted block onto the cloth.

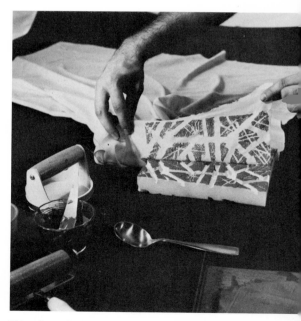

Flip the whole thing over so that the cloth lies on top of the block, and burnish the surface with a barren or the back of a spoon. Lift off the cloth, and repeat this process until the fabric is completely covered.

Hand-printed cloth serves handsomely in an arrangement, as a kerchief, or as dress material.

A RELIEF PANEL OF POLYSTYRENE FOAM AND TWO-PART EPOXY

Materials and Equipment

> polystyrene foam
> soldering pencil or a blunt instrument
>   for cutting
> several tubes of two-part epoxy cement
> sand
> lacquer thinner

Procedures

When carving your design into the polystyrene foam, it is possible to use any number of methods. Heat-carving, a blunt instrument for pressing into the soft foam, or sharp tools will all work admirably.

Be certain to utilize the full thickness by carving the foam at different levels. The relief will be clear in the finished panel and the use of different depths adds considerably to the final piece.

Mix several tubes of two-part epoxy cement with about 40 percent sand. Blend plastic and sand thoroughly. Then press the mixture into the channels in the foam, and spread sand-filled epoxy evenly over the top. Unlike polyester resin, which will dissolve polystyrene foam, epoxy will not affect this temporary, disposable mold.

When the epoxy hardens completely, pour lacquer thinner on the foam to dissolve it. The lacquer will not affect the hard epoxy. Make certain that you have adequate ventilation to draw off the fumes of the lacquer thinner.

Heat-carve a piece of polystyrene foam. Try to carve to different levels with the soldering pencil since the final piece will be in relief.

Mix several tubes of two-part epoxy glue in a paper cup.

Add 40 percent sand (by volume) to the glue.

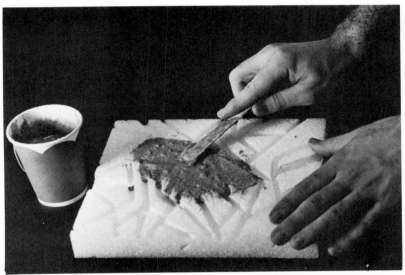

Press the mixture into the channels of the foam, and spread more sand-filled epoxy over the top of the foam to form a backing.

When the epoxy cures, pour lacquer over the foam. This will dissolve the foam without harming the epoxy.

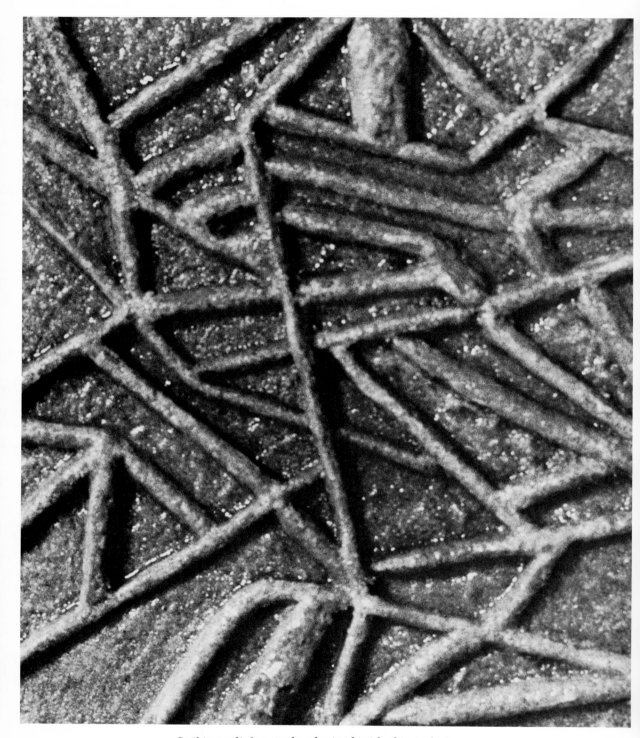

Striking reliefs may be obtained with this technique.

IN THE TWENTIETH CENTURY, great strides have been made in developing the giant man-made molecules we know as plastics. Industrialists, artists, and craftsmen have begun to explore the myriad applications of these materials. Working with dozens of commercially available plastics such as polyester resin, acrylic, fusible thermoplastics and plastic foams, designers and arists are beginning to scratch the surface of the potential of plastics both in the utilitarian and aesthetic veins. But only of late have the craftsmen and laymen begun to even consider the plastic medium beyond its often basic industrial role.

From the early industrial uses of plastics for making those horrid "baby dolls" and "plastic flowers," the general public came to recognize and associate plastic materials as something fragile, limited, and temporal. We hope that through this book the reader has come to see the true values of plastics. Today's plastics are as diverse in numbers as in function: flexible or rigid, fusible or heat resistant, strong as steel or biodegradable. In just the last few decades, plastics have been created which truly merit their "flexible" name.

We hope that by using this text craftsmen have come to understand some of the intrinsic properties peculiar to the plastic medium. Once the artisan realizes what his material can do, his designs can then better suit his working medium. Plastics certainly have more diverse properties and capabilities than any other craft material. But to best utilize these advantages, craftsmen must learn to design projects in a plastics image. Plastics are not meant to imitate other substances such as glass, wood, or cement. Just as one would never treat glass as wood in crafts, the craftsman should never treat plastics as anything but plastics. The projects in this book emphasize this need for reorienting design to *plastics*, recognizing these polymers for what they are and the fabulous things they are able to do.

6

TOWARD A FUTURE

197

This print shows one striking optical possibility offered the printmaking craftsman through these materials.

Plastics in their craft form are underdeveloped. The field is open for artisans to experiment. Exploration in this medium, which should bring the greatest sense of accomplishment to the craftsman, can also lead to very personal results dictated by the craftsman's own creative spirit—tempered by both your talents and the potential of plastics. The plastic elements of color, texture, shape, and sheer inbred vitality make creating in the plastics realm an overwhelmingly exciting experience. There is no end of possibilities for the medium, if the craftsman keeps on experimenting.

We hope that the reader-craftsman will not simply take each design and project in this book and duplicate them. Imagination used in designing plastic forms yields more satisfactory results than copying our designs. For example, try to apply the acrylic modeling paste to picture frames or boxes. Thousands of forms other than seashells may be cast in RTV molds. Tesserae panels needn't depict just cityscapes. Fish mobiles of fusible thermoplastics may evolve into butterflies. Polyester-resin-filled particle board tables can lead to polyester designs on walls, panels, room dividers . . . the applications and possibilities are endless once the basic plastic principles and techniques are understood and practiced. Your craft forms can be startlingly beautiful, but more importantly, they are justified by the great fun of creating with plastics.

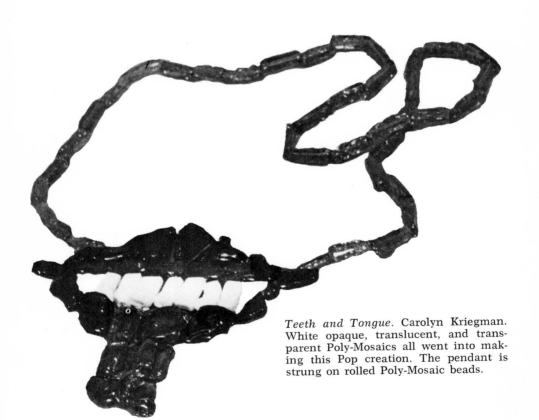

Teeth and Tongue. Carolyn Kriegman. White opaque, translucent, and transparent Poly-Mosaics all went into making this Pop creation. The pendant is strung on rolled Poly-Mosaic beads.

Cook, J. Gordon. *Your Guide to Plastics*. England: Merrow Publishing, 1968.

Garret, Lillian. *Visual Design*. New York: Reinhold Publishing, 1967.

Lucite Design Handbook. Wilmington, Delaware: E. I. du Pont de Nemours & Co., 1968.

Modern Plastics Encyclopedia. New York: McGraw-Hill Publications, 1970–71.

Moholy-Nagy, L. *Vision in Motion*. Chicago: Paul Teobald, 1947.

Moseley, Spencer, Pauline Johnson, and Hazel Koenig. *Crafts Design*. Belmont, California: Wadsworth Publishing, 1963.

Newman, Thelma R. *Creative Candlemaking*. New York: Crown Publishers, Inc., 1972.

———. *Plastics as an Art Form*. Philadelphia: Chilton Books, Revised Edition, 1969.

———. *Plastics as Design Form*. Philadelphia: Chilton Books, 1972.
Roukes, Nicholas. *Crafts in Plastics*. New York: Watson-Guptill Publications, 1970.

BIBLIOGRAPHY

Acetone
   a solvent used to clean up uncured polyester resin.

Acrylic
   a synthetic resin formed under heat and pressure into sheets, tubes, and rods. Acrylic is available in a variety of colors and finishes including mirrored finish. Common trade names are *Plexiglas, Lucite,* and *Acrylite.*

Blow-molding
   a forming operation in which air pressure forces heated plastic into a mold.

Casting
   to form an object by pouring liquid resin into a mold.

Casting Resin
   usually a clear, water-white polyester used extensively by artists and craftsmen.

Catalyst
   a chemical used to initiate the curing process. For polyester resins the most common catalyst is methyl ethyl ketone (MEK) peroxide.

Cementing
   joining plastics with solvents or adhesives.

Collage
   a technique of composing a work of art by combining materials not normally associated with one another.

Cure
   or *set* is the process by which the physical properties of a plastic change. In polyester resin the cure is effected by the addition of a catalyst which changes the plastic from a liquid to a solid.

Decoupage
   the technique of decorating a surface with paper cutouts.

Delamination
   the separation of layers in a laminate usually of fiberglass.

Embedment
   an object within a casting or a lamination. The resin is usually clear or transparent.

GLOSSARY

Epoxy
a plastic that can take the place of polyester, shrinks less, and is often used as an adhesive. It is available in two-part (catalyst and resin) kits.

Exotherm
heat generated by a chemical reaction, usually resulting in a resin curing.

Fiberglass
melted glass is spun into fibers and made into woven or chopped strand mats.

Flocking
the application of glue and a soft, velvet-like powder of synthetic fiber that coats the area to a soft matte finish.

FRP
fiberglass-reinforced polyester resin.

Fillers
are usually inert materials that are added to plastic resins to change their properties in some way. Often, fillers will be added to make resin more thixotropic or stronger.

Gel
an intermediate stage in the curing process of resin evidenced by a gelatin-like appearance. In the gel state the resin has taken shape, but it is not yet hot or fully cured.

Gesso
gypsum, or plaster of Paris, prepared with glue for use as a surface painting.

Impasto
a technique in which the medium employed has a thickness that extends away from the surface in highly textured effects.

Lamination
the process of impregnating an absorbent material, often fiberglass, with resin and allowing it to cure.

Laminating Resin
a resin used as a binder for fiberglass or other absorbent materials.

Latex
a flexible organic compound often used as a mold or as a resist material.

Light Box
a five-sided enclosure that houses a light source. The light is directed out of the box so that it defines transparent plastic forms.

Light Piping
the ability of acrylic to transmit light from one end to another.

Masking
the process of covering part of a surface to protect it from scratches or paint while another part of the surface is being worked.

Mold-release Agent
a lubricant used to coat surfaces to prevent resins from sticking.

Mylar®
trademark of E. I. du Pont de Nemours for polyester film useful as a separating film for polyester resin.

Opaque
nontransparent.

Parting Agent
see *mold-release agent.*

Pigment
a nonsoluble colorant. Pigments are usually associated with opaque colors.

Plastic
any substance that can be formed or deformed under heat and pressure.

Plastic Memory
the quality of some thermoplastics that will return to their original shape after reheating.

Polyester Resin
a thermosetting resin with a syrupy consistency.

Polystyrene
a thermoplastic.

PVC
polyvinyl chloride.

Pot-life
the length of time after the addition of a catalyst that a plastic will remain workable. This is not to be confused with *shelf-life.*

Relief
the projection of an ornament from the principal surface.

Resist

the process of keeping dyes from attacking fabrics by coating the fabric.

Set

the process of converting a liquid resin to a solid state by curing.

Shelf-life

the length of time that a resin may be stored and still remain workable.

Silk-Screen Printing

a printing process which uses a taut woven fabric as a stencil.

Solvent

a substance that dissolves other substances.

Storage Life

see *shelf-life*.

Tack-free

a surface that will not mark when touched.

Thermoplastic

a material that will soften when heated and harden when cooled. A thermoplastic material may be repeatedly heated, softened, and reshaped.

Thermosetting Plastic

a material that becomes a solid due to chemical changes and may not be readily transformed to its original state. Once a thermosetting material assumes its shape, it is considered permanent.

Thixotropic

is the ability of a liquid to resist the pull of gravity. The addition of certain fillers thickens resins and transforms them into a paste form that will not run when applied to vertical surfaces.

Translucent

allowing light to pass through.

Transparent

clear, allowing one to see through to the other side of the object.

Tusche

a substance used in silk-screen printing as a resist.

Undercut

protuberances that lock a cured form into its mold and prevent its removal.

Working Life

see *pot-life*.

MANUFACTURERS USUALLY do not sell small amounts but will be happy to send you product information. When inquiring of manufacturers about the sale of small quantities please ask them for their nearest source to your location.

ADHESIVES FOR PLASTICS

Adhesive Products Corp.
    1660 Boone Avenue
    Bronx, New York 10460
Many different adhesives.

Columbia Cement Co.
    159 Hanse
    Freeport, New York 11520
Quik Stik, rubber cement for urethane foam.

Eastman Chemical Products, Inc.
    Chemicals Division
    Kingsport, Tenn. 37662
Eastman 910 will glue almost anything. Exceptionally strong.

Guard Coating and Chemical Corp.
    58 John Jay Avenue
    Kearney, New Jersey 07032
Cements for: acrylics, Mylars, nylons, styrenes, PVAs, PVCs, epoxies, and polyesters.

Rezolin Division of
Hexcel Corporation
    20701 Nordhoff Street
    Chatsworth, Calif. 91311
Cements for epoxy, acrylic, and polyester.

Schwartz Chemical Co., Inc.
    50-01 Second Street
    Long Island City, New York 11101
Solvent cements.

CATALYST

Catalyst may be obtained from all jobbers of polyester resin.

Lucidol Division
Wallace and Tiernan Inc.
    1740 Military Road
    Buffalo, New York 14217
MEK Peroxide.

SOURCES OF SUPPLY

Reichold Chemicals, Inc.
   RCI Building
   White Plains, New York 10602
MEK Peroxide.

COLOR

Color may be obtained from all jobbers of polyester resin.

Chempico Pigments and Dispersions Co.
   P.O. Box 203
   South Orange, New Jersey 07079
Polyester color pastes.

Ferro Corp.
   Color Division
   Cleveland, Ohio 44105

Patent Chemical Inc.
   335 McLean Boulevard
   Paterson, New Jersey 07504

Plastics Molders Supply Co., Inc.
   75 South Avenue
   Fanwood, New Jersey 07023

FOAMS

Styrofoam may be purchased at any 5 & 10.

Artfoam
   100 East Montauk Highway
   Lindenhurst, New York 11757
Urethane foam in blocks of different sizes.

FILLERS

Cabot Corp.
   125 High Street
   Boston, Mass. 02110
Cab-O-Sil.

Carey-Canadian Mines Ltd.
   320 S. Wayne Avenue
   Cincinnati, Ohio 45215
Asbestos.

Diamond Alkali Co.
   300 Union Commerce Building
   Cleveland, Ohio 44115
Calcium carbonate.

Plymouth Fibers Co., Inc.
   Traffic and Palmetto Streets
   Brooklyn, New York 11227
Cotton flock.

FILM

E. I. du Pont de Nemours & Co., Inc.
   Wilmington, Delaware 19898
Mylar film.

FINISHES

Ditzler Automotive Finishes
   Detroit, Mich. 48204
Acrylic lacquer for spray coating.

PPG Industries, Inc.
   1 Gateway Center
   Pittsburgh, Pa. 15222
"Durethane 600" elastomeric lacquer and "Durethane 100" elastomeric lacquer thermosetting enamel, both for use over urethane foam.

MACHINES AND ACCESSORIES

Bits

AAA Saw and Tool Service and Supply Co.
   1401-07 Washington Blvd.
   Chicago, Ill. 60607
Router bits.

Henry L. Hanson Co.
   25 Union Street
   Worcester, Mass. 01608
High speed drills for acrylic.

Saw Blades

DoAll Dart-Precision
   254 No. Laurel Avenue
   Des Plaines, Ill. 60016
Band saw blades.

Lemmon & Snoap
   2618 Thornwood S.W.
   Grand Rapids, Mich. 48506
Carbide-tipped circular saw blades.

Polishing Equipment

Divine Brothers Co.
Hardware Products Division
    200 Seward Avenue
    Utica, New York 13503
Complete line of buffing and polishing machinery and wheels and compounds.

Foam Cutting Machines

Dura-Tech Corp.
    1555 N.W. First Avenue
    Boca Raton, Florida 33432
Hot-wire cutters.

Safety Masks

Acme Protection Equipment Co.
    1201 Kalamazoo Street
    South Haven, Michigan 49090

Spring and Toggle Clamps

Adjustable Clamp Co.
    417 No. Ashland Avenue
    Chicago, Ill. 60622

Lapeer Mfg. Co.
    1144 W. Baltimore
    Detroit, Mich. 48202

Strip Heaters

Briscoe Mfg. Co.
    Columbus, Ohio 43216
"Briskeat RH-36" heating element.

Electric Hotpack Co., Inc.
    5083 Cottman Street
    Philadelphia, Pa. 19135

General Electric Co.
    1 Progress Road
    Shelbyville, Ind. 46176

MISCELLANEOUS

Hand Cleaner

Ayerst Laboratories
    Department A
    685 Third Avenue
    New York, New York 10017
"Kerocleanse": removes resins from hands.
"Kerodex #71": blocks skin against irritants.

Jewelry Findings

Allcraft Tool and Supply Company
    215 Park Avenue
    Hicksville, New York 11801

Lamp Parts

Lamp Products
    P.O. Box 34
    Elma, New York 14059

Masks and Tapes

Borden Chemical Co.
    369 Madison Avenue
    New York, New York 10017
Clear "Mylar" tape.

J. L. N. Smythe Co.
    1300 West Lehigh Avenue
    Philadelphia, Pa. 19132
"Clearmask."

Spraylat
    1 Park Avenue
    New York, New York 10016
A water-soluble latex that can be brushed on. Dries in 45 minutes and may be peeled off when dry.

3M Company
    St. Paul, Minnesota 55101
Masking paper and protective tape.

Metal Frames

Contract Products Corp.
    636 Broadway
    New York, New York 10012
Extruded metal frame units, 8" to 40" long, in aluminum or gold finish.

MOLD MATERIALS

Adhesive Products Corp.
    1660 Boone Avenue
    Bronx, New York 10460
S-T-R-E-T-C-H-Y vinyl.

Dow Corning Corp.
    Midland, Mich. 48640
RTV silicone "Silastic."

Flexible Products Co.
    1007 Industrial Park Drive
    Marietta, Ga. 30061
Vinyl mold materials.

General Electric Co.
    1 River Road
    Schenectady, New York 12306
RTV silicone.

PAINT FOR PLASTICS

Glidden Co.
    11001 Madison Avenue
    Cleveland, Ohio 44102
"Glidden" acrylic sign finishes.

Keystone Refining Co., Inc.
    4821-31 Garden Street
    Philadelphia, Pa. 19137
"Grip-Flex."

Wyandotte Paint Products Co.
    P.O. Box 255
    Norcross, Ga. 30071
"Grip-Flex" and "Grip-Mask."

PLASTIC FINDINGS

Ace Plastic Co.
    91-30 Van Wyck Expressway
    Jamaica, New York 11435
Balls, rods, and tubes of acrylic.

Hastings Plastics Inc.
    1704 Colorado Avenue
    Santa Monica, California 90404
A complete range of plastics and supplies.

Industrial Plastics
    324 Canal Street
    New York, New York 10013
Full range of plastic resins, sheets, findings,
and supplies.

POLISHES, SANDPAPERS, AND COMPOUNDS

Permatex Co., Inc.
    P. O. Box 1350
    West Palm Beach, Florida 33402
"Permatex" plastic cleaner.

Surefire Products Co.
    6445 Bandini Blvd.
    Los Angeles, Calif. 90022
"Surefire" cleaner and scratch remover.

The Butcher Polish Co.
    Boston, Mass. 02148
Butcher's white diamond wax.

Matchless Metal Polish Co.
    Glen Ridge, N.J. 07028
Flannel buffs and several buffing compounds.

United Laboratories
    E. Linden Avenue
    Linden, New Jersey 07036
Muslin buffs and compound.

Carborundum Co.
    Niagara Falls, New York 14302
Wet or dry silicon-carbide sanding belts.

PLASTIC MOSAIC TILES

Ain Plastics
    65 Fourth Avenue
    New York, New York 10003

Boin Arts & Crafts Company
    91 Morris Street
    Morristown, N.J. 07960 and
    75 South Palm Avenue
    Sarasota, Florida 33577

CCM: Arts & Crafts, Inc.
    9520 Baltimore Avenue
    College Park, Maryland 20740

Dick Blick Co.
    Box 1267
    Galesburg, Ill. 61401

Economy Arts and Crafts
    47-11 Francis Lewis Blvd.
    Flushing, New York 11361

Model Craft Hobbies
    314 Fifth Avenue
    New York, N.Y. 10001

NASCO
    Fort Atkinson, Wisc. 53538

Poly-Dec Co., Inc.
    P. O. Box 541
    Bayonne, New Jersey 07002
"Poly-Mosaic" tiles, versatile, heat-fusible,
gluable ¾"-square tiles.

Sax-Arts & Crafts
    207 N. Milwaukee Street
    Milwaukee, Wisc. 53202

PLASTIC PAINTABLE MEDIUMS AND GLAZES

Brocado, Inc.
    Chicago, Ill. 60608
"Mod-Podge" decoupage glaze.

California Products Corp.
New Masters Fine Arts Division
    169 Waverly Street
    Cambridge, Mass. 02139
Acrylic vinyl copolymer gesso and modeling paste.

M. Grumbacher, Inc.
    460 West 34th Street
    New York, New York 10001
"Hyplar" acrylic polymer latex emulsion paste.

Hunt Manufacturing Co.
New Masters Fine Art Division
    Statesville, N.C. 28677
"Vanguard" acrylic polymer paint, gesso, and modeling paste.

Permanent Pigments
    Cincinnati, Ohio 45201
"Liquitex" polymer medium, gesso, and modeling paste.

PLASTIC PELLETS

Poly-Dec Co., Inc.
    P. O. Box 541
    Bayonne, New Jersey 07002
"Dec-Ets," fusible thermoplastic pellets. Will sell small quantities.

Shell Oil Co.
Plastics Division
    110 West 51st Street
    New York, New York 10020

PLASTIC PUTTIES

Devcon Corp.
    Danvers, Mass. 01923
Plastic steel and epoxy bond, steel- and aluminum-filled epoxy pastes.

Sculpmetal Co.
    701 Investment Building
    Pittsburgh, Pa. 15222
Plastic steel.

REINFORCEMENTS

Burlington Glass Fabrics
    1550 Broadway
    New York, New York 10018
Fiberglass.

Western Fibrous Glass Products
    739 Bryant Street
    San Francisco, Calif. 94107
Fiberglass.

RELEASE AGENTS

Dow Corning
    Midland, Mich. 48640
Silicone release paper.

Price Driscoll Corp.
    75 Milbar Road
    Farmingdale, New York 11735
General-purpose mold releases for epoxy and polyester resins.

RESINS AND SHEETING

Ain Plastics
    65 Fourth Avenue
    New York, New York 10003
A wide range of sheets, resins, and plastic findings.

American Acrylic Corp.
    173 Marine Street
    Farmingdale, New York 11735

American Cyanamid Co.
Plastics and Resins Division
    Wallingford, Conn. 06492
"Laminac" polyester resin.

Cadillac Plastics and Chemical Co.
    15841 Second Ave., P. O. Box 810
    Detroit, Mich. 48232
Polyester resin, "Plexiglas" acrylic, and an assortment of many other plastic products, available throughout North America.

Glidden Co.
    Baltimore, Maryland 21226
"Glidpol" polyester resin.

Industrial Plastics
    324 Canal Street
    New York, New York 10013
A jobber of a complete range of plastic resins and findings as well as blow-molded acrylic domes in various dimensions.

Koppers Co., Inc.
Tar and Chemical Division
    Koppers Building
    Pittsburgh, Pa. 15219
Polyester resin.

Model Craft Hobbies
    314 Fifth Avenue
    New York, N.Y. 10001
Polyester resin, molds, and various related
findings.

Polyproducts Corporation
    13810 Nelson Avenue
    Detroit, Michigan 48227
Suppliers of a complete line of resins, foam
systems, fillers, reinforcements, mold materials, and related equipment.

PPG Industries
Coatings and Resins Division
    1 Gateway Center
    Pittsburgh, Pa. 15222
"Selectron" polyester resin.

Reichold Chemicals, Inc.
    RCI Building
    White Plains, New York 10602
"Polylite" polyester resin.

Rohm & Hass Co.
    Sixth and Market Streets
    Philadelphia, Pa. 19106
"Plexiglas" acrylic and "Plexiglas" acrylic
mirror.

World of Plastics
    1129 S. Elmora Avenue
    Elizabeth, New Jersey 07202

SILK-SCREEN SUPPLIES

Advance Process Supplies Co.
    400 N. Noble
    Chicago, Ill. 60622

Naz-Dar Company
    1087 North Branch
    Chicago, Ill. 60622

Ulano Graphic Arts Supplies, Inc.
    610 Dean Street
    Brooklyn, New York 11238

SOLVENTS

National Solvent Corp.
    3751 Jennings Road
    Cleveland, Ohio 44109

Shell Chemical Co.
    110 West 51st Street
    New York, New York 10020
Acetone.

Union Carbide Co.
Chemicals and Plastics Division
    270 Park Avenue
    New York, New York 10017

STAINLESS-STEEL STRIPPING

Fred F. Wilcox Co., Inc.
    Box 1056
    Des Moines, Iowa 50311
"Form-A-Frame."

INDEX

(*Italic* figures refer to illustrations.)

DAVID WALDON

Snakes on a Plane

Thunder's Mouth Press New York

TO MY MOTHER, CINDERELLA WALDON,
WHO LIKES NEITHER SNAKES NOR PLANES

Snakes on a Plane: *The Guide to the Internet Ssssssensation*

Copyright © 2006 by David Waldon

Published in the United States by

Thunder's Mouth Press
An imprint of Avalon Publishing Group, Inc.
245 West 17th Street, 11th floor
New York, NY 10011
www.thundersmouth.com

AVALON
publishing group incorporated

First printing, August 2006

Library of Congress Cataloging-in-Publication Data is available.

ISBN-10: 1-56025-971-X
ISBN-13: 978-1-56025-971-8

9 8 7 6 5 4 3 2 1

Interior design by Pauline Neuwirth, Neuwirth & Associates

Printed in the United States of America
Distributed by Publishers Group West

"For behold, I send among you serpents, vipers against which there is no charm, and they shall bite you, said the Lord."
—Jeremiah 8.17

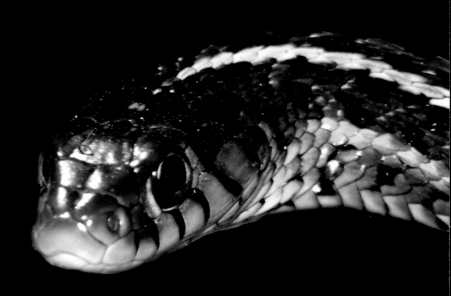

"I'VE GOT A PROBLEM. . . .
I'VE GOT A HANDFUL OF SNAKE
AND A HANDFUL OF PLANE."

INTRODUCTION

For sixty-two-year-old Monty Coles, Memorial Day weekend was a great opportunity to indulge in his longtime hobby as a pilot. He hadn't had a lot of chances to take his single-engine Piper Cherokee out for a spin recently, especially since he replaced that one engine with a new model. But the weather was good in Charleston, West Virginia, on that late Saturday morning in May, and Coles had the day off from his job selling kitchen cabinets. So he drove to the local airport and made preparations to take to the skies.

Coles' flight plan was simple: lift off, take some pictures of the view, and then land in the small southern Ohio town of Gallipolis to pick up some fuel. And the actual journey was simple—at first. But just as Coles was about to begin his approach for landing, he suddenly discovered that he wasn't the only occupant of his plane.

"I was scanning the instrument panel when this little head appeared in a hole in there," recalls Coles. "And I went, 'This isn't a good sign.'"

It was immediately obvious to Coles that the stowaway was a snake, mostly likely a resident of the hangar in Charleston who had fallen into the Cherokee from the roof. Quickly Coles looked for something to grab the intruder with. Finding nothing to do the job and upon the snake extending itself out of the hole by about four inches, Coles went to Plan B, reaching for a handheld radio and smacking the creature upside the noggin. All this achieved was the radio's batteries flung all over the place and the snake knocked down onto Coles' feet. It was then when the pilot realized the enormity of his situation. For this was no

MONTY COLES TRIUMPHANT AFTER HIS IN-AIR BATTLE: SAMUEL L. JACKSON HAS NOTHING ON HIM.

Photo by Paul Arbgoast.

tyke, but a four-and-a-half foot black snake who was just as displeased about the predicament as Coles.

"It was flopping around, and I was kicking like mad," says Coles. "And I just thought, 'Well, I'll just open the door and let him find his way out. Well, before I get to the door handle, he had shot up that side of the plane, and I just grabbed him right behind the head and held on."

Black snakes (which, by the way, are sometimes called pilot black snakes) are not venomous, but are constrictors, and this one lived up to its classification by coiling around Coles' arm and squeezing tight, while Coles was squeezing the

Snakes on a

FOR MORE THAN a decade, Paul Dergarabedian has been watching the Hollywood bottom line. As the president of Exhibitor Relations, Dergarabedian has reported on and analyzed the financial performance of every major studio release, and many minor ones. He's seen projected blockbusters fall on their asses and "sleepers" rouse the industry. But even Dergarabedian is taken aback by *Snakes on a Plane*, admitting in an interview (from, naturally, his car) that "it's not often that you have a movie that can take on a life of its own like this. We're talking about a moderately budgeted horror film, basically. We're not talking about a $100-150 million movie."

Q: Are you surprised that New Line didn't move the release date up to take advantage of the publicity—and maybe to short-circuit any chance for a premature dip in buzz?

A: I think it's good that they've stuck with the release date. Maybe it will just create more anticipation. But it is sort of a double-edged sword because you don't want to dilute the excitement by waiting too long to have the movie enter the marketplace. On the other hand, New Line has got to be loving this. You're talking about a lot of free publicity.

Q: The Internet activity is at a fever pitch now, but there's been some level of heat on this film for nearly a year now.

A: I think the minute that title hit the streets, it created an instant buzz . . . if you're a filmmaker, you have to be loving this. The only downside is that so much of it is out of the control of the marketing department of the studio. Usually marketing departments at studios are notorious for wanting to have complete control over everything. But this, in a way, is a blessing, because to have this many people talking about it, all of this buzz going on on the Internet—I just hope that the opening of the movie can live up to all of this hype.

Q: Is *Snakes on a Plane* review-proof at this point?

A: I think so. Because no one is going to not go because of a bad review. These types of movies don't get good reviews, anyway. And a movie called *Snakes on a Plane*, if it were to get good reviews, it might kill the credibility of the movie.

Q: New Line has not become litigious when it came to what was going on online, unlike what some other studios

DAVID R. ELLIS (PHOTO FROM 2004),
THE RINGMASTER OF THE "SNAKES" PIT.

Spreadsheet

have done the past. Do you think this could set a precedent of sorts, especially if "SoaP" does score well at the box office?

A: It's almost unprecedented to have a movie get this kind of pre-release attention that's not necessarily manufactured by the studio, and where the studio is not trying to stop anyone, really, from doing any of it. They're saying, "Let's embrace this and enjoy the fact that we're getting this much free publicity." Hopefully, it will turn out to be money in the bank for the studio.

Q: Bottom line—how will "SoaP" do at the box office?

A: This is a movie that certainly will have a box office, both domestically and abroad, that will be very strong. The DVD sales are pretty much of a foregone conclusion, as this will be a cult favorite. Horror films in general have had a very strong track record at the box office over the last five years, and this would be among the most high profile of those releases. It will truly be one of those films that makes a ton of money for the studio. And then think of the possibilities—you could have *Snakes on a Train*—you can transfer that title into all types of situations or different animals. It may open up a lot of possibilities. *Lizards on a Whatever*. One thing is that I will guarantee you that they will never show this as an in-flight movie.

Photo by David Livingston/Getty images.

Photo by Evan Agostini/Getty Images.

Photo by Peter Kramer/Getty Images.

CO-STARS FLEX ALEXANDER, RACHEL BLANCHARD AND JULIANNA MARGULIES—DID ANY OF THEM HAVE ANY IDEA WHAT "SOAP" WOULD TURN INTO? PROBABLY NOT.

snake's neck in return. Oh, and Coles still had a landing to worry about, being about six miles out of Gallipolis.

"There were several planes practicing in the pattern—it's a non-controlled airport," Coles said. "(So) I called ahead, and I said, 'I'd appreciate a straight-in on Runway Five with a priority; I've got a problem.'" The other pilots complied, and when one asked Coles what his problem was, he said, "Well, I've got a handful of snake and a handful of plane."

In the end, Coles made a smooth landing in Gallipolis, so smooth that a friend who witnessed the culmination of the flight suggested that he travel with a snake at all times, because that was the best landing he had seen Coles make. After briefly displaying his worthy opponent, Coles let the snake loose in a field by the runway, none the worse for wear other than a blooded nose. "The snake now resides in Ohio," he says. In fact, everyone involved was safe and sound—well, expect for the rat or mouse that's now a lump in the snake's midsection.

On another Saturday almost two months before Coles' flight, I received a call from a literary agent in New Jersey. He had seen a posting I had made on a writing jobs' board from three years before and wanted to know if I would be interested in writing a book proposal dealing with the high level of Internet activity surrounding a movie that was to be released in August called *Snakes on a Plane*. I already was familiar with the action-thriller, mostly through my capacity as an entertainment journalist, so I knew the basic premise of the movie. (Actually, anyone who had heard the film's distinctive title already knew its premise.) I knew that *Snakes on a Plane* starred Samuel L. Jackson as FBI agent Neville Flynn, whose mission of escorting a murder witness from Hawaii to the site of the trial in Los Angeles grows quite complicated when a hit is put on the witness in midair—in the form of hundreds of deadly snakes that had been smuggled onboard the 747. And I knew that there had been an intense reaction to the film from a group of Web denizens who were totally stoked about the movie, its storyline, and the apparent fact that a major Hollywood studio—New Line Cinema—had gone through with letting such a movie be made. I had even glimpsed a few of the news articles about the ongoing hysteria, and heard a tongue-in-cheek report about such on the usually soberly austere National Public Radio.

But I had no idea exactly how much was going on involving *Snakes on a Plane*— or "SoaP," for those in the know—until I agreed to this out-of-the-blue assignment. Frankly, my mind was blown, and that's not an easy thing to do considering the number of shocking entertainment-related developments I had witnessed or covered over the years. Actually, it wasn't so much the level of fan interest that was surrounding *Snakes*—

extreme enthusiasm had accompanied other movies in the past, such as the *Star Wars* series; superhero franchises such as *Superman* and *Batman* and *Spider-Man*, best-selling books that made the transition to film such as the *Lord of the Rings* trilogy and the *Harry Potter* collection, *The DaVinci Code* and even *The Passion of the Christ*. But with the exception of the first *Star Wars* in 1977, all of those examples had one common trait—they already were well known long before they hit the screens. Relationships between the material and teeming masses had been established. Crowds knew what they were going crazy about. *Snakes on a Plane*, on the other hand, had no history with the public. There was just its kooky name, its kooky plot, and an iconic star who seemed tailor-made to take on such an audacious project—and who seemed to know that.

In fact, Jackson, an actor who has specialized in playing strong-willed characters with a knowing mischievous twinkle in his eye, got in on the joke soon after he signed on to do "SoaP." He took delight in telling reporters than he took the lead in the movie before he had even read the script, relying on the name of the film. And last August, when word circulated that New Line had changed the title to the benign *Pacific Air 121*, Jackson publicly disputed that move and announcing that the movie he would be appearing in would be called *Snakes on a Plane* come hell or high water.

SAMUEL L. JACKSON (IN PHOTO FROM 2000). ONLY A SNAKE—OR A FEW HUNDRED—WOULD MESS WITH A DUDE LIKE HIM.
Photo by Dirck Halstead/Time Life Pictures/Getty Images.

It was around that same time when the hysteria about "SoaP," which had first been announced the previous fall, really exploded, in part because of a blog entry by a screenwriter named Josh Friedman, who co-wrote Tom Cruise's rendition of *War of the Worlds* and had a part in converting James Ellroy's book about the Black Dahlia murder into a film version starring Hilary Swank that will be out in the fall of 2006. Currently, though, Friedman's biggest claim to fame may be in revealing to the world that, months earlier, he had been offered a job to work on a script called *Snakes on a Plane*, and that he immediately fell in love with the concept and its title, that he had taken to use that title as a convenient phrase to convey the idea that, well, shit happens—and how he implored the New Line executives, whatever they did, not to tinker with that title, because that's what the movie was. (As Friedman himself wrote, to become perhaps the first to echo what may be the most popular movie quote of the still-young 21st century, "As the great Sam Jackson would say: There are motherfucking snakes on the motherfucking plane.")

The only reason that Friedman didn't stick with the project was that he got indications that New Line was going to do what he implored them not to—change the film's title to something more generic. Once that was confirmed, he lost interest in *Pacific Flight 121* and soon moved on to other professional matters. His blog of August 21, 2005, that related this tale was mostly to celebrate news that "SoaP" was back, but it ended with an addendum, an encounter he had several weeks after he dropped out of the project:

> Weeks later I am sitting in a lobby waiting to have a meeting with a producer who has kept me waiting an hour because he is "catching up" with Paris Hilton. . . . Sitting next to me is a special effects team who's working on one of the producer's other movies. They have been waiting almost two hours and I have been bumped in line ahead of them. I feel bad about this and give them a sheepish smile and shrug. One of them says: "Whattya gonna do?" The other one shakes her head and says, "Snakes on a Plane . . ."
> I fall off my chair.

The movie title as catch phrase also isn't that entirely uncommon (see *Chinatown*), but again, that occurrence usually doesn't happen until after the movie has been released. This was a title that already had entered the lexicon just weeks after it had been all but killed by the people who were making the movie. But such is the power of *Snakes on a Plane* to become part of the language in the form of an utterance that can convey so much in so few words. It's a phrase that I, as a man who has lived with another person's liver inside of him for the past seventeen years, can relate to. (It's also a phrase that Friedman, who declined to be interviewed for this book, has grasped hold to in recent months, as he is recovering from cancer surgery. Before his operation, though, he wrote a post of the "ultimate words" we all leave behind. Guess what his were?)

All of these factors—Friedman's comments, Jackson's advocacy, the crazy title and out-there plot—have combined to create the motion-picture equivalent of the "perfect storm," a movie whose popularity was powered in large part by groups of people who were moved to act by themselves to express their appreciation, sight unseen, of its existence. These gestures of expression have come in many forms, from Photoshopped posters and original illustrations to parody short films and theme songs, to T-shirts and hands and silicon bracelets, and beyond. With the help of the new wave of do-it-yourself Web tools and sites such as YouTube, MySpace, and Cafepress, fans of "SoaP" have again shown the tremendous power of the Internet to spread the word about all sorts of matters, important or otherwise (a Google search of the phrase will turn up over 5.4 million hits)—and to spread it beyond the confines of cyberspace. Stories about "SoaP" have appeared in almost every major media outlet, have practically become regular installments on the daily cable shows of Keith Olbermann and Stephen Colbert, who report on the phenomenon as if they still can't believe it's actually happening. No less than Stephen King has declared that *Snakes on a Plane* will be the sleeper hit of the summer, a prediction that has become more of a done deal with each passing day.

And New Line—what does the studio think of this? That may be the most revolutionary part of this whole slithery saga. In an era when major studios have used threats of legal action to prevent fan sites from encroaching too closely onto their intellectual property, the company that brought *The Lord of the Rings* and *Austin Powers* to the big screen has not been screaming bloody murder about the proliferation of unauthorized "SoaP" material. Quite the opposite, in fact. When the official Web site launched, it featured little more than a link that rotated to a different fan page a week. When more content became available on snakesonaplane.com, included were tools that could be used to build new sites or enhance existing ones—icons, backgrounds, even a banner that featured a countdown to "SoaP's" August 18 release. Some merchants have reported that they have sold their "SoaP" items to members of the production team and New Line staffers. The studio joined with the online community site TagWorld to stage a contest to choose a song from an up-and-coming act to appear in the movie and on the soundtrack. And in the most high-profile testament that New Line was paying attention to what was going on, the brass OK'ed in March five days of extra production time so that elements culled from the fans' input could be incorporated into the mix. Being that many of these elements consisted of more gore, more nudity, and especially much more profanity, these new scenes all but threw out New Line's initial plans for a more marketable PG-13 rating. But the studio executives and the film's producers had the advantage of knowing what the audience wanted, and they weren't about to not give it to them.

This book is not a detailed deconstruction of the making of *Snakes on a Plane*; that's what special-edition DVDs are for. Nor will it cover every minute detail of the unadulterated hype that has surrounded the movie, for a variety of reasons. (For one, a lot of the online stuff does use scenes, stills and images from the actual movie—and while New Line isn't suing over any of that, we don't want to take any chances here.) What it is is a look at some of the folks who have contributed to transforming "SoaP" from just another late summer action flick into a tent post for pop culture—and maybe the future of motion-picture marketing. Whenever possible, this book gives a personality and a face to their work, and gives them the opportunity to speak for themselves about what they've done, why they did it, and what *Snakes on a Plane* means to them. It also shows that while there are different reasons why the people chronicled here were drawn to "SoaP"—or, in a few cases, why they aren't that enthused about the movie—they all agree on one thing: this is the kind of thing they haven't seen before. After all, it's snakes . . . on a plane.

Back to Monty Coles, the West Virginia pilot who got so much attention over the uninvited visitor to his cockpit. He marvels at the attention his little adventure garnered—attention he likely would have never received had *Snakes on a Plane* not been burning the Internet wires. He wasn't even aware that such a film was pending until he got calls from the Associated Press and ABC News, among others, about his fight with the cold-blooded squatter. "It was busy," he says. "We did *Good Morning America* at 7 o'clock." But Coles—who now checks under his instrument panel with a long-handled mirror as part of his flight preparations—has had just about his share of the snake-on-plane experience. "I probably doubt if I will go see it," he said. "I don't mind snakes. But that was enough for a while." Although, should New Line call him up with an invite to what will likely be a lavish premiere for "SoaP," well . . . "That would be an interesting vacation," replies Coles. Just as long as someone else is doing the flying.

SNAKES ON PLANES AS CONCEPTUALIZED BY KATIE ANN HEADLEY, AGE 7, OF CINCINNATI, OHIO.

Snakes on Blogs and Fan Art

BRIAN FINKELSTEIN

> > > washington, DC

> > > snakes on a blog (http:www.snakesonablog.com)

Brian Finkelstein was not a snake person. In fact, his one encounter with a slithery specimen was memorable for all the wrong reasons. "As a kid, I ran across one near a pond once, and I ran away from it," he says. "That's pretty much the extent of my experience."

BRIAN FINKELSTEIN—
NO, HE'S NOT
HUNTING FOR
SNAKES.

At least, his experience with the real McCoy. These days, Finkelstein has snakes on the brain—or at least *Snakes on a Plane* on the brain, thanks to his "SoaP"-related Web site. His is neither the first nor the only "Snakes on a Blog" in existence, but it's the most popular one going today, with hits numbering over 600,000 and a widening array of "Snakes" material being posted there on a daily basis. And as a result, the Georgetown University law student has become almost as much of a celebrity among the movie's fan base as Samuel L. Jackson himself, complete with the resulting publicity. Most articles dealing with the "SoaP" crazy include quotes from Finkelstein, who has become a good judge of character when it comes to dealing with journalists.

"Every once in a while you hit a reporter who seems bored and totally uninterested, and they think it's kind of beneath them, and then it's horrible," says Finkelstein, who says the ratio of "good" reporters to the "bad" is about 70-30. Another side effect of all the attention surrounding him, he admits, is just a touch of guilt. "I think it's kind of unfair because a lot of people have done a lot more than I have. I think I've made one comic early on because I was bored and felt like a jerk for not putting anything up there. And that's about it. I'm doing nothing of actual creative ability. I've done very little, so I don't deserve that much credit. So I appreciate people knowing, but there are other people as well. So I'll take what I can get."

And Finkelstein means that, though not in a selfish way. See, his "Snakes on a Blog" did not begin as just another place for "SoaP" devotees to congregate and share their stuff with each other. From the time Finkelstein launched his site, he had a singular goal.

"My mission, which I thought was kind of a fun one, was to try to get myself invited to the premiere. I've never been to a Hollywood premiere, and I don't know what the process is like, I don't know what the process is for getting invited, but it seemed like something that was doable and fun and interesting. So I started the Web page both to get myself invited and to track the progress of trying to get myself invited."

Finkelstein's site evolved almost by default. "I was kind of using everything else as space filler because, honestly, there wasn't that much going on with me trying to get myself invited. And, you know, how much can you possibly write about that. So I started picking up on stuff that was going on online, and cataloging it, and it just kind of grew. And as more people became interested in it, the more content there was and the more interest there was. And it kind of snowballed."

And that snowball became a mountain for Finkelstein when he started getting the phone calls from New Line Cinema. "It wasn't even people who were in charge at New Line," he says. "It was more like, once in a while, someone would call and say, 'Oh, you're doing such a good job, we like what you're doing.' That anyone from the studio would contact Finkelstein with good tidings remains a shock to the Webmaster. "The first time I talked to New Line, the first question I asked was—actually, the first question I ask all the New Line people every time somebody calls from there—is, 'Are you going to sue me?' They laugh, they say, 'No, of course not.' I am very appreciative that one studio recognizes the value of not suing their audience, of saying 'This is where the money is coming from' and that they're not going to attack it."

Maybe the brass at New Line is having too much fun browsing through Finkelstein's site to care about attacking it. He admits that, when it comes to posting submissions from the masses, his standards aren't particularly high—"Anything that shows any kind of real talent outside of the Internet always impresses me," he says—but the quality and/or ingenuity does show through more often than not. Finkelstein is a particular fan of the work of DCLugi (aka David Coyne—more on him later in the book) and of items such as "Snakes on a Sudoku," a reptile-tinged variation on the ancient Chinese numbers puzzle. More recent entries onto the blog are the stick-figure animations of an artist named StikNstein, who has clever and often demented takes on the film. "I think they're fun and quick and small, and they're unique," says Finkelstein. "You don't see anything else like them."

Maybe what's impressed Finkelstein the most about the "Snakes" experience, though, is the camaraderie that interest in the film has engendered throughout the Internet. There's no one-upmanship between competing "SoaP" sites about who has the best stuff to show off, he notes.

"I don't think there's any rivalry. I felt a little bit guilty because I used the name 'Snakes on a Blog' and somebody had used it before me, and they stopped using it and kind of passed away from the crowd. So I'm certainly not going to say that somebody else can't use it after me since I was so unoriginal in the first place. It's

by FRANCIS HEANEY and FRANK LONGO
authors of THE SUDOKU CODE

WHAT BETTER WAY TO IMPROVE ON A COMPLEX JAPANESE PUZZLE OF NUMBERS AND LOGIC THAN TO PLACE SNAKES IN THE VICINITY? THIS PUZZLE IS FROM THE KEEN MINDS OF FRANCIS HEANEY AND FRANK LONGO; A "SNAKES ON A SUDOKU" BOOK BY FRANCIS HEANEY AND CONCEPTIS PUZZLES WILL BE PUBLISHED THIS MONTH BY STERLING PUBLISHING.

SNAKES ON A CONTEST II: DEADLINE LOOMING

June 13th, 2006 at 8:16 am

Last chance to enter the second contest.

2 Comments
Permalink

88 Navigation

NAVIGATION

My Quest
Contact Snakes on a Blog
Sign the Petitition
The Bootlegged Teaser
The Best Video Trailer

hard for me to hold a grudge about that. Everyone's having such a good time that it's hard to imagine people getting really upset about anything."

Then there's the movie itself: With anticipation about what *Snakes on a Plane* will actually be like, Finkelstein has his opinions. He doesn't care as much if the film is actually good or fits more snugly into the "so bad it's good" category. He just wants it to be entertaining, just like the buzz surrounding it has been.

"I think there's a very fine line, and the studio seems to be aware of it, that they need to walk here for this to be good," he says earnestly. "What it needs to do is match the title. It needs to have a sense of seriousness but yet have a kind of absurdity built in. There's no joke in the title. The title is what it is. But it's funny because it's so straightforward and honest and so clear. The movie needs to run that same line where there's no acknowledging that they're doing something kind of goofy here. It needs to be what it is—*Snakes on a Plane*, no joke, and yet still kind of funny in its own absurd way. And hopefully, because they went back and shot five days of footage to kind of make the movie match fan expectations, New Line understands that that's what they're going for, and they're going to be able to hit that target. It's a tough target to hit, but hopefully they can do it."

Meanwhile, there's still time before the film is released—more time for Snakes on a Blog to expand even further. One thing Finkelstein plans to do is help organize get-togethers of like-minded fans to meet up and attend opening night as groups. As for him—well, if all goes well, he will have already seen the flick by the time August 18 rolls around. Yeah, his premiere dreams are still alive.

"I don't have the tickets in my hand yet, so I can't say that I'm definitely going there," he says with a hint of anticipation. "But I think I'm in pretty good shape at this point. It would be hard to imagine from a PR point of view them not inviting me to do that."

WILL JOHNSON

> > > Raleigh, North Carolina
> > > stiknstein (www.stiknstein.com)

A BOY AND HIS DOG: WILL "STIKNSTEIN" JOHNSON AND HIS BEST FRIEND, MOLLY.

If you are lucky enough to be financially secure when the time comes to retire from the rat race, many options lay in front of you. You could be like Warren Buffett and donate much of your money to charitable foundations—though it helps to be Warren Buffett and be worth nearly $50 billion. Or, if you're a fifty-seven-year-old meat cutter from Raleigh, North Carolina, named Will Johnson, you can devote your time to more artistic ventures such as creating animations of stick figures doing violent things to each other.

If you're Will Johnson, that is.

Please to be meeting the man who goes by the online moniker "StikNstein." His is a most curious art that is called, fittingly, stick death. (And no, I'm not making this up. Not believing? Just go to Google or Wikipedia.) Stick death is kind of just that—the depiction of mindless violence upon stick men, usually with an equally twisted gag thrown in for good measure. "I wanted to play with it in a more contextual way," Johnson says, "and *Snakes on a Plane* was perfect."

Johnson stumbled upon the film while preparing to launch his own site. "My interest was piqued with the movie title," he says. "I would suppose you have to have a certain twisted perspective to appreciate people who see the subtle power in the concept. But I guess I'm one of them." A further examination of the burgeoning "SoaP" phenomenon convinced Johnson that it would be fun to, in his way, poke a stick at the situation: "Once I learned a little of the background and the way the enthusiasm for the movie spread virally across the Internet, I figured the concept was perfect for expression via stick death animation."

His feelings were proven correct when he submitted his first "SoaP" stick death animation to Brian Finkelstein's Snakes on a Blog. They proved to be such a hit that Johnson has sent in several more since then. It's a bit of a departure from the political subject matter that Johnson usually tackles, but he's glad for the opportunity to flex his creative muscles on a topic he so obviously is getting a kick out of.

"I think it's valuable for all of us to cultivate a simple appreciation of the absurd," he says. "I believe it is one facet that can enrich your life as well as make you roll your eyes and smile. I believe people take life too seriously for the most part. For me, the fans' perspective on the movie is more fun than the movie itself. Irony and absurdity tend to be best exemplified in two ways: the extreme or the subtle. *Snakes on a Plane* seems to provide an outlet for both."

Want to do your own stick deaths, "SoaP"-style or otherwise? Johnson used a free-ware program called Pivot Stick Animation to create his masterpieces. It works just as standard animation does, but in a way that won't have you pulling your hair out. Just create one frame and then use your cursor to slightly advance the action from frame-to-frame. Johnson reports that it takes him about an hour to create a 40-second animation. Piece of cake. The Windows application can be downloaded at http://www.snapfiles.com/get/stickfigure.html.

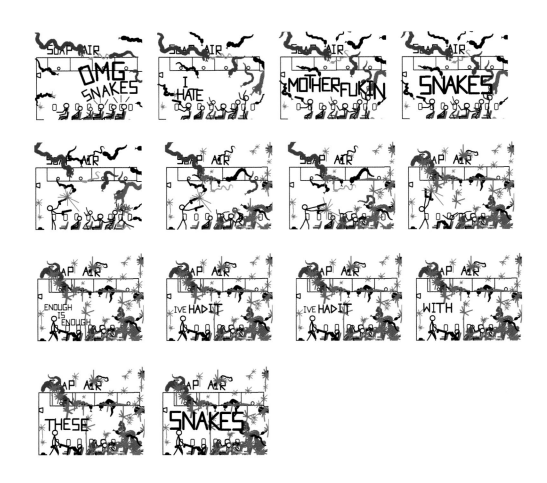

SHAY PIERCE

> > > Austin, Texas

**SNAKESONAPLANIAC
EXTRAORDINARE SHAY PIERCE.**
Courtesy of Shay Pierce

Brian Finkelstein's first contest at Snakes on a Blog was to determine what the online fans of *Snakes on a Plane* should call themselves and be called. He accepted 115 different suggestions and determined the finalists from the most frequently contributed choices. They ranged from the simple (SoaPers) to the clever (SoaP Scum) to the, er, blunt (Motherfuckers—Samuel L. would approve). The winner, though, after more than 1,400 votes were cast, was Snakesonaplaniac (or Snakes on a Planiac, for those who don't like run-on sentences, or words for that matter).

The champion, the person who first sent in Snakesonaplaniac as his suggestion, was Shay Pierce of Austin, Texas. He presents himself as what most would assume would be the typical "SoaP" fan—a young man who works as a programmer at Midway Games, one of the leading supplier of video games for the XBox and Playstation consoles. When he first heard about the film, he was incredulous.

"I think I was thinking, 'No way someone's actually going to make a movie with this title. It's too good to be true,' " recalls Pierce. Once he came across the story of how Samuel L. Jackson fought to keep the original title, he was sold. "Samuel L. Jackson got it," he says firmly, "He knew that it was the best title ever. He knew how absurd it was, and he loved it, because he also knew how fun it could be."

For Pierce, the phrase he championed for the contest was a no-brainer. "For me, everything is about the title *Snakes on a Plane*," Pierce says. "It's the best title of all time. When we thought it was going to be changed to *Pacific Flight 121* or even *S.O.A.P.*, we were in an uproar. I don't even like to abbreviate the title—why pass up a chance to say the phrase *Snakes on a Plane*? It's inherently fun to say."

Pierce, who posts about the movie frequently on his blog (http://iqpierce.livejournal.com) won a *Snakes* teaser poster and a T-shirt for his way with words, and his phrase proved to be the inspiration for a new logo design by fellow Planiac Claire Schaeffer (more on her later). But all of his prizes pale in comparison to his desire to see the finished film. "I've always said that it didn't matter whether the movie turned out to be utter garbage or the most exciting action film ever made," he says. "But I have to admit this isn't entirely true. I'm looking forward to seeing the various ways they play with the premise—there's a lot you can do with such a concept.

"I think this is going to be a very fun action flick, probably with a slightly absurd sensibility—and definitely with the best title of all time."

MAX PACHECO

> > > New Bedford, Massachusetts

Brian Finklestetin's second Snakes on a Blog contest involve having Planiacs sending in photos of themselves wearing "SoaP" T-shirts or other merchandise in outlandish situations. The winner, Max Pacheco, took the crown not only with his clear devotion to the movie, but also by choosing a background that proves that Americans still know how to build sturdy houses that can take a lickin' and keep on tickin'.

photo by Cynthia Pacheco.

In fact, while no one was around when Pacheco and his mother took his prize-winning photos (though neighbors came by and asked him about his sign), "there were people upstairs with the lights on," when he drove by the place recently. Pacheco doesn't know all of the details about how the abode ended up Pisa style, except that the damage was caused by a car accident. "I hope they never repair it and that it stands as a monument of why people should drive carefully," he adds.

Pacheco, who majors in English communication at Emmanuel College in Boston, was informed of *Snakes on a Plane* by the same friend who told him about the slanted house. He became so excited about the film that he plans to break his personal taboo against seeing movies in theaters in order to watch "SoaP" as God intended—in a large room with a bunch of rowdy and excited people.

"The other day my friend looked at the pilot hat I borrowed to wear when I first see *Snakes on a Plane*, and he asked me if I thought the whole thing had gone too far, and I said no," says Pacheco. "I think there's something beautiful about people having so much fun at the expense of a serious movie after so many serious movies have taken advantage of people by taking their money and not having a good movie to offer in return. So many people are getting a good laugh out of 'SoaP' that aren't even going to see it, and those that are going to see it will like it no matter what as long as Sam Jackson swears."

Pacheco also admires the candor used in marketing the film. "You never know whether a movie is going to be good or not nowadays," he says. "If all advertisements are trying to make a movie look good, then it's hard to figure out what's actually crap. But a title like *Snakes on a Plane* gives moviegoers the honesty they need these days. I hope this title revolution catches on. If only *Contact* had been titled *You Don't Actually See the Alien*.

STEPHANIE WASEK

> > > pottstown, pennsylvania
> > > snakes on a blog (http://community.livejournal.com/snakesonablog/)

Although Brian Finkelstein's Snakes on a Blog has received the lion's share of publicity, Stephanie Wasek, associate editor of *Outpatient Surgery* magazine, has her own, nearly-as-(in)famous "SoaP" site on LiveJournal.com. You can tell them apart by the lowercase letters in the title, just in case you get them confused.

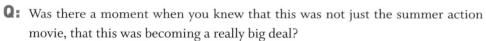

STEPHANIE DRESSES FOR THE OCCASION.
Courtesy of Stephanie Wasek

Q: How did the *Snakes on a Plane* craze start for you?

A: I found out about the movie sometime around last August. I go to school [at the University of Maryland's University College], and one of my classes was a desktop publishing class. We had to make up stuff for a newsletter, and instead of just using the fake stuff that the teacher gave us, I was going to make a newsletter that was all about *Snakes on a Plane*. So I started scouring the Internet for stuff, and I sent it to a couple of my friends, and they were, like, "Dude, you really have to do something with this 'cause this is just hilarious." So I started a LiveJournal community for it, and two of my friends joined, and it was just the three of us posting little things for each other, and suddenly people just started joining. It's taken on a life of its own.

Q: Was there a moment when you knew that this was not just the summer action movie, that this was becoming a really big deal?

A: I guess it was about sometime in March when I realized that people were posting every single day, that there was something new every single day to talk about on *Snakes on a Plane*. And I realized that there were 200 people there. And around that time was when the *Philadelphia Inquirer* contacted me, and that kind of made it no longer just an Internet thing, that there were people outside of the Internet who knew about it, and that was kind of strange.

Q: What's been the best part of this experience for you?

A: The Internet is just so chocked full of very, very funny people, and very creative people. And this is something that people feel they can somehow contribute to it. They have this idea, they post it somewhere, and suddenly they're part of the whole thing. And I think most people get drawn into it the same way. Suddenly they've created something, and other people have seen it and liked it and commented on it, and suddenly you're part of it, and you just feel like you identify with *Snakes on a Plane*.

STEPHANIE WASEK'S SNAKES ON A BLOG

Q: Has New Line contacted you yet about your blog?

A: As a result of the *Inquirer* article, New Line's local p.r. got in touch with me. I was going to hold a party and have as many people as wanted to come, and see if we could get whatever group rates they may have had at local theaters, and I was going to see if I could rent out a nearby conference room at a hotel and just have food and contests and stuff. But they apparently are interested in trying to work with me with all that. So I'm, like, "Hey, if you want to help me with a party, that's fine."

Q: Does *Snakes on a Plane* have to be any good quality-wise for you to enjoy it?

A: I'm stuck. On the one hand, if it's really bad, that's kind of awesome. And if it's really good, that's also kind of awesome. I just don't want it be fully mediocre. That's the worst thing it could possibly be. If it were just strictly mediocre, that would be kind of a letdown. But it is review-proof for me. I don't care what the critics say. I'm going to go see it on opening day, and I'm going to be there with friends or family and everybody else who is now part of this because they couldn't help but get caught up in it too.

Q: One more thing—how do you feel about snakes in general?

A: It all depends on the situation. I like poisonous snakes from afar. I like poisonous snakes on National Geographic Channel, where they belong. They don't belong in my carry-ons.

TWO OF THE WINNING ENTRIES IN STEPHANIE'S CONTEST FOR THE BEST "SOAP" ICON. THE "PLANIEST" CHAMPION COMES FROM "LOZENGER8"; THE "TEXTIEST" FROM JESSILYN DOWNS.

VORI SALZMAN

> > > Rock Hill, South Carolina
> > > http://community.livejournal.com/snakesonablog/20207.html

Vori Salzman is into many different things. She loves reading and writing, biology and British comedy, horror movies and Japanese rock music. She's also into animals, including snakes. Which is probably kind of obvious, considering she's in this book. But Salzman, an art student, took her appreciation of snakes, and *Snakes on a Plane*, to an entirely new level. Literally.

She found out about "SoaP" in early March from one of her Winthrop University classmates. "He said, 'So, you know they're making a movie called *Snakes on a Plane*? . . . And it's about snakes on a plane." Salzman wasn't quite sure what to make of it, even after doing the Google thing to look up this strange incarnation. "I couldn't believe it was real," she says. "My disbelief was equally balanced by pure elation; would anyone truly make something so simple, so brilliant? It seemed like a joke, or maybe completely idiotic."

And that's what sucked Salzman in—in enough to embark on what may seem like either an ambitious idea or a very, very silly one. While on a cross-country trip in late March from Charlotte to Los Angeles (with a layover in Dallas-Fort Worth), the budding artist composed a photo essay about . . . snakes on a plane (and in airports). Armed with a couple of plastic snakes purchased at the local Wal-Mart and a camera she admits wasn't exactly high-tech, Salzman took gleeful photos of the rubber reptiles in conspicuously normal circumstances. Then, being the enterprising woman of the 21st century, she posted them on Stephanie Wasek's blog for all to see.

Why did "SoaP" captivate her so? Consider her earlier remark about the brilliant and the idiotic. "The entire issue straddles the intellectual line between annoyingly obvious and brilliantly understated," Salzman says. "It pulls no punches. It's stripped down, lacking even the padding of a metaphorical title. The first reaction is always '. . .That's it?' Yes, that's it. After a pause, the next response shows just how fine that line is. They always say either 'That's stupid . . .' or 'Oh my God, brilliant . . .' We, as a media-soaked culture, have been bombarded by catchy, metaphorical, loose-cannon flicks for years. *Memento*, *Rain Man*, *The Shining*, *The Butterfly Effect*, *Mission: Impossible*… But guess what: *Snakes on a Plane*. It doesn't matter what the actual film is like. Nobody really cares. The fact is that they *made* it."

By the way, Salzman says she will be attending the movie with friends, though she doesn't say whether she will be taking a camera or not. One kind of hopes she does, as she plans to arrange for "various people [to be] dressing up in the roles of serpents or airplanes. It's hard to find patterns for airplane costumes, but we'll do our best. We're all art students, after all."

DISTURBING, GARRULOUS SALESMAN WITH A PYRAMID SCHEME, I SURREPTITIOUSLY GLANCED AROUND FOR ANY SORT OF RELIEF. THERE IT WAS; RIGHT ACROSS THE TINY AISLE OF THE CRAMPED, FREEZING PLANE. THE WOMAN THERE WAS READING A NOVEL. HOLDING HER PLACE WAS A LITTLE SNAKE BOOKMARK. I TOLD MYSELF I WOULDN'T LEAVE THE FLIGHT WITHOUT DOCUMENTATION OF SNAKES ON A PLANE.

AFTER THE SUN ROSE, WARMING THE PLANE, THEY STARTED EMERGING. FROM THE DEPTHS OF MY CARRY-ON THEY CREPT, UNDULATING, DOWN THE AISLE.

GRANTED, IT WASN'T A VERY LONG FLIGHT, BUT AFTER YOU LOOK THROUGH THE SAFETY CARD THE SECOND OR THIRD TIME AND FIND ALL THE TYPOS IN SKYMALL, YOU GET BORED—AND CRANKY, AS ONE SNAKE DEMONSTRATED.

I COLLAPSED INTO A FOOD COURT IN THE DFW AIRPORT, AN OVERPRICED CHICKEN WRAP AND AN HOUR UNTIL MY NEXT FLIGHT'S DEPARTURE BEFORE ME. THE PERSISTENT SERPENTS CRAWLED UP THE TABLE AND CIRCLED MY WRAP.

THEY FINALLY PERFORMED A VIABLE SERVICE BY GUARDING ME FROM THE WANDERING TRAVELERS WHO PROWLED DFW AT THE UNGODLY HOUR OF 8:45 AM. ALTHOUGH, NOW THAT I THINK ABOUT IT, MAYBE THEY WERE JUST GUARDING MY FOOD.

IN DALLAS, THE WEATHER WAS VERY CHILL AND WINDY. THE SNAKES EMERGED ONLY ONCE THEY WERE WARM AND COZY INSIDE THE AIRPORT. AFTER CHECKING OUT THE SADDLES, COWBOY HATS AND T-SHIRTS IN THE GIFT SHOP, THE SNAKES RELAXED ON MY LUGGAGE.

A CLOSER LOOK REVEALS THAT PERHAPS THE SNAKE HAS HIS OWN AGENDA. WHAT'S HE GOING TO DO ONCE HE GETS TO LA?

THIS SNAKE HARASSED A COUPLE OF SPANISH-SPEAKING BUSINESSMEN WHILE WAITING FOR OUR PLANE TO BOARD. THEY DIDN'T SEEM TO NOTICE.

THERE WERE 28 ROWS ON THE PLANE TO LA. I WAS SEATED IN ROW 27. THE SNAKES WERE ANNOYED AT THIS AND CRAWLED AROUND INDIGNANTLY. THEY WERE ONLY SOOTHED WHEN THE PRETTY FLIGHT ATTENDANT GAVE THEM THEIR OWN SPRITE.

WHEN THE SPRITE WAS GONE, HOWEVER . . .

ONLY THROUGH A STROKE OF LUCK WAS I ABLE TO CAPTURE THIS PHOTO. THE GUY IN FRONT OF ME WAS WEARING HUGE HEADPHONES AND LEANING SLIGHTLY FORWARD, SO THE SNAKE'S TAIL DIDN'T BUMP THE BACK OF HIS HEAD. LOOKING AROUND, I SAW THAT NO ONE WAS WATCHING MY PHOTOGRAPHY SESSION. WERE THEY TOO PETRIFIED WITH FEAR?

HONESTLY, ONCE YOU'VE READ THE SAFETY CARD A COUPLE OF TIMES AND BROWSED THE PROVIDED MAGAZINE, THERE'S NOTHING LEFT BUT THE RECENT ISSUE OF SKYMALL.

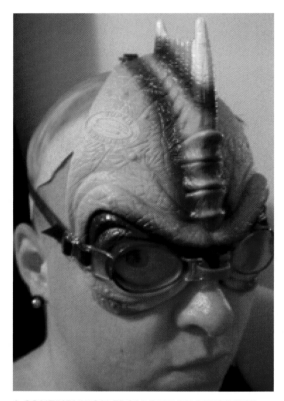

A CONTRIBUTION FROM ONE OF CAROLYN'S TRIBE MEMBERS, SCREEN NAME "SCHWARTZ". THE PHOTO IS OF SCHWARTZ TRYING OUT HER SNAKE HEAD.

CAROLYN SANS SNAKE COSTUME.

It's not exactly a new idea, the attendance of a movie screening while dressed as a character from said film. As the *Star Wars* franchise was revived for better or worse in the late '90s, hordes of die-hards dressed as Jedi Knights could be seen tromping toward theaters where the segments of the new trilogy were premiering. The same could be said for *Harry Potter* movies (little wizards complete with wands and stuffed owls) and *Lord of the Rings* flicks (hobbits, orcs, and everything in between). And don't even get me started on the midnight screenings of *The Rocky Horror Picture Show*, maybe the king (queen?) of participatory cinema.

Enter a freelance Web site developer from Oakland who goes by the nom de Internet "Medusa." (She gives her real name as Carolyn C.; the initial is to keep her online and offline lives a bit separate.) A dedicated traveler on the information superhighway, Medusa first learned about the existence of *Snakes on a Plane* on one of the several message boards she keeps tabs on. And, after doing some research and figuring out that the movie was the real deal, she created her own "SoaP"-dedicated space on Tribe.net, a service that builds Web-based communities through friends near and far. But Medusa's site wasn't simply to pay heed to the "Snakes" experience. No, her plan goes one step further than that. She wants to develop a movement that will have people attend the first screenings of the movie . . .

. . . in groups . . .

. . . dressed like snakes. *

For Medusa, a woman of wit and intelligence who approaches the "SoaP" phenomenon from a anthropological level, it was the best way she could think of to get involved. "My whole context on this is I am very interested in these sorts of street theater, costume-based bits," she says. "I've gone to Burning Man for years"—Burning Man being the annual week-long get-together of vibrant self-expression that takes place in the Nevada desert—"and a lot of my friends

---

* Pilots' caps optional.

CAROLYN'S WEB SITE

also are very interested in these sorts of Renaissance faire, Burning Man-type of spontaneous, 'let's get dressed up and go out in public and be in a character just because it's fun' things. And any opportunity to do that sort of thing is really compelling and interesting. And I know I have a number of friends who also enjoy that kind of thing, which is why I thought, 'Well, I have the means here to get together a bunch of people who would actually go through the effort of making an elaborate costume and enjoy going out in public and acting silly and getting attention for it.' "

In the beginning, the plan was for just Medusa and her local pack of friends to don the guise of reptiles and head to their neighborhood theater. Now, though, ambitions have been broadened—a bit. As of mid-June, she has forty-one signed-on members of her Tribe, including people she didn't even know. And while she has no idea how many of them, or how many more, will go all-in on this experiment in fun, she feels a responsibility to make it as easy as possible for those who want to take part to do just that. Accordingly, Medusa plans to introduce a section that will offer costume advice.

"I want to do my own research on a variety of ways that someone can make their own snake costume at home," Medusa says. A fashion designer friend, online name "Skittlegrinder," has offered to chip in. "She wants to dress as a sidewinder and actually walk sideways, undulating, up to the door of the theater. I want to dress as a queen cobra and make some type of a cape like my cobra hood is expanded. And I thought that if some people wanted to be rattlesnakes, they could just tie a baby rattle to their tail and just have it drag along behind them."

Comparisons to other situations when fans dress to the nines to see their favorite flicks, in Medusa's eyes, don't quite hit the mark. "When people go to see *Star Wars* or *Harry Potter*, they're like a really dorky fan, and they do it in a *Dungeons & Dragons* kind of way," she says. "Whereas I think the *Snakes on a Plane* thing is more of a mocking but not-negative way of celebrating the ridiculousness of this movie." And she credits that ridiculousness, and the embracing of such by, among others, Samuel L. Jackson, as one reason for her excitement about "SoaP."

"When I read that he chose to be in the movie based solely on the title and that he didn't even read the script . . . and apparently when they tried to change the title in mid-production, he said, 'No, you can not do that, it just has to be this title'—that is just so great. I love that. It shows a certain level of silliness on his part that he has fun with his job or maybe doesn't take his career too overly seriously in a sort of egotistical way—that he is having fun with it."

Medusa is so invested into making her dream come true, she's not even annoyed by those who claim that the entire "SoaP" spectacle is just supplying New

Line Cinema with free advertising. "OK, sure, maybe I am," she admits. "But people are doing that every day. On a certain level it's, like, 'Hey, they had the balls to go out and make this movie and not even try to code it in something . . . like a real title. Maybe they deserve to make money even though it's probably going to be a horrifically bad movie.' Although it might be kind of funny."

What is definitely funny is that, after presenting her plan for what could be the country's largest exhibition of street theater ever, Medusa forgot one little wrinkle—whether "SoaP's" release would conflict with this year's Burning Man event. A quick check of the calendar reveals that they are ten days part, leaving Medusa free and clear to become a cobra for a night, when everything goes. "We're very unshy, we're very goofy in public,'" she says of herself and fellow snakes-in-crime. "We'll walk up to strangers and hiss at them or snakebite them or whatever we're going to do as snakes."

ONE OF THE visual highlights of Carolyn's site is a simple but distinctive drawing by Robert Reeves. His explanation:

The 'thought' behind this cartoon was to embrace the simplicity of the 'SoaP' meme (what made it such a hit in the first place) and move away from the hype and the over-analysis and yet also try and grab on its coat-tails and become a part of it all it has become—the D.I.Y. ethic meets the post-ironic lifestyle and gets a blog.

The buzz about the forthcoming film, in my opinion, stems from a feeling that an Internet (sub)culture has joined with main-stream Hollywood and an ad-hoc network of people have helped make a cult film starting from the beginning instead of finding and adopting an existing movie. Instead of being marketed to and being told what is 'hip,' the inmates have finally taken over the asylum.

HAYLEY "PIP" WOZNY

> > > Richmond, Virginia
> > > snakes on a Fic (http://community.livejournal.com/snakesonafic)

Courtesy of Hayley Wozny

Web sites such as YouTube, MySpace and Flickr are fairly new examples of the Internet as interactive portal, places where the average bear can express his or her own creativity at will. But before any of them arrived on the horizon, there was fan fiction. For those of you unfamiliar with the practice, think of fan fiction as the modern form of oral tradition, only with a bit of a head start. They are tales based on favorite movies and TV shows, taking a sliver or a slice or a huge chunk from those productions and weaving them into directions all the writers' own. They can take a variety of forms. They can be reverential to the source material, parodies of the original intent, or—especially in the case of certain science-fiction programs—erotic in nature. This particularly applies in the case of what is known as "slash" fiction, the intimate pairing of two characters of the same gender. (Think of the unspoken passion between Kirk and Spock, and you have the general idea. If not, I can't help you.)

It's unlikely that any slash stories will result from *Snakes on a Plane*, unless some author gets overly ambitious about the feelings between Samuel L. Jackson and a rattlesnake. But it's very possible that at some point the fans of "SoaP" will put fingers to keyboard and type up some wild and whimsical adventures based on the ninety minutes or so of spectacle they have just witnesses. In fact, not only is it possible, it's downright probable. Actually, it's already happening as we speak, at what can basically be called the *Snakes on a Plane* Fan Fiction page, or "Snakes on a Fic."

The site is the brainchild of Hayley "Pip" Wozny, a perky young woman from Virginia who goes by the screen name of "artfuldodger." She first learned about "Snakes on a Plane" last winter from a fellow student at Virginia Commonwealth University, where is a junior who majors in English. Noticing the hoopla surrounding the film, Wozny soon came up with the idea for a fan fiction site but hesitated. She was pushed into making the leap by one of her professors. "She had a *Snakes on a Plane* poster up in her office," explains Wozny, "and she insisted that if I created the community, she would write a story for it."

And the professor did, under the name "gracelesscurran." (Wozny's work also shows up on her page, a short story told from the perspective of the cat in the pet carrier who meets a snake-related fate in the film's initial teaser.) Wozny is the first to admit that "Snakes on a Fic" isn't the most sizzling "SoaP" site out there, but approaches it as an investment in the future. "I'm expecting that after the movie comes out—well, I'm hoping, anyway—that after the movie comes out, I

will become amazingly popular." But the fact that there are any stories up there, weeks before the film is seen by human eyes, is something of a marvel—though not so much so by the Webmistress. "Honestly, I don't think you really need anything else other than the title of this movie," she says. "It doesn't need the tagline, it doesn't need anything. It's just—snakes on a plane. Snakes—on a plane."

No matter how many fan fictions eventually end up on her site, Wozny is just pleased to be part of a bit of Internet history. She sees the "brouhaha" over "SoaP" as a reaction to the fact "that Hollywood takes itself so incredibly seriously with movies. Everyone goes to see movies that take themselves seriously, and then you have this—*Snakes on a Plane*. It's just asking for people to shake their heads and go, 'Wait a minute, what?' Maybe Hollywood has decided, 'How far can we actually get people to take this stuff seriously?' It's kind of ridiculous."

Ridiculous, but cool. And even cooler for Wozny was the reaction she saw the "SoaP" trailer got at the *X-Men: The Last Stand* screening at her local theater. "That was the loudest that theater got all night," she says. Sounds like she made a sound investment.

Hayley Wozny's "SoaP" fan fiction:

Fluffykins' No Good, Horrible, Very Rotten [Last] Day

They put me in a crate. Alone. Alone and afraid. "Fluffykins" they once called me, but now, now I felt as though I should be re-named "Alone," for that was what I was. A poor, frightened cat in the bowels of airplane in the sky.

Alone, I ate my meager rations of chow. Alone, I licked myself each day, often for hours at a time to occupy myself. And I thought of the ways I could escape from my dark prison, my metaphorical abyss within this plane. There had to be a way out. There had to be. When

I saw the creature, I was to the point of desperation where anyone would have sufficed. Anyone. And that was my downfall. My fatal weakness. I thought I could trust him. His voice was so smooth. So calming. So tender, even. He offered me a way out, said he knew a way to leave my confinement and be free once again! Freedom! The word was like catnip to my senses, like buttery cream to my tongue. Oh, how I craved freedom from my cage. He told me that he would show me the way out, but that first I had to let him in.

Oh, that forked tongue, how it lied! The pressure came suddenly, silently, and was so deadly. The one I called "friend," the one I thought of as my savior, betrayed me. The feeling of hurt overwhelmed me as I realized what a snake—literally—I had let into my cage. And there was still no way out. And now even the light leaking in through the metal bars was hidden by the slithering form of a snake. A snake. That was on the plane.

I wanted to get out, to warn my owners of what frightful beasts had somehow come to be on the airplane. But then I remembered who had left me in this cage all by myself to begin with. My owners. No, I decided. If I was going to die by the might of this snake, I didn't want to die alone. If I would die, so would they. And all to these snakes. On a plane.

Meow. Avenge my death! Mrow!

Snakes

FAMED ANIMAL WRANGLER Jules Sylvester has worked with critters on 340 films, including *Congo*, *The Freshman* and *Arachnophobia*, but the avuncular Brit admits that he never had as much fun as he had handling the stars of the show for *Snakes on a Plane*. Sylvester had so much fun, in fact, that's he's letting us in on a few secrets from the set—at least, when it comes to the snakes. Like, for example, what he thought when he first heard the crazy title. "I started laughing," says Sylvester, "and I went, 'I hope they never change the title, because it's one of those things where you know exactly what you're getting.' "

OTHER SLITHERY TREATS:

- Sylvester's company, Reptile Rentals Inc., supplied 450 snakes to the movie, most of which were transported from L.A. to the Vancouver set by van because of the strict regulations regarding air transport of serpents. Ironic, eh?

- Despite the number of snakes used, few were dangerous. Most—but not all—of the venomous snakes were of the CG or animatronic variety, and Samuel L. Jackson almost never worked with the real things due to the action involved with his scenes.

- Snakes have a great union, as they only worked a few hours a week. "When the snakes get shagged out after three or four hours of shooting, I put them aside and get the second team in," says Sylvester. And their payment for a job well done? One frozen mouse per week.

- Contrary to popular opinion, snakes can't be trained. They did what they did on the set—some crawled, some climbed, some wrapped themselves around things. "It's just pure management on my part," says Sylvester.

- Sylvester did just as much work, if not more, with the humans on the set, constantly warning the extras to watch their footing lest they step on a fellow cast member. A typical instruction: "If you've got five snakes in your lap, don't stand up and take off running; you stay there and you scream bloody murder, but your feet stay locked in position. Because if they fall at your feet and you start tramping on them, you will tread on one of them, and I will be really mad at you."

on the Set

Samuel L. Jackson took a shine to his co-stars, spending time in the snake room between scenes. On the other hand, Julianna Margulies "didn't like snakes," says Sylvester. "We kept the snakes away from her. I think she went, 'Oh, I'll just do the CGI and work with the animatronic ones.' Which was fine, because she had to look scared anyway. She was scared enough for everybody, I think."

Oh, and what does Sylvester think of the crazy Internet buzz? Admiration of the film and its fans aside, this animal guy reminds that there's more to life than snakes . . . on a plane. "I think it's just mind-boggling," he says. "I don't mean to be rude, but they really need to get a life."

JULES SYLVESTER POSES WITH KITTY THE PYTHON—OR IS IT THE OTHER WAY AROUND?

Photo courtesy of Jules Sylvester

JEFFREY ROWLAND

> > > east Hampton, massachusetts
> > > overcompensating (http://www.overcompensating.com)
> > > Topatoco (http://topatoco.com)

JEFFREY ROWLAND IN CARTOON FORM, ALONG WITH HIS "SNAKES" T-SHIRTS.
Courtesy of Jeffrey Rowland.

In the world of the *Snakes on a Plane* fan base, Jeffrey Rowland would be what you call a "double threat." He is the talent behind one of the first examples of a "SoaP"-oriented piece of fan art, and the designer of one of the first homemade T-shirts based on the movie. And as a purveyor of slithery fun and frolic on the Internet, Rowland is quite protective of the movie's momentum among the public.

"The only thing I'm afraid of now is that people are going to be tired of the movie before it actually comes out," he says. "Because it's almost become saturated. I mean, it's out there, and it's so big that everyone knows what you're talking about when you talk about *Snakes on a Plane*."

Rowland first heard talk about the film from his friend and fellow artist Meredith Gran. "She told me that there's a movie coming out with Samuel L. Jackson called *Snakes on a Plane*. And it's just perfect, just the literalness of it is what kind of made it funny," he says. "It's, like, the worst thing that could possibly happen. Just being on a plane is bad enough, but being on a plane full of snakes is just really, really bad. And just the way that the title was so literal, you were just automatically laughing like idiots."

Inspiration followed soon afterwards in the form of an edition of Rowland's online comic strip, Overcompensating. It's actually one of two he produces on a regular basis. The other one, Wigu, is about "this family that is on the run from the shadow government that is in league with extraterrestrials and all that kind of stuff. That's my real artistic outlet thing. But I do Overcompensating as something that's just there every day, because it's fun. I like taking little things that happened in my day and just either really exaggerating them or playing them down, whatever the case may be."

So, when Rowland drew a story in which Samuel L. Jackson, wielding a light saber, tells him about *Snakes on a Plane* in his own forceful matter, he was only exaggerating. "I wish he did," says Rowland with a smile. "I mean, maybe [he did] in a dream or something like that. It just materialized there on the spot."

A few days ago, so did the idea for a T-shirt. Rowland, who runs a clothing business called Topatoco, was involved in the aviation industry in a previous life, and still had some plane diagrams lying around. "I had one of the cockpit, and so I basically did a trace of a couple of snakes," he explains. Thus was born the design of snakes actually flying a plane. It was an instant smash, becoming Rowland's top

JEFFREY MEETS SAMUEL L. JACKSON IN ROWLAND'S WEB COMIC "OVERCOMPENSATING."

seller, just as his "SoaP" comic has gathered more hits than any of his other images. The rush has been so great that it sometimes takes Rowland a few weeks to satisfy the demands of his customers, which has led to the curious result of him being able to tell the difference between longtime fans of his stuff and those who discovered him via "SoaP." "The people who know me because of my comics, they're a little bit more patient than the people who just see the shirt on the site and buy it, and have no idea that I do comics as well. Those people can be a bit impatient at times."

And as for worrying about if or when New Line Cinema would ever put the kibosh on Rowland's work, those fears went out the window long ago, and for good reason. "I probably have sold at least a thousand dollars of merchandise to people with newline.com e-mail addresses," he says of his "competition." He's of the mindset that New Line knew immediately that it had a bit of a fan-generated sensation behind them and knew how to act accordingly. "They saw that there was all this activity, all of this Internet buzz about a movie that they hadn't actually spent a dime on promotion for yet. And you never see that. But I think they were cool enough to let us market the movie for them.

"I think a lot more studios are coming to embrace the automatic viral marketing. If they have a good enough idea, word of mouth is almost the most legitimate type of promotion you can get. People started talking about this movie because they thought it was a brilliantly ridiculous concept—and there you have it. . . . It's almost been an all word-of-mouth promotion, and that's kind of the most legitimate kind of advertising. Some people have accused me of being on New Line's payroll and being part of this viral marketing thing, but no—it's just part of this really funny idea, and I'm really glad that somebody had the sense of humor to actually do that and make it a reality and that people thought it was a good enough idea to do something ridiculous like that. 'Cause it's a ridiculous movie. I hope it is."

But what, prey tell, if it's not ridiculous, if it actually garners rave reviews? "Given the title, I think if it gets a four-star review, it's going to [be because] it's hit its point precisely, which means that it's called *Snakes on a Plane*, and it needs to be completely over the top and ridiculously violent and have Samuel L. Jackson just doing what he does best, which is yelling and Tasering snakes on the plane."

JEFFREY FADEN

> > > santa cruz, california

> > > jeffreyatw.com (http://www.jeffreyatw.com/comics.shtml)

**JEFFREY FADEN—
HE MEANS BUSINESS.**
Courtesy of Jeffrey Faden.

Jeffrey Faden attends the University of California at Santa Cruz, where he majors in linguistics, which is the study of human language. Something like that usually entails a strong ability to communicate. Jeffrey does that on a regular basis with his array of online comics, including CAR, and it was an edition of that, drawn in September of 2005, that became one of the first fan-produced renditions of *Snakes on a Plane*.

Now Jeffrey has something to say about his strip and what has happened in the nearly one year since he first heard about *Snakes on a Plane*. It's a little different from many of the other testimonials in this book, so I felt that it should be digested in full, in his own words.

"Having been on the Internet for a while, I've come to discover the rate at which memes spread. I know where they're found, who spreads them, and usually how long it takes to reach certain demographics. I try not to exercise any sense of superiority when it turns out I've found about some quirky or downright hilarious media long before anyone else has—but I try to create awareness about things I find anyway, so I can spread the word about things I find worth mentioning—or at least I can say I was there before the thing got completely blown out of proportion.

My comic, CAR, was just a daily outlet for me—I wasn't really doing it for anyone but myself, so I didn't care too much about the quality of the work (hence the copy-paste nature of the strip)—but I still had fans and people getting laughs out of it. Since a few other Web comics I had read were making comics about this new film, I thought I'd jump on the bandwagon and try to contribute my two cents. But due to lack of creativity on my part and utter absurdity of the subject itself, I couldn't think of anything.

So I guess this comic is one of the few cases where I really just mention something for the sake of riding on its own value—at least in my opinion, I'm not adding anything of humorous value to *Snakes on a Plane*—but just mentioning it because it's just such a strange phenomenon, and I really just wanted to get it out of the way since I was sure I would hear a whole bunch about it in the coming year.

And of course, I was right. Now there's bootleg *Snakes on a Plane* merchandise, endless parodies, random people at my university screaming

"MOTHERFUCKING SNAKES ON A PLANE!" and more, all much to my chagrin. Personally I still plan on seeing the movie, but even at the time of making the strip in the summer of 2005, I was already so burnt out on *Snakes on a Plane* jokes that it's not all that funny to me anymore.

I guess that's the problem with Internet "superiority."

—Jeffrey Faden, June 2006

JODY RADZIK

JODY RADZIK, SNAKE CHARMER.
Courtesy of Jody Radzik.

Shortly after the *Snakes on a Plane* teaser poster made its debut in March, directed David Ellis told *Entertainment Weekly*, with some level of pride, that the film's distinctive logo of two snake intertwined around an airplane had its roots in some of the fan art that had been circulating throughout the Internet. Ellis didn't go into details about which specific illustration had been mined for "SoaP's" official logo, but regular visitors to the Los Angeles-based celebrity gossip site Defamer had their ideas.

They remembered when a photo of a brightly colored snake crawling around a model airplane had been posted there. That offbeat objet d'art was the brainchild of Jody Radzik, a New Mexico-based graphic designer and self-declared "snake geek." He had been a big fan of Defamer for a while, even corresponding directly with that site's editor, Mark Lisanti. That relationship came into major play last September when Radzik, who runs his own snake-related blog, went on one of his usual serpent hunts. "It was one of my life's dreams to capture a Sonoran mountain kingsnake," he says, and he did just that, catching a three-year-old female of the species. He took it back to Santa Fe and then had a brainstorm: "I got the idea to send a photo to Mark with the snake on a toy plane, as he was writing quite often about the movie."

A brief posing session produced two sparkling shots of the kingsnake before the fussy model escaped from the tank that was holding her. When Radzik sent the pictures to Lisanti, he wasn't counting on them ending up on Defamer, but was pleased to see it there—not so much because of the movie, but rather because he wanted to bring traffic to another one of his sites, a blog calls Guruphiliac (http://guruphiliac.org) that does for (or to?) spiritual gurus what Defamer does for (or to) superstars. Actually, it doesn't take much for Radzik to reveal that, despite his lifelong affection for snakes, he's not that keen about the upcoming film that will highlight them.

"It will be two hours of seeing snakes do things that they just wouldn't do in that situation," he says. "Snakes on a plane would do anything they could to stay *away* from the people on the plane with them. They'd all go hide, wedging themselves into whatever crevices they could find until they felt safe. The bottom line is that snakes just want to be warm, safe and fed. They could care less about anything else, including a bunch of screaming people on a plane with them."

Still, Radzik admits to being "stoked" about the chance that his photo may have influenced the marketing for a major motion picture. And although he's not planning on seeing *Snakes on a Plane*, he says he may change his mind—"if New Line flies me out for the premiere," he says.

Web site citations:

http://www.defamer.com/hollywood/snakes-on-a-plane/snakes-on-a-plane-the-home-version-126083.php

http://www.defamer.com/hollywood/snakes-on-a-plane/snakes-on-a-plane-the-logo-162301.php

http://www.ew.com/ew/report/0,6115,1175748_1_0_,00.html

SNAKEPLANE
Photo by Jody Radzik

ROBERT BABCOCK

> > > Lexington, Kentucky

Snakes
on a

Plane

**ROBERT BABCOCK'S
GEOMETRIC RENDITION OF
"SNAKES ON A PLANE."**

Anyone can put together a snazzy graphic using the wonder application Photoshop. In fact, plenty of people have. Alas, although many of these works are delightful and clever, just about all of them are off limits in this book due to copyright situations. So when a truly original take on "SoaP" turns up, it's worthy of notice and attention, even if it's gobsmackingly simple.

Robert Babcock probably wasn't the first to come up with the pun that there was more than one kind of plane a snake could be on. But he was one of the only ones to go with it when it came to turning the idea into an actual illustration. "I was doing a lot of 3D solid modeling work for an analysis at work, and geometric planes played a heavy role in what I was doing," he says. So he used an application called InkScape to create the nifty color image of snakes riding the surface of a three-dimensional plane, where nobody gets any peanuts. Eventually he posted it to the alternative humor Web site Fark.com.

"The whole *Snakes on a Plane* phenomenon has been something I've really enjoyed," Babcock says. "The discussions and in-jokes all over the place now are a lot of fun. I think the no-nonsense nature of the title and obvious plot was a welcome change from the norm, and that the director and cast—at least in the case of Samuel L. Jackson—have wholeheartedly embraced the furor surrounding it has only made it that much better. It's just refreshing to have a movie that looks to be good, mindless fun and that realizes that from the get-go. It will be interesting to see whether *Snakes on a Plane* becomes this decade's 'cult' film in the future—if it's either so completely over-the-top, like the *Evil Dead* series, or played very seriously while obviously being completely absurd, like *Buckaroo Banzai*, I can definitely see it happening."

Now that's high praise—not to mention a great equation for fun!

(Sorry, I couldn't resist.)

[For a taste of other Photoshop creations i.e. "SoaP," go to Fark.com and prepare to stare in wonder.]

Snakes on Parody Movies

"SNAKES ON AN ELEVATOR"

> > > Directed by Alexander Kieft

> > > starring Dwight Smith (Agent Marc), Patricia Kelly (Agent Flynn), Mischa Stephens (Lewis Gainsborough), Dermot Delude-Dix (Man with a suitcase)

DIRECTOR ALEXANDER KIEFT.
Photo by Andrew Rindfleisch

When Swarthmore College students aren't taking courses like "Sex, Sin, and Kin in Early Modern Europe," they're trying to outthink Hollywood. Take Alexander Kieft and his cinematic contribution to the "SoaP" craze, "Snakes on an Elevator." "[Alex said] 'We need to make a spoof for this film before it gets big, before they put out a preview for it, and then we'll market this film as the independent student film that inspired the major motion-picture,' " says Mischa Stephens, who plays the frightened court witness in "Elevator" and also composed the short's music.

The breakthrough took place where most college breakthroughs occur— in the cafeteria. "One night they were serving steak at the cafeteria, and someone said, 'Hey— steaks on a plate!'" Stephens says. "And then we thought, 'Oh, what other kinds of ridiculous things could carry this? What would be the more ridiculous place to find snakes?' 'Oh, an elevator.' "

So on Abraham Lincoln's birthday, Kieft, Stephens and their collaborators made a little history of their own in an empty Swarthmore classroom. They started shooting at 11 AM. and finished at 2 AM, says Stephens, "because there were classes in the morning." They didn't even take the time to write a script, since many of the cast had backgrounds in improv. "That's what was so much fun about it," says Stephens of the free-form dialogue. "We were just playing with clichés."

The payoff, of course, are the snakes, ensconced in the suitcase of the assassin (Dermot Delude-Dix) who is sharing the elevator with the witness and the two FBI agents (Dwight Smith, Patricia Kelly) charged with keeping him alive for the short trip to the courtroom. Since snake wranglers apparently are in short supply at Swarthmore, there are no snakes to be seen in the movie. Kieft had prepared for that contingency with the short's very premise. "If the lights go out, it doesn't matter if you can see the snakes or not; we can do that with sound effects," he says. "Some people who actually stick it out and watch the whole thing get a kick out of it and kind of see that that's part of the whole joke, that there aren't any real snakes, that we just did it in an elevator without anything."

Post-production took about a week and included Stephens' writing of the video's score. "My only composing experience was in high school," he says. He stuck with the improvisation theme when it came to preparing the music, and got indirect guidance from his director. "Alex was modeling his shooting sort of like *24* or *Lost* so I took inspiration from the music of those shows with very solitary note stuff."

In August 2006, New Line Cinema will release its highly anticipated blockbuster thriller, tentatively titled PACIFIC AIR FLIGHT 121.

This is the original independent film that served as the basis for PACIFIC AIR FLIGHT 121.

NOTE: THIS ISN'T REALLY TRUE. BUT IT SURE SOUNDS SNAZZY, DOESN'T IT?

AGENT MARC (DWIGHT SMITH) TRIES TO PUT SOME SENSE INTO HIS RELUCTANT WITNESS (MISCHA STEPHENS) BY STARING AT HIM INTENSELY.

THE WITNESS STARES BACK. HEY, IT'S A STAREDOWN CONTEST!

LEWIS THINKS HE'S A DEAD MAN IF HE TESTIFIES.

HAVE NO FEAR—AGENT FLYNN (PATRICIA KELLY) IS HERE. (FLYNN . . . ISN'T THAT THE NAME OF SAMUEL L. JACKSON'S CHARACTER IN "SOAP"? HEY, THAT'S CLEVER!)

STAIRS? WHO TAKES THE STAIRS ANY-MORE?

HEY, LET'S TAKE THE ELEVATOR INSTEAD . . .

THIS IS WHEN THE FORBIDDING MUSIC STARTS.

WOW, I WONDER WHAT'S GOING TO HAPPEN NEXT?

SNAKES ON AN ELEVATOR

SNAKES, MOTHERFUCKER!

The entire thing was done, in fitting homemade style, using Apple's GarageBand program. "My favorite part of the movie is when the elevator door opens and you sort of here those 'duh-duuuh' notes," Stephens says.

Available at both YouTube.com and its own dedicated site (http://www.snakeso-nanelevator.com), "Elevator" has received mostly positive reviews from the public (and a mention in *BusinessWeek*), though Kieft has found some scattered negative reaction to the film's length (fairly massive when it comes to "SoaP" shorts) and to the fact that the video "didn't have enough actual snakes in it." A few bad apples, though, haven't spoiled his spot in the lore of this awesomely titled B-movie.

"The fun aspect of ['SoaP'] is that you know exactly what you're going to get out of it—as long as there actually are snakes and a plane," Kieft says. "This could be the worst movie ever made, and everyone would still enjoy it because that's what you're expecting— the worst movie ever made."

Whatever "SoaP" may do at the box office, "Elevator" has already helped Kieft's career. He showed it when applying for his current gig teaching film and video part-time at a private high school. Despite that promising start, Kieft's not sure if he's gunning for David Ellis's job, "I really haven't figured out exactly what I'm going to be doing," Kieft says. "I'm not hugely big on the idea of going out west, but I do have some friends who are doing that, and it's a possibility down the road." If he does move to L.A., we advise him to watch out for the real snakes.

"SNAKES ON A PLANE FAKE TRAILER"

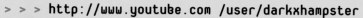

> > > http://www.youtube.com /user/darkxhampster
> > > Directed by Parker Hicks
> > > Starring: Parker Hicks (pilot/kid playing recorder), Forrest Hicks (guy 1), Justin Edwards (guy 2/flight attendant)

He's only 15 years old, but Parker Hicks already has already done almost thirty short films with his friends. Parker definitely has the chops to go far in this business, as his Arabian Nights-inspired fake trailer for *Snakes on a Plane*, amply demonstrates. With his twin brother Forrest, friend Justin Edwards (he's the flight attendant in the wig) and the family camcorder in tow, Parker has put his own spin on the "SoaP" story, including a musical twist ending we'd bet Samuel L. Jackson didn't think of.

Q: How would you describe your style as a director?

A: Well, when I was 6, I liked Steven Spielberg, so I pretty much tried following what he does.

Q: When you started filming, where did you want the direction of your trailer to go?

A: I just wanted to make the undercurrent of the movie like a comedy— to have it seem serious while the whole thing was going to be funny.

Q: Your friend Justin plays the flight attendant. Did you guys draw straws to see who was going to play that role?

A: Well, I really wasn't going to do any part except for the pilot, and my brother was supposed to be getting the drinks for them. So it pretty much worked out that he had gone to the bathroom, and since he was gone he could have played the flight attendant.

Q: How did you think of the end where you tried to solve the snake problem by charming them with music?

A: I just thought about the people being so stupid on that plane, and of something they could do that would actually draw the snakes toward them. And that was one of the things that the Arabian guys did to tame the snakes.

Q: Where did you find the stuffed attack snake?

A: I actually got it from a carnival that was in town.

"ATTENTION, PASSENGERS. WE HAVE TURNED ON THE 'FASTEN YOUR SEAT BELTS' SIGN BECAUSE THERE ARE SNAKES . . . ON THE PLANE."

TWO GUYS (JUSTIN AND FORREST) SITTING AROUND, SUSPECTING NOTHING . . .

EVEN THOUGH—WELL, YOU CAN SEE . . .

"I'LL HAVE A COKE . . ."

BUT HE WASN'T EXPECTING THIS!

PARKER CHANNELS HIS INNER SAM JACKSON.

MORE SNAKE CARNAGE.

WILL MUSIC SOOTHE THE SAVAGE BEAST?

GUESS NOT.

"SNAKES ON A PLANE: HOW HOLLYWOOD REALLY WORKS"

> > > directed by David Levy
> > > written by Trevor Ryan
> > > starring: Trevor Ryan (Trevor), David Levy (Assistant)

In the golden age of Hollywood, where all dreams come true, the biggest nightmare was the "casting couch," in which comely starlets would find their innocence suddenly destroyed during a meeting with a lecherous producer. These days, the biggest nightmare is that a heartfelt screenplay will have its innocence suddenly destroyed by lecherous producers bent on molding these stories to their own will—usually by squeezing the emotion and tenderness out of them to make way for lots of machine gun action and exploding spaceships.

As budding Tinseltown producers, Trevor Ryan and David Levy don't know anything about the first example—they're good boys, really!—but what about the second? Well, whether it's full of truth or not, Ryan and Levy's short film "Snakes on a Plane: How Hollywood Really Works" does deliver a giddy but pungent observation of, well, how things may really work in Hollywood.

Ryan and Levy each have day jobs—Trevor works for a producer at Warner Brothers, while David runs an independent shop called Periscope Entertainment and just presented his first feature, a drama called *Lying* that stars Chloë Sevigny and Leelee Sobieski. But as a duo, they are The Doomed Planet (http://www.the-doomedplanet.com), a comedy team that specializes in the types of short films that they put together when both were attending college in upstate New York. When both of them landed in the entertainment industry in L.A., getting the old act together again was an act of self-expression. "We tried writing a screenplay one day," says Levy. "And then we realized that it would take so much effort to get a feature off the ground that halfway through the screenplay, we just thought, 'Why don't we start a Web site like everyone else is doing and start making these shorts?' So we figured we start a Web site, and we had a camera, so we set up The Doomed Planet and got into the Internet Web content game—not for benefits; just more as a creative outlet."

Snakes on a Plane entered their lives when someone sent Ryan a link to the teaser on YouTube.com. He thought the film was a parody itself, but was then shaken back to reality when he went to the Internet Movie Database and found it was actually happening. He filled his partner in on his discovery, and soon the pair was focused on making their own video based on "SoaP." They decide to stick with what they knew—the behind-the-scene labyrinth of getting a motion picture past the concept stage and into some form of actual production. Or, as Levy says with giddy bluntness, "You go from *The Diary of Anne Frank* all the way to *Snakes on a Plane*, which I think is literally so popular because it is *Snakes on a Plane*."

In the film, Ryan plays a smooth-talking producer, complete with earphone, eager about making a movie based on the time-honored story of the brave Jewish Dutch girls who hit from the Nazis in her attic for years. (He calls it "*Schindler's List* meets *Panic Room*.") But . . . he has one or two changes he'd like to make. Like changing the whole "stagnant secret hideout thing" into a plane to rev up the action. And then, of course, you have to get rid of the Nazis ("Nazis, aircraft . . . Hindenburg . . . a little soon"), but they can be replaced with . . . snakes. Because you don't have to worry about them since they aren't exactly "slithering into movie theaters and coughing up big bucks." Oh, and then, instead of having a young Jewish girl hiding from snakes, why not a big "African American" guy fighting the snakes? You get the picture.

When asked if he based his characterization on any one producer, Ryan defers just like any smart guy who wants his career in Hollywood to progress would. Actually, he does allow that the entire film is a form of "mishmash, a conglomeration of conversations I've overheard and have been part of." He also admits to a touch of risk taking, as the movie was shot inside the office of longtime movie big shot Denise Di Novi (*Batman Returns*)—without permission. "It was a Sunday night," says Ryan. "We went in, and we went past the security guards with this equipment, and set up all the lights. And I went, 'I hope that Denise doesn't come into the office tonight.' "

If Ryan was on any hook, he quickly came off of it when Di Novi saw the finished product and gave it a thumbs-up. And the Planet guys did it all in good fun. "Everything is right there in the title—there's snakes, and they're on a plane," says Ryan. "That's, like, all there is." And then thinking how the people may have come to this movie, starting off with something that's really deep and complex and feeding to the Hollywood [mind trust], which has the tendency to do just this sort of thing."

Still, Ryan and Levy weren't poking a sharp stick at the movie machine as much as they were getting into the spirit of the joy "SoaP" has generated. And that joy has spread beyond the fans, as Levy found out while taking a boat trip when he was in Cannes for *Lying*.

"I looked up, and Sam Jackson stepped on the boat with me," says Levy. "And I got to go to Sam Jackson and tell him how excited I was to see *Snakes on a Plane*, and then fill him in that I was one of the people who put something on YouTube based on it. I had one minute, maybe less, conversation, but it kind of brought the whole experience full circle. And you could tell that he was soaking it in, that he wasn't taking it for granted. He was doing the 'Hi, how are you' smile, but then, when *Snakes on a Plane* was mentioned, he lit up. You could tell that all this has been a fun run for him."

Believe it or not, that hasn't been the most surreal thing Levy and Ryan have dealt with in terms of "SoaP" and their short film. That happened right after *X-Men: The Last Stand* hit the theaters, complete with the first full *Snakes* trailer. "Some people have told us that they saw our film that we made about it," says Ryan with proud bemusement, "and then when the trailer came out, they went, 'Oh, my God, Trevor and Dave have really made a film!' Now that may be high praise or low praise, but it's definitely something—and in the land of making movies, that's often all that matters."

Snakes on a Plane:

How Hollywood Really Works

We're NOT kidding

TITLE CARD FOR THE DOOMED PLANET'S SNAKES SPOOF

AS A FINELY COIFED AGENT, TREVOR RYAN PREPARES TO DEMONSTRATE THE ART OF THE SPIEL.

FIRST, KNOW YOUR MATERIAL FROM FRONT TO BACK.

THEN, LEARN TO MASTER YOUR HAND GESTURES, LIKE THIS . . .

. . . AND THIS

FINALLY, ALWAYS LOOK DETERMINED, EVEN WHEN YOU'RE ON THE PHONE AND NO ONE CAN SEE YOU. PLANET

DON'T FORGET THOSE HAND GESTURES!

COYNE'S BONO IMPRESSION, INCLUDING COOL SHADES.

How has jumping onto the *Snakes on a Plane* bandwagon treated David Coyne? Not so badly, if you consider that the budding actor, filmmaker, and musician just snagged an invitation from New Line Cinema to attend some events surrounding the August release of "SoaP," including the premiere itself. Not bad for a fledgling performer who readily admits that he took on his homemade projects as a way to generate publicity for himself—"as any smart struggling actor would," he adds.

Coyne is no stranger to some level of spotlight. He's done stand-up comedy and acting for years, and has even done some on-air hosting for the Discovery and the Independent Film Channel. His forté, though, may be impersonations, a skill that's seen to full effect in his series of self-made short films that are available on YouTube.com. On one clip, Coyne can been seen in the guise of Kevin Spacey-as-Lex Luthor à la *Superman Returns*; on another he assumes the dual roles of Christopher Walken and Jack Nicholson as the two icons share a lunch. And then there are the two "SoaP" jewels in his crown. In a video he calls "Snakes on a Plane Early Auditions," Coyne reprises his Nicholson and Walken guises and throws in some Robert DeNiro and Joe Pesci in a skit involving top actors trying out for the role that Samuel L. Jackson eventually landed. Profanity, naturally, rules the day. His other "SoaP" film takes a radically different track, a spiritual ode to Jackson in which Coyne, this time playing the sunglasses-wearing Bono, sings his heart out to the actor in the music video "Someone Tell Sam Jackson He's My Bro."

Coyne first learned about "SoaP" when his co-workers and frequent collaborators, Nathanial Perry and Chris Rohan, created their infamous audio trailer that helped to spark the online momentum for the movie. His planning for the audition clip was clear from the beginning. "I knew right off that Walken and Jack would be in it," he says. "Pesci and De Niro were also on my mind as I'd just finished a short flick involving those two impressions." Then there was the cameo by no less than Beaker, the thin and whiny lab assistant made famous on *The Muppet Show*. "Beaker actually shot his own stuff and added it to the piece," Coyne says with a wink. "I was upset at first, but when I saw the footage I couldn't deny that he's a genius."

That clip got Coyne, a tall fellow with a flexible face that comes in handy when it comes to impersonations, a lot of attention. "I knew that if there was already an audience for the film, I could offer something of entertainment value," he says. His films "received an overwhelming positive response not just from 'SoaP' fans, but many folks just looking for a laugh. It's funny, I've been doing this kind of thing for years but I've only just started taking advantage of the Internet." The resulting publicity has earned him a mention in *Rolling Stone* and, now, the notice of New Line. He already had done a jokey tune called "SoaPSong" that was played over the loudspeakers during the film's re-shoots, but, Coyne says, "I think they were more taken with the music video 'Someone Tell Sam Jackson He's My Bro' than any of the other stuff. At first just gave me a genuine pat on the back. Now they've invited me to the premiere and want to show me a good time."

As for the attention "SoaP" has garnered, Coyne is philosophical. "As a filmmaker myself, I think these are interesting times," he says. "I'm nearly addicted to posting short clips on the Net because of the immediate viewer response. I imagine that the big studios will keep an ear open for what the fans are looking for more than ever—especially when the voice of the fans can be so loud and clear via the Web. There's good and bad in it. It's great to get feedback and requests. At the same time, you want to do what turns you on and hope there is an audience for it. That's how I've been operating."

That's great. Now say it like Chris Walken would.

COYNE AS BOBBY DE NIRO: "I don't mean nobody no disrespect, but I thought you should know—you've got fuckin' snakes on this fuckin' plane."

COYNE AS CHRISTOPHER WALKEN: "I'll fight a snake! I don't care?"

COYNE AS JACK NICHOLSON: "Oh my God, look how many snakes are on this fuckin' plane!"

COYNE AS JOE PESCI: "What the fuck with all these fuckin' snakes here, eh? They're all over the fuckin' place!"

SoaP Precursors

1 FER-DE-LANCE

The fer-de-lance is one of the nastiest snakes from South America—and that's saying something, considering some of the creepy-crawlies that inhabit the Amazon. (And we're not even talking about the military dictators.) Not only is it chock full of deadly venom, it's quite aggressive and ornery. And in 1974, it—or, rather, they—got to be the star of its own B-movie, surprisingly called *Fer-de-Lance*. It's about the things that can go wrong when a bunch of prepubescent killer snakes get loose aboard a U.S. Navy submarine called, you guessed it (or maybe not), the *Fer-de-Lance*. They get there courtesy of a bonehead sailor (played by Frank Bonner, aka WKRP in Cincinnati's Herb Tarlek!) who thought it would way cool to bring a bunch of snakes onto a vessel that is named after them—get it? Well, Bonner/Tarlek sure gets it soon after the "babies" escape from their holding pen and slither amok among the crew. The resulting carnage leads to a devastating accident underwater that leaves all of the officers dead and only a ragtag group let by David Janssen (in his usual role as the Reluctant Hero), Hope Lange, and the black guy from *Hogan's Heroes* to save the boat, kill the snakes, and keep their dignity.

I wish I could tell you that this movie is as god-awful as it sounds, but the truth is that *Fer-de-Lance* has been out of print for so long that even eBay doesn't have a copy available. But if "SoaP" makes any amount of money, don't be surprised if a new print of this turkey makes to the bargain DVD bin. Good for us.

2 SATURDAY NIGHT LIVE

Even it's now into its fourth decade, *Saturday Night Live* still has the ability to be groundbreaking, whether it's the original Not-Ready-For-Primetime Players in 1975 or the "Lazy Sunday" digital short from 2005. And sometimes, the effects of a *SNL* spot aren't evident for years afterward.

The last sketch of the February 7, 1998 episode featured show regulars Will Ferrell, Cheri Oteri, and Tim Meadows, along with host John Goodman, in the scenario of a routine flight being disrupted by a lunatic pilot (Ferrell) proclaiming that he has released a cobra inside the jet plane. The cobra, which looks like it was bought at some Times Square gift shop for about 75 cents, proceeds to bite everyone it encounters, Ferrell announces in his creepy but placid voice that more cobras are now doing their thing, and the plane finally crashed into a fireball—from which the main cobra emerges to announce to the audience its intention to dominate the world. Or something like that. The cobra, by the way, was voiced by Oteri—or was it Molly Shannon?—doing some screechy snake-type thing.

If you cruise the Internet looking opinion about this bit, you'll find there is no consensus about the quality of what has become known as the "cobra skit." Some think it was brilliantly surreal while other call it yet another sign of the creative bankruptcy of *SNL*. But no one thought much more about it until *Snakes on a Plane* turned up. Now it's seen as a piece of television archeology, a sign that the *SNL* writers at that time had the uncanny ability to see into the future. Or maybe they were just really, really lucky. Or desperate to fill out the ninety-minute time slot

P.S. Note presence of current "SNL" regular Kenan Thompson and former regular David Koechner among the "SoaP" cast. Seriously, if there's a cameo by John Goodman, we're gonna die.

③ TAIL STING

Just like *Snakes on a Plane*, the title of *Tail Sting* kind of says it all. No, it's not as crystal clear as "SoaP" in terms of explaining what the movie is about in just a couple of words, but it's obvious from the words *Tail Sting* that this won't be an exercise in subtlety .

Made in 2001 (and "made" may be a nice term in this case), *Tail Sting* has a plane as its chosen venue o' horrors, but instead of a swam of snakes, the enemy within this time is a pack of ugly, genetically engineered scorpions. Why—why, you may ask, are scorpions on a plane carrying actual passengers, you may ask. Well, for the greater good, naturally. They're the brainchild of a forward-thinking female scientist (who is also, of course, gorgeous) who has a plan of using the gnarly insects to find a cure for a dread disease. But through a series of mishaps that include corporate espionage, stowaways, and sheer dumb luck, the scorpions are released from their container to mutate, grow, and sting their hearts out. It's up to Beautiful Scientist Lady and her unlikely cohort, the Forlorn Widower Pilot, to figure out how to round up the varmints and save the plane and the day from Certain Doom.

Doom indeed. Movies such as *Tail Sting* are, in some way, the lifeblood of the film industry, if only because with grade-Z material such as this, it gives some bright-eyed kid in Duluth hope that if someone can get something like that released, then anything is possible in Hollywood. And we do mean everything, including, yes, a sequel to *Tail Sting*. 2005's *Stinger* involved evil scorpions on a Navy submarine. Back to square one, in a way—or square zero in another.

NATHANIAL PERRY
AND CHRIS ROHAN

> > > bethesda, maryland
> > > subatomic warp (http://www.subatomicwarp.com)

You won't see the names Nathanial Perry and Chris Rohan in the credits when *Snakes on a Plane* hits studios—at least, not that we know of. At this point, nothing about "SoaP" should surprise anyone. Maybe the producers will sneak in an acknowledgment for the Maryland pair that created the spoofy, expletive-heavy audio trailer "introducing" the movie to the public—and the clip widely seen as one of the main motivators behind New Line giving the go-ahead to the five days of re-shoots that changed "SoaP" from late summer action-flick to small but significant milestone in recent Hollywood history. But if Perry and Cohen haven't gotten a tip of the hat once the final reel runs out, neither of them will raise a fuss. Frankly, the honor was all theirs.

"I don't care," says Perry of whether he thinks he deserves any praise from the studio. "Chris and I set this up just for the hell of it. It was just a really fun thing to do. If they want to give us money, I'm more than happy to take it—I'll take money any day of the week. But I really don't care. All of this is going to make me want to see the movie twice as much as I wanted to before."

The two friends work together at Graphic Audio, a company that does post-production on audio books and also produces trailers for those projects. Thus, they were perfectly equipped to tackle the sideline of poking fun at a film whose title and plotline left both Perry and Rohan with a generous feeling of bemusement. After being urged on by fellow employee Matt Webb, It was Rohan who sketched out the script on the very September day both found out about "SoaP." "It probably took about ten minutes to write down something rough on paper," he says, "and then I went to the booth and did the voice of the announcer and the bad guy." Rohan's villain, a lisping, sneering cad who comes up with the "brilliant" idea of smuggling serpents onto a flight, sounds like a mix between Kim Jong-Il from *Team America: World Police* and Evil Betty from the martial-arts spoof *Kung Pow*, with maybe a dash of Dr. Evil thrown in for good measure. "There are a lot of just really bad villain comedy voices," Rohan says.

Someone, though, had to give profane voice to Samuel L. Jackson, an assignment that Rohan wasn't even going to attempt to pull off. Perry stepped up to that plate. "I was basically thinking of the mindset of *Pulp Fiction*, but pretty much mocking Dave Chappelle's style of doing him," he says about his method of prepa-

ration. "I just started getting angry and yelling all the lines." With a cameo from another of their Graphic Audio co-workers, Nanette Savard, they were done. "She didn't even know what she was doing at the time," says Rohan of Savard's bit as a flight attendant who catches the wrath of the hilariously enraged Jackson.

Once completed, the trailer didn't hit the public immediately. "For a while it just sat there on my computer," Rohan says. "It was just something that we had done, and we let it sit there." Then in November, Webb decided to post the clip to his Web site, Subatomic Warp. Someone linked it to the Internet Movie Database, adds Rohan, and "eventually it got linked again and again and again, and it just kind of blew up."

Naturally, neither Rohan nor Perry had any idea that their work would be incorporated in any way into the actual film. They learned about the turn of events in March along with the rest of the outside world.

"I found that kind of stunning and odd," says Rohan.

"I think I came in late that day, and Chris came up and said, 'How do you feel about the fact that the trailer changed the movie?'" recalls Perry. "I was just speechless about it. It was definitely a great moment."

More was to come. Both Perry and Rohan have been quoted in several of the news articles about the fan frenzy, and there were more personal rewards as well. "My girlfriend was taking me to her school and practically showing me off, and I had to show one guy my driver's license and do the voice," says Rohan about his "fifteen minutes of fame." And Perry sheepishly beams about the party he went to a couple of weeks ago. "When I got there, they stopped the music and played the audio trailer," as if it was his entrance music. "That was kind of awkward, but funny at the same time," says Perry.

The guys are looking forward to seeing "SoaP"—eventually. ("I actually really don't like to go watch movies in the theaters," says Rohan, "so I might just wait for the DVD.") And even though they really weren't in the movie's writing room, they have their opinions about why everyone cars so much about the feature.

"Because it's different," Rohan says. "It's telling you exactly what the movie is about, which is a major strength. And it invites its own satire. It's a really genius idea to just call the movie *Snakes on a Plane* because you either want to see it, or you don't. And it seems kind of limited when you think about it, but then again, they only have to go for an hour and a half, and it can just be a thriller. Just sit down, watch the movie, have fun, turn your mind off—*way* off—and enjoy the movie."

"It's already turned into a cult classic," adds Perry. "You just know that there are going to be snakes, there are going to on a plane, they're going to be attacking people, and you hope to see them get back on the ground safely. I'm pretty sure there will be some good comedy in it and everything, and there will probably be some pretty good horror as well."

And even though they think their role in the *Snakes* experience has been cool, they also keep things in perspective. Rohan compares himself to yet another co-worker, David Coyne, who had done several "SoaP" parodies, both audio and video. (Funny bits from Coyne, Rohan and Perry can be heard on their humor site NutsAFlame.com.) "He tried to really peddle himself as an actor and funny man, like he is," says Rohan. "But I didn't have anything to sell when I did this. I just did it."

"But it's still nice to go back and say, 'Oh, look at what I did.' "

P.S. Regarding the reports that a specific line from Rohan and Perry's trailer made it into during the re-shoots—you know, the one in which Samuel L. Jackson uses multi-syllabic colorful metaphors to express his displeasure at the snakes? Well, that kind of goes the way of "Play It Again, Sam." "It's not a direct quote from the trailer," says Rohan. "It's similar to a lot of quotes from the trailer. I went through it, because I hadn't heard it in a long time, and no, it's not there. But that's OK."

SNAKES ON A PLANE AUDIO TRAILER

Chris Rohan
Nathanial Perry
Nanette Savard

MUSIC: Alien Encounters

> Announcer 2: Snakes on a Plane

SFX: Snake hiss

> Announcer: After the events of September 11th, the nation did it's best to keep the population safe from terror. Security was tightened to ensure that those horrible events never occurred again. They failed.

COS: Evil Lair

REVERB: Conference Hall

> Terrorist 1: We cannot use weapons or explosives. Security is too tight.

> Terrorist 2: We need a better method.

> Terrorist 1: Seemingly harmless until it's too late.

> Terrorist Boss: Gentleman...I have already solved the problem. We do not need any weapons. We have...snakes.

SFX: Snake rattle

> Terrorist 2: Snakes?

> Terrorist Boss: Yes, snakes. First I will put my army of

snakes into a box. Then I will put that box on a plane. Then I will release the snakes! And there will be SNAKES!!!

MUSIC: Sharp fade out

Terrorist Boss: ...On the plane!!!

(PAUSE)

Terrorist Boss: And...then...that will happen...

(PAUSE)

Terrorist Boss: And I will RULE THE WORLD!!! (Evil Laugh)

SFX Snake rattle

MUSIC: Fade in

Terrorist 1: They will let you put snakes on a plane?

Terrorist Boss: Of course. No one suspects the snake. (Shorter evil laugh)

SFX: Snake hiss

END REVERB

Announcer: There plan would have worked...

COS: Airport

AMBIENCE: Airport terminal. Snakes in background.

Terminal Lady: I'm sorry no pets are allowed on the plane.

Terrorist Boss: (coughing, nervous and trying to cover accent) But these are just snakes.

Terminal Lady: Oh, ok then!

Terrorist Boss: (evil laugh covered up with coughing) Thank you.

END AMBIENCE

MUSIC TRANSITION: Alien Encounters / So Sick

Announcer: But they didn't count on one thing...

COS: Airplane

SLJ: Stewardess, get me my mulla fuckin' Coke! I'm mulla fuckin' Samuel L Jackson you mulla fucker!

Announcer: The one and only bad mulla fucker, Samuel L Jackson, was on the plane.

SFX: Snake hiss

SLJ: What the...

SFX: Two pistol shots, snake death

SLJ: ...fuckin' bitch! Stewardess! What the fuck is this mulla fuckin' snake doin' in my mulla fuckin' Coke mulla fucker?

Stewardess: Thank god you saved...(scream of pain)

SFX: Pistol shot, blood gush

SLJ: Get me my mulla fuckin' Coke bitch!

SFX: Body fall

Announcer: And he's throwin a badass mulla fuckin' hissy fit.

AMBIENCE: Snake noises

SFXQ: Pounding fist impacts on *

SLJ: * What the...*What the *fuck *mulla *fuckin' *fuckin' *hell? I did not ask for mulla fuckin' snakes on my mulla fuckin' plane! * Fuckin'...Fuckin' *bullshit!

END AMBIENCE

Announcer: The tension is climbing.

SFX: Chain gun firing on snakes

Terrorist Boss: NOOOO! That badass mulla fucker is ruining all my evil plan! I need more snakes! (Drawn out, powerful evil laugh)

SFX: Snake Hiss

SFXQ: Punching snakes and snake reaction on *

SLJ: You mulla fuckin' *snakes are *fuckin' *ruining my *fuckin' *flight!

SFX: Snake death

SLJ: Fuck!

Announcer: And he still hasn't gotten his Coke.

SFX: Total destruction of surroundings under following line

SFXQ: Pounding fist impacts on *

SLJ: (Unintelligible stream of cursing) I *want my *fuckin' *Coke!

Terrorist Boss: You will never have your Coke. (Evil laugh)

SFX: Snake hiss

(PAUSE)

Announcer: That's...pretty much the plot

SFX: Snake noises

SLJ: Why are there fuckin' snakes on a plane?

Announcer: Snakes on a Plane. Starts Friday unfortunately in theaters everywhere.

SFX: Snake hiss

MUSIC: Fade out

Snakes on T-Shirts

CHRIS BUCCELLA

> > > Poughkeepsie, New York
> > > Damnation-Inc (http://www.damnation-inc.com)

WEB PAGE FOR DAMNATION-INC.COM

CHRIS BUCCELLA—WOULD YOU BUY A T-SHIRT FROM THIS MAN? A LOT OF PEOPLE ARE.

It's sleek, it's simple, and it says it all: Snakes + Plane = *Snakes on a Plane*. Put that equation into graphics form, and you have the hottest formula this side of Einstein. And it came to Chris Buccella not in a dream, but rather in the shower.

Back up to last October, when Buccella, then a senior at Marist College in Poughkeepsie, New York, first found out about the buzz. "I read the Web comic Overcompensating," he says, "and he [Jeffrey Rowland] had mentioned *Snakes on a Plane* in that, so I went on the IMDb and looked it up, and I went, 'Wow, they're actually calling this movie *Snakes on a Plane*? It's probably a working title or something.' " Later on that evening, while in the shower, an epiphany came to Buccella. "I got a great idea, because that's where great ideas come from. And it was 'Snakes + Plane = *Snakes on a Plane*.'"

A great idea for a new T-shirt, thought Buccella, who already was helping to get an online merchant called Damnation-Inc off the ground. So he quickly converted his concept into design form and presented to his friends, who approved. After that, he went public, producing just a few to begin with. "As a college student, I really didn't have a lot of working capital," he says. "But I could buy a couple dozen one-color 'Snakes' shirts, which I did."

At the time he put his shirts on sale, Buccella was still under the impression that *Snakes on a Plane* was in fact just the working title for the forthcoming movie. That idea was swiftly erased a few weeks later. "This order came in for a T-shirt from one of the producers of *Snakes on a Plane*. And said, 'The movie's going to be called *Snakes on a Plane*.' And that's when I was, like, 'This is a real thing, for real?' "

Very real. And soon after that, Buccella's enterprise became a very real thing as well. The original design sold so well (one order came from as far away as Copenhagen), it financed other "SoaP" variations, including the black-on-green "Snakes on a Stealth" variation and, for the ladies, a pink "I love Snakes on a Plane" design. And then there's perhaps the jewel in Buccella's crown o' T-shirts—the black "red-letter" version.

"The shirt came out because a lot of people had wanted one in black," says the designer. "But instead of just releasing the original one in black, I thought, 'With the black, we'll make it the special edition one, what else can I make special about it? Oh, I'll put the "MF" in the middle, for "Snakes on a Motherfuckin' Plane."'"

CHRIS' ORIGINAL DESIGN

Photo by Harry McIntyre.

SNAKES ON A STEALTH T-SHIRT.

Photo by Harry McIntyre.

INTERACTIVE STICKER.

SNAKES ON A _____

Photo by Harry McIntyre.

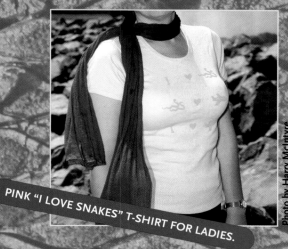

PINK "I LOVE SNAKES" T-SHIRT FOR LADIES.

Photo by Harry McIntyre.

WRISTBANDS.

Photo by Harry McIntyre.

Photo by Kevin Winter/Getty Images.

SAMUEL L. JACKSON AT THE MTV MOVIE AWARDS, PROUDLY BEARING THE FRUITS OF BUCCELLA'S LABORS.

YEAH, BUCCELLA WENT THERE. HE IS SELLING SNAKES IN A CAN. BUT DON'T BLAME HIM; BLAME TRADITION. "I WAS THINKING OF RELATED MERCHANDISE, AND THERE'S NOTHING LAMER THAN THE SNAKE IN THE CAN TRICK," HE SAYS. "SO I DECIDED TO OFFER THEM AS AN ACCESSORY." NOW, HE MARVELS AT HIS INGENUITY – OR SOMETHING LIKE THAT: "IT'S JUST REALLY FUNNY TO ME THAT I HAVE A CASE OF SNAKES IN A CAN SITTING HERE, AND PEOPLE CAN BUY THEM."

A shirt fitting for Samuel L. Jackson, Buccella also thought. Indeed, the Web page that features the special edition shirt, unlike the other shirts, has no picture of a person modeling it. Instead, there's a space holder that says, "Reserved for Samuel L. Jackson." "I didn't think anybody else was qualified except for Samuel L. Jackson to do it," Buccella says. "And I couldn't hire him or anything; I was just kind of hoping that he'd get one somehow. And then orders came in from a couple of people saying, 'I'm ordering an extra one to give to Samuel L.' And I go, 'OK, you're his hairdresser's assistant or his veterinarian's receptionist or something.' "

Well, one of those orders may have been legit, because Jackson turned up to the MTV Movie Awards in June proudly wearing Buccella's MF shirt. It was a red-letter day for Buccella. "That's icing on the cake," he says. But don't expect to see Samuel L. modeling the garb on the Damination-inc site. "I probably can't afford rights to the photographs; I'm still looking into that. But the fact that he did it is pretty gratifying."

What do you think of the reaction to the movie? "When they made it official that it was going to stay *Snakes on a Plane*, that was the first sign that the online community kind of had a voice as to the direction that this film was going. And later they re-shot some scenes for key phrases for Samuel L. Jackson. So it makes me wonder if this is something that's going to continue into the future where film studios really listen to fan input, or is this a one-off thing because of such a crazy title with the star power of Samuel L. Jackson coming together?"

Is this movie review-proof? Will it be a success whether it's good or bad? "I would say that it is review-proof. People are going to see it based on the title and based on the hype that has happened already. It should have a great opening week-end. That being said, it had better be pretty bad or pretty good. If it's mediocre, it's not going to do very well. Fans will want it to be either so bad that they can get some pretty good dumb quotes out of it, or surprisingly good that they can be astonished that a doomed-to-failure movie was actually pretty decent."

LUKE ALLEN HACKNEY

> > > East Lansing, Michigan
> > > Scary Lion, a subsidiary of RetroDuck
       (http://www.scarylion.com)

What a difference a shirt makes—or, to be exact two. Longtime friends Luke Allen Hackney, Adam Van Lente, and Sean Maday have run RetroDuck, a T-shirt company based out of East Lansing, Michigan that sells both vintage and modern designs, for three years. Earlier this years the business produced a spinoff, Scary Lion, with Hackney in charge of its creative content. And then *Snakes on a Plane* arrived on the scene.

"I'm not really sure where I first saw it, which is kind of the wonder of the Internet," says Hackney, who has built an impressive career as a journalist even as he pursues his degree at Wayne State University. "Like, how many different blogs talk about the same things? But as soon as I saw it, I knew it was going to be a meme that people latched onto, and it just seemed like we had to do it. It's just the idea of the movie was funny to me. And I was talking to a friend of mine online, like, 'We've got to make these shirts,' and I kind of talked about a couple of possibilities, and I called Adam and I was, like, 'We need to do these today.' "

And so it was done. Hackney came up with two "SoaP" concepts—one PG-rated, one a definite R, and both full of appropriate whimsy. It took Hackney "probably about ten, fifteen minutes" to create the designs, but the results have been fruitful. "They single-handedly took out of the red," says Hackney, almost two months to the day after Scary Lion was launched. "The 'I've had it with these snakes' shirts sell better, just about double." Among those making purchases: "Soap" executive producer George Waud. "He bought shirts from us, so he was either buying them to look at them to try to cease and desist us, or he actually likes them." So far, it seems to be the latter. "I guess it doesn't surprise me because, just from how much it has taken off, they realize that the only way this movie is going to make any money is if it becomes a camp hit, I guess. And all of this free publicity is free publicity when it comes down to it."

SCARY LION HOME PAGE

(L TO R) LUKE ALLEN HACKNEY AND ADAM VAN LENTE WITH A FRIEND, WHO IS NEITHER LION NOR DUCK (NOR SNAKE, FOR THAT MATTER).
Photo courtesy of RetroDuck.com.

WE CAN DO THIS THE EASY WAY . . .

. . . OR THE HARD WAY.

Q: Do you see New Line's hands-off policy in terms of the fan frenzy as a trend or a one-shot deal?

A: I think it sets a precedent based on what's going on around this movie a few months before it even comes out. Honestly, I'd probably say that it sets a precedent. If it does extraordinary well, the only people they have to thank for that is the Internet. And if it does terribly, maybe they won't go back.

Q: Do you think that *Snakes on a Plane* has to actually be a good movie do extraordinary well?

A: If you look at recorded history, these movies probably don't do that well, and it's kind of weird that this one has the ability to do well. There's a lot of people like me, and I have no idea what generation you would classify us as—I mean, camp has a lot of appeal to us, and that's part of the reason, I think, that this thing has been so big on the Internet. It just looks awful. I don't think anybody would say this is going to be a good movie. It's a ridiculous movie, you know, with a ridiculous title. I think there are a lot of people like us that just find some kind of humor in that. What's really funny is that Adam used to work at a video store out here in Michigan, in our home town, and at the end of the night he and another person who used to work there looked for just the most awful, terrible looking box in the store, and that's what we'd would watch that night. So we've always just been kind of into just really terrible movies. They're funny, you know. It's entertaining. There's been a few that were just so bad that we turned them off, but usually it gets to the point where you're laughing pretty hysterically just from how awful it really is.

Q: Will you be in line opening night to see this movie?

A: Oh, yeah. We're going to be pissed drunk, and we're going to see it.

JEREMY KALGREEN

> > > columbus, ohio
> > > Amorphia Apparel (http://amorphia-apparel.com)

To get an idea of the type of easy-going guy Jeremy Kalgreen is, you have to know about his part-time job, the gig he has other than his T-shirt business, Amorphia Apparel. He delivers pizzas—110 miles away from his home in Columbus, Ohio. "I work two days a week at this pizza place," Kalgreen says. Why the extra-long commute? "It's where I grew up," he replies. "It's really just an excuse to go up there and visit with my friends on the weekend from high school and be nostalgic and have fun there."

Having fun is definitely a theme for Kalgeen, one that translates into his line of T-shirt designs. And that includes his rendition of the *Snakes on a Plane* theme, a whimsically-designed cobra, complete with hood, pilot's cap and wings, proving that he's been in the air more than a few times. The look came to him quite easily. "I did it in two hours," says Kalgreen, who has a background in photography but is otherwise an admitted novice when it comes to graphic design. "When I decided to do the shirt, I just went out on my porch, listened to some music and thought, 'How do I do this?' And I think I had a mental image of the snake done in that style."

Kalgreen found out about *Snakes on a Plane* via the subversive humor Web site Fark.com, which has a section devoted to off-kilter new stories. "It was an interview with Samuel L. Jackson," he says. "He was doing some promotional stuff for whatever he was pushing at the time, and the person interviewing him asked him what he had coming up, what his future plans were. And he just went on this rant about this movie that he was making, and they want to change the title, and the only reason that he did it was because of the title, which was *Snakes on a Plane*. And just the idea that Samuel L. Jackson was making this, that he took the movie just because of the title, and because of that title—it was just perfect."

The next move was, perhaps, inevitable. "I started seeing the T-shirts pop up, and other things started to go from there, and it became one of the things to wear," says Kalgreen. "I was just opening my T-shirt shop, and—you know, it seemed to me like this sort of sitting around the campfire, telling ghost stories, trying to top the other guy thing. There were a lot of genuinely talented designers doing their shirts, and the next person would come out with one to try to top those, and then the next person, and so on. So I figured that I might as well open my store and that it would be fun to try to participate in this."

AMORPHIA APPAREL WEB PAGE

JEREMY KALGREEN—DON'T READ ANYTHING INTO THIS PHOTO; HE WAS JUST EXPERIMENTING.
Photo by Jeremy Kalgreen.

CLOSE UP OF JEREMY'S "SOAP" LOGO.

Fun, and a bit profitable as well. Kalgreen says he hasn't done a lot of advertising for his store—for example, he doesn't tend to wear his garb when he's on delivery duty—but says that the "SoaP" merchandise has done well for him. He gives a lot of credit to the posting about his site on Brian Finkelstein's Snakes on a Blog several weeks ago. "That was a huge wave of traffic then that I still get business from," he says.

As the film approaches, Kalgreen hasn't ruled out creating another "SoaP" design before the release date. He has, though, ruled one idea out: "I don't think I'll be doing *Snakes on a Pizza* or anything like that"

Q: What do you make of all of this attention over a movie that no one has ever seen yet?

A: I think it's tapped into something primal. It's almost majestic. It would be like if you were just walking down the street and you saw a mountain Yeti coming down from the hills, where it's something that you look at, and you see it surveying all of the land standing on top of whatever, and you know that this is primitive, but it just looks so noble while it's up there. . . . It's all about trying to manipulate the audience. You go see a trailer for a movie and it looks great, but then you go to see the movie, and you see that the trailer is totally misleading. But I believe with *Snakes on a Plane*, there is no way I'm going to leave that theater and not be given snakes on a plane. It's just so straightforward, so ridiculous. And I love bad movies, I love B-movies. Some of my favorite are B-movies. We have Bad Movie Night all the time, and this is like a pre-made bad movie that's up my alley.

Q: But if the "SoaP" gets three- or four-star reviews, will you be disappointed?

A: If it got three- or four-star reviews, I would be shocked, but I would be more than willing to roll with it that way. If it turns out that it's a great movie, then more power to it. Maybe it will encourage [marketing] people to take a more direct and less artificial role.

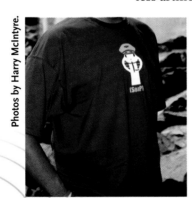

Photos by Harry McIntyre.

MEN'S T-SHIRT.

WOMAN'S T-SHIRT.

MESSENGER BAG, THE BEST TO TRANSPORT SNAKES WITH (SNAKES NOT INCLUDED).

JIM LORD

> > > Memphis, Tennessee
> > > Teesed.com (http://www.cafepress.com/teased/)

When it comes to barbecue, the secret is in the sauce. And when it comes to cool T-shirts, the secret is in the idea. Jim Lord has learned that the easy way. His Cafepress site, Teesed.com, began as a convenience for the Memphis native and his friends. "We're on a barbecue team for the World Barbecue Competition, and we were looking for a place where we could buy fifteen shirts," explains Lord. "And in most places you had to buy a whole bunch of something. So we came across Cafepress and found we could upload our logo and just print the 15 shirts that we wanted for a pretty good price."

JIM LORD'S WEB PAGE

Lord liked the experience so much, he established Teesed as a full-fledged online store on Cafepress, where he created logos for sale on T-shirts and other products to the general public. It was at Cafepress where he happened upon *Snakes on a Plane*.

"There's a message board on Cafepress for shopkeepers, and one of the areas is called 'Trends and Buzz,' " says Lord. "And in that section, someone posted about this new movie called *Snakes on a Plane*, that it was getting all kinds of underground hype. So I clicked around a couple of things and started looking at it, and you could sense that it was going to be some type of cult hit, just from looking at the marketing and all the different people posting about it. And I came across Snakes on a Blog and saw that someone had a T-shirt up and realized that, hey, it's a great idea.

Within two days, Lord had thrown his snake design into the vipers' nest. His first concept was Snakes on a Shirt, which was followed soon after by his more aggressive "Rattle This!" look, which had an additional touch—well, two, if you count the nuance of "SoaP"-centric profanity. The letters have the texture of snakeskin. "We did that with Photoshop and played around with different textures," says Lord. "I realized that that would lend a little bit to the snakeskin look."

Sales have been steady, though not through the roof; Lord points out, correctly, that there is some stiff competition out there when it comes to "Snake" attire. "It's not like everyone is beating down my door to get them because there are a lot of different shirts out there, but I've sold quite a few—probably three or four a week. It's nothing major, but without having seen anything about it, I wouldn't have had a shirt up at all."

And before you ask the obvious question—no, Lord's never barbecued a snake, but he's eaten one in the past. "Tastes like chicken," he reports about his plate of roasted rattler. And what kind of sauce would he recommended for preparing the delicacy? "I think you have to go kind of light on the sauce," says Lord. "You want to get the flavor of the snake. Otherwise, what's the point?"

Q: Did you think that *Snakes on a Plane* had to have been a hoax when you first heard about it?

A: Well, my thinking was that we've kind of seen so many serious movies and big-budget movies planning to be box-office hits that people are just so ready for a movie you don't have to think about, that's just utter nonsense, campy, over-the-top type of stuff. And just reading about Samuel L. Jackson's comments about the movie, about the script and the title—reading about all those things, you can just tell that this was a *Pulp Fiction*-type of over-the-top movie, and I think a lot of people are ready for that.

Q: Will you go to see the movie on August 18th?

A: I don't know if it will be shown here in Memphis. If it comes out here, I don't know if I'll make it for opening night, but I'll definitely be seeing it. But I'm not an opening-night kind of guy. I like to be in a theater where I can pick my seat and enjoy and not have to worry about fifteen people sitting around me talking.

HEY, LOOK, IT'S SNAKES ON A SHIRT!

WHO ARE YOU LOOKING AT?

JAKE WACHHOLZ

> > > Amherst, Ohio
> > > snakes in a Drain et al
> > > (http://www.cafepress.com/jakesonaplane)

Take a look at Jake Wachholz, and it's clear that he is not a serious man. Take a look at his T-shirts, and that opinion is solidified. His line of "SoaP"-inspired T-shirts definitely emphasizes fun over fear, whimsy instead of terror. They also prove that while a mind is a terrible thing to waste, a sense of humor—and wordplay—is just as important to maintain.

JAKE WACHHOLZ: "WHERE ARE MY SNAKES AT?"
Courtesy of Jake Wachholz.

Wachholz, who lives in Amherst, Ohio, and is currently between jobs, first found out about *Snakes on a Plane* the old-fashioned way—a friend told him about it. "He was, like, 'Have you ever heard of a movie called *Snakes on a Plane*?'" says Wachholz. "And he was, like, 'Bet you don't know what it's about.' 'Um, snakes on a plane?' So that was pretty much it. We checked out the trailer online, and I was, like, way excited. And then I heard they were going to change the name to *Flight 121* or something, and that Samuel L. Jackson wasn't going to do it if they changed it and that the only reason he signed on was the title, which is excellent because there needs to be more humor in Hollywood, and I think this works perfectly for him."

Neither Jackson nor the film itself seemed to be primarily on Wachholz' mind later on when he was hanging out with his friend, his girlfriend, and a few other chums. "We were just sitting around, and I started just saying *Snakes on a Plane*, and whatever rhymed with 'plane' after that. And we were just constantly making up new things. And then I was thinking to myself that there should be shirts printed, and if nobody buys them, I don't care; it's just funny that they're there. So I went home, I Photoshopped on the shirts, just put them out there and then showed my friends. And I didn't tell them that it was me. I don't know if they knew or not, but either way, I wanted other people to share the humor that we were having."

Besides, Wachholz continues, "I was just jealous of everyone already having their own thing on there."

Now Wachholz has plenty out there. Thanks to the rhyming skills of himself and his pals, his Cafepress site (unofficially called "Jakes on a Plane"; originally called "Snakes in Places That They Shouldn't Be") includes some ten variations on the same theme. There's Snakes in a Drain, Snakes in the Rain, Snakes in Maine (with a mariner's beard and a lobster)—who knew snakes could get into so many sticky situations. A few border on the truly surreal, such as the distinctive Snakes Hussein—which originally was going to be really, really surreal. "I was going to try to see if I could merge a snake and Hussein together, but the simpler, the better," says Wachholz.

Snakes...

His top-selling design is Snakes on a Drain; his girlfriend's favorite design is Snakes on Maine. And there were a few ideas that he didn't go threw with—yet. "We had thought about Snakes That Use Gain or Snakes on Rogaine," he says. And maybe—yeah, he may be going there. "(Snakes on) Cocaine . . . with this little white line over where his nose is." Well, he already has Snakes on Mary Jane—why not go all the way?

Q: You're a part of the *Snakes on a Plane* frenzy, but what do you make of the frenzy over a film that no one has seen yet?

A: From everything that I've seen on the Internet and from my friends, I'm just way excited. It doesn't even have to be good. It's just that the title alone sells it.

Q: What do you think a movie like this says about the state of Hollywood? Do you see this as a bit of refreshing candor or as a trend or what?

A: I hope it's a trend. It's a way that they can not so much poke fun at themselves, but show that not everything has to be 100 percent serious, that they can just do goofy things like this for the fans and show that the audience members are not complete idiots.

Q: If it is a serious movie, though, will you be disappointed?

A: Well, judging by the way the graphics look and everything, and they that they're using parts that they saw on the Internet from the fans and such, I don't think it's going to be that serious.

Q: You and your friends will all get together opening night to see it?

A: Oh, yeah. We'll wear snake costumes and plane costumes. I'll try my best to get a snake costume, and then there will be a plane costume. And I'll ride my friend's back or vice versa. We'll see what we can do.

ASHLEY ANDERSON

> > > Port Wentworth, Georgia
> > > Pixelism's premier place of purchases
> > > (http://www.cafepress.com/kid_a)

When Georgia freelance artist Ashley Anderson created his "SoaP" design, a play on another catchy slogan of similar meaning, someone could have made the connection that he was tying the two together. After all, the connection between "Snakes on a Plane" and "Shit Happens" is easy to make. But that wasn't quite what Anderson had in mind when it came to his original reasoning.

"When I came up with the idea for the shirt, I tried to think about what it could mean," says Anderson. "And for me, I decided that it meant not that the situation in the movie was what was referred to with the term 'shit,' but rather the movie itself." That fits in with when through Anderson's head when he first learned about "SoaP." "When I heard it was going to be a real movie, I thought it was a pretty fair depiction of the nature of Hollywood—the depths that they would go to just make money off of ticket sales. I was pretty amazed that they would let such a terrible, terrible movie with such an unclever title make it even past consideration, much less let Samuel L. Jackson star in it—or rather that he would want to star in it."

After that, the idea for Anderson's logo came quite naturally to him. "Sketch a lot on my sketch pad, and a lot of my shirt ideas come from wordplay. I think it was just thinking about the "shit happens" sticker, and also it just popped into my head to black out the last three letters of 'shit,' and put 'Snakes on a Plane' right there."

And, by the way, Anderson is looking forward to seeing "SoaP" when it is released. "I'm pretty sure my friends and all going to get together and see the movie, and I think we might even try to make some signs to take with us," he says. "Instead of picketing the movie, we might be picketing *for* the movie, like when we're standing in line to get tickets." But he's not exactly sugar-coating things when he theorizes what the audience of the flick will be looking for. "I'm expecting that this film will bring a lot of people in just because so many people have heard about how bad it should be. I'm sure there are going to be some people whose taste is so bad for the reason that most of us go see decent movies. But I'm imagining that most of the profits for this movie will come from people who just want to see the train wreck."

ASHLEY ANDERSON'S WEB SITE FOR SELLING T-SHIRTS.

ASHLEY ANDERSON.
Courtesy of Ashley Anderson.

Q: How did you first found out about *Snakes on a Plane*?
A: I can't remember the exact place or name of the Web site. I was hanging out at

BLACK T-SHIRT

WHITE LADIES' T-SHIRT.

Photos by Harry McIntyre.

one of my friend's house one night, and he asked me if I had heard about *Snakes on a Plane*, and I was, like, "No, what the heck is that?" He showed me this Web site where someone had done all these different parodies of just the title of *Snakes on a Plane*. There were about forty different versions. It was really hilarious. And people who saw the Web site could submit their own contributions. That's how I found out about it.

Q: To what do you credit the frenzy around the movie?

A: I think it's partly due to the mainstream, as well as what you would call the underground, celebrity of Samuel L. Jackson. He's a great actor, but he's never really had a big part outside of *Pulp Fiction*." He's never won an Oscar even though he's a fairly decent actor. And so I think part of it just deals with his unique popularity, because I don't know anyone who doesn't like Samuel L. Jackson. And I heard that when he was interviewed about the film, he actually said that he didn't even read the script—he just saw the title and said, "I'm in, but if you change the title of this film, I'm going to quit." So I think it's partly due to Samuel L. Jackson's unique and very strong popularity, and it's also due to the fact that Samuel L. Jackson used his popularity and his power as a star to kind of back these people into a corner as far as [them saying], "We're changing this terrible title of the film." And also, just the Internet buzz—the Internet has a power as a media tool that's very grassroots. All of that makes me want to see this movie.

CLAIRE SCHAEFFER

> > > st. petersburg, florida
> > > shelf life
(http://www.cafepress.com/shelflifeshop/)

Claire Schaeffer is not dealing with snakes on a plane at this very moment, but rather with something not as dangerous but maybe more aggravating—traffic on a Tampa freeway. It's getaway day, and Schaeffer is stuck in her car trying to do just that. But despite the situation, her mood is gregarious, especially when the subject is her favorite actor and the crazy film he's starring in.

Schaeffer first learned about *Snakes on a Plane*—well, she's quite sure. "I believe I either read it on a blog, or someone posted about it on a message board," she tries to recall. "I just remember reading it and going, 'Well, that's a real kick! People are either going to love it or not get it.' " At the time, she already had an online store at Cafepress up and going, so inspiration wasn't too far away. "I started looking around, and I found that people were already talking about [the movie]. And I'm a big Samuel Jackson fan, so I said to myself, 'OK, I have to make a shirt.' "

STILL LIFE WEB PAGE

At first she created two designs—a spoof logo with the self-descriptive name "Snakes on a Helicopter" and a retro piece Schaeffer calls her "Betty" motif—as in "And then Betty said, 'There were muthafuckin' snakes on the plane.' " One sold better than the other—guess which one. "[The retro one] is my top seller," she says. The helicopter design, she reasons, may not be doing as well, "because it's kind of a joke on the movie, and people who are fans of the movie really want something that's about the movie."

The fans that come to Schaeffer's site now have plenty of options to choose from, as she has no less than ten different designs to choose from. You can go mystical with a yin-yang T-shirt (her second-best selling logo), one that proudly proclaims that the wearer is a "Snakesonaplaniac," or Schaeffer's personal favorite, what she calls her "Jackie Brown" ode in honor of another one of Jackson's notable films. Today, she expresses surprise that she came up with so many ideas.

CLAIRE SCHAEFFER.
Courtesy of Claire Schaeffer.

"I lost track of the count," she says. "I started with two different designs, and then I would think of something and say, 'You know, I need to add that.' 'Oh, *that* would make a great shirt.' And it just kind of carried away from there. The more I was reading about it, the more people were talking about it, I thought, 'Well, there are going to be some people who don't want "motherfuckin" on their shirt,' so I should make something for people who like the idea of the movie, but don't want to have profanity on their shirt. And then there were some who sent in a request

BASIC "SOAP" DESIGN.

AN OUTFIT FOR LITTLE SNAKES!

CLAIRE'S MOST POPULAR DESIGN.

CLAIRE'S LEAST POPULAR DESIGN.

"JACKIE BROWN" DESIGN.

SNAKES AND PLANES IN HARMONY,

for children's gear, and I said OK, so I took one of my designs and redid it in primary colors, and there's no profanity on that one."

Schaeffer's working in the fields of marketing and advertising could explain her fertile mind when it comes to "SoaP" stuff. And while she thinks her design choices have hit their limit, she already has had time—maybe because of the still-show traffic—to think about where Jackson and his wiggly adversaries should be going if the word "sequel" comes up. "Snakes in Space," she says. "That's the one I want to see. That one could be very interesting." Especially in terms of T-shirts.

Q: Why do you think *Snakes on a Plane* caught on in the way that it has?

A: In the days before the Internet, this wouldn't have happened. But I think it's a combination of both highly campy and highly simple, and no one would ever think that anyone in marketing would use such an obvious name for a movie. And then I also think it has to do with Samuel Jackson being in it, and just looking at some of his past, really strong characters and the type of language that he uses with them, it's just a lot of fun to play around with Samuel Jackson fighting snakes. I do think that his role is a large part of it.

Q: Do you think that this movie would have even been made without his participation?

A: It wouldn't have the same attraction to me if he weren't in it, no. That's a big part of it to me. Even when he is doing serious work, there's a lightness about his work, a sense of humor with which he can really approach these things. It's just the kind of movie where he goes, "OK, I'm going to be fighting snakes," and I don't think there are too many actors who can do that and have people enjoy it.

Q: What about New Line allowing all of this unauthorized activity going on around their film?

A: New Line Cinema has been so gracious about allowing fan fiction and fan art to exist. A lot of companies wouldn't have done that.

Q: Will you wear one of your T-shirts when you go to see the film?

A: Well, I'd be crazy not to, wouldn't I?

THE AUTHOR DOES HIS BEST FEDERLINE TO DISPLAY APPROPRIATE "SOAP" HEADWEAR.

ONE FOR THE ROAD.

Snakes
on (Almost)
Everything Else

TONY BROWN

> > > worcester, massachusetts
> > > searching for clairty (http://
chryslerpoetlivejournal.com

Snakes on a Plane has come in many shapes and sizes. Here's a prime example—behold, a poem about "SoaP." But it may not be what you're expecting.

TONY BROWN IN PERFORMANCE.
Courtesy of Tony Brown

SNAKES ON A PLANE

by Tony Brown (aka "chryslerpoet")

I woke up tonight after a nap
and looked at myself:
fat again, in limbo again, still medicated, still
underemployed. Smoking again. Drinking
too much, and snappish and boorish to boot.
Tomorrow's my birthday. I'm nearly 50.
The TV and the magazines tell me
it's all Snakes On A Plane from now on—
you know, where you're waiting for something to kill you
and you've got nowhere to go.
So why for the first time
do I like what I see?

Maybe because of this:

There's a black dog in the corner who keeps
looking at me. Right now, he's chained up
and there's no drool, he might be asleep but
with eyes that dark it's hard to tell.

I know this dog.
I've known him for years. He doesn't bite like a snake—
no quick nerve-freeze, no sudden fall—
no, the dog clamps down
and holds on till you're dragged to the ground,
and he'll follow you around all the time waiting
for his chance to do it.
I used to worry about that.
I could care less now.

The way I look at it:
at this age I'm well into the second half.
Whatever bites me, bites me.
If I get depressed, I'm skipping the suicide
because there's isn't all that long to wait.

And if there are snakes
on this motherfucking plane,
motherfucker, please—at least I'm flying.

The architect of this tome, Tony Brown, lives in Worcester, Massachusetts. By trade he's an independent consultant who specializes in management training. At his core, though, he's a poet, a spoken-word artist, and a man with more on his mind that just Samuel L. Jackson blowing up snakes real good. Indeed, as with most poet worth their weight in life lessons, there's a lot going on inside his soul. And he's more than willing to explain his motivation and his place in "SoaP" lore. "I think the *Snakes on a Plane* phenomenon needs some documentation," Brown says succinctly.

Q: Not only did you write a poem based on *Snakes on a Plane*, you didn't really use the plot of the film as the basis. You used the other meaning of the term.

A: The thing is that I'm as fascinated as everybody else with the phenomenon. We all make jokes about it, and I make jokes about it. But the image of being trapped and being unable to escape something . . . I had just turned forty-six, and a lot of the stuff that's in the poem is true. I'm in the process of getting a divorce, my life's been going through an awful lot of changes. And the metaphor really spoke to me of something that was—underneath all of that, that really gets into a primal fear, which is the whole idea of being out of control of your fate, and not being able to get away with it. That's sort of where I took that from.
    Plus my little homage to Mr. Jackson at the end.

Q: That also reminded me of Dylan Thomas—"Do not go gently into that good night . . . Rage, rage against the dying of the light."

A: That's exactly where I was going with it, is working in that kind of Dylan Thomas vein about "So what? You still have to live."

Q: Did writing the poem make you feel better at all about your life?

A: That's strong. This is what I do. I'm a poet. I write and publish them and read and perform them. I think a lot of times I try to use poetry to work out how I'm doing.

Does it make me feel better? No, but it was accurate. And, certainly, that little bit of defiance at the end—yeah, it was an accurate statement of where I stood at the moment. And from that point of view, being able to put a name on it, yes, it made me feel better.

Q: Have you read this poem in public?

A: Absolutely.

Q: And what's been the reaction to it?

A: It's very popular. [Laughs] It's funny—every time I read it—I've done it a few times—and every time I read it somewhere, number one, people know the poem ahead of time, having read it on the Web or something like that. And number two, a lot of people will start yelling "Snakes on a Poet" or "Poets on a Snakes." Because so much of the audience, when I read it, is familiar with the concept that the minute I announce the title, people are, like, "Ahhh!" It gets a good reaction. It's interesting because I wrote it, and I put it out there, and when I originally put it out on my blog, I made the comment that I was sort of facetiously trying to be the first person to write a poem. And it really seems to have struck a nerve with people. I get comments about it all the time. I really do. I think people expect a funny poem, and it's not a funny poem. I took one image out of it, and there is some humor in there, but it's not really a funny poem. It's a poem about facing your own mortality. And it does strike a nerve with people.

Q: When you first heard about the movie, did you think it was the real thing, or did you think it was a hoax?

A: The person who first told me about it told me it was a real idea that sounded like a parody. And it was a person I trusted, so I went and looked it up, and I was, like, "You've got to be kidding me." And it struck me that the amount of attention that's being given to a movie that nobody has ever seen—I'll be honest, I don't know if it's going to be any good, I don't know if the movie's going to be interesting. I'm going to go on opening night and see it, I'll tell you that. I'll make my decisions then. But obviously it's struck a nerve with people. The story has struck a nerve. And have to say that I'm looking forward to it in whatever way it comes.

MATT BARR

> > > Kansas City, Missouri
> > > http://www.snakesonablog.com/2006/05/20/snakes-
on-a-kindergarten-class-ii

MR. MATT, THE
TEACHER

In this day and age of frequent worries about education, we want our kids to have teachers who are totally committed to nurturing their minds, who want to be their friends as much as their role models—who are willing to talk to them about wacky movies and run around wearing gorilla suits and silly T-shirts ...

But I'm getting ahead of the story. Let's start here—once upon a time in the far away land called Kansas City, there was a young man named Matt Barr. To his class of precocious kindergarten students at the Lavonna Peterson Montessori School, he was Mr. Matt, smiling teacher and school principal, always willing to pull out all the stops to reach his kids with lessons on a myriad of topics, whether it was through song, dance, or the building of a Roman aqueduct.

One day Mr. Matt was reading one of his favorite magazines, *Wired*, when he read an article about a strange new movie. "There were no pictures—just words about Samuel L. Jackson being in *Snakes on a Plane*, and that was about it," Barr says. "And I went on the Internet and found something on it, and it looked, to me, pretty bad, the whole idea of it." But when he found out about the contest that New Line Cinema was having to choose a song from a lesser-known band to be on the "SoaP" soundtrack, "I just became totally obsessed with it," says Barr.

While in the Roman Aqueduct Supplies aisle at the local Costco, Mr. Matt met a fellow aspiring musician. Together they wrote a song for the competition using the name of Cleopatra's favorite serpent, Asp. The teacher-slash-musician also got help from another source—his precocious young aqueduct builders. "The kids were asking me what I was singing, and I was asking them to help me out, so they just starting singing, 'Snakes on a plane,'" he says. "And I went, 'OK, that's the chorus—you guys helped me out! Thanks!' So that's how they got involved with it."

His students' interest inspired a script revision that even the MPAA wouldn't demand: a G-rated version of *Snakes on a Plane*. Take out the famous twelve-letter word, and it's possible, declares Mr. Matt, "We studied world history and evolution, so I had to take a lot of controversial things and make them OK for kids, so this wasn't too big of a leap from what I normally do."

Mr. Matt started with what he knew about "SoaP"—the initial premise, the stills that had turned up online—and went from there. His primary motivation was to engage his kids with items and names that they were familiar with. The kids helped, just as they had with his song. "I originally wrote it as a Mary-Kate and Ashley movie," Mr. Matt said of the film being seen on the plane, "but there

were so many boys in my class, they said, "'No, we want *Harry Potter*!' So *Harry Potter* it was. And the students also chose the menu for the Hawaiian portion of the story. "We talked about the type of things they eat in Hawaii, and I asked about the type of thing they'd eat on the plane," says Mr. Matt. "and they just went, 'Pineappled ham!'"

Throughout the process, Mr. Matt saw his story as not only entertaining for his students, but also informative. He made a point to name the back-stabbing cop Benedict Arnold, "because I wanted them to understand people from history who had been termed traitors." And when the children wanted to have hundreds of snakes invade the plane, Mr. Matt prepared a diagram of the inside of a jet so he could show his kids how the creatures would make it from the cargo hold to the passenger cabin. They got it all, he says: "They're pretty advanced."

Eventually the students took things up a notch by creating their own little "Snakes" tunes, many of which will be recorded and burned onto a CD for the parents to oooh and coo about. And speaking of the parents, since it's highly unlikely any them will want to expose their children to a blood-soaked thriller (not to mention Mr. Jackson's vocabulary), what do they think of what's going on inside the classroom? "They're not as into it as I am," says Mr. Matt, who will show his class a greatly sanitized version of the film when it hits DVD. "But they're fine with me talking to them about it. They know me as their teacher, and I do all of this crazy stuff, so they're pretty used to it."

About the only "Snakes" activity Mr. Matt's class hasn't taken part in is an actual visit by an actual snake. "The pet stores won't let me borrow one," he says. Many of the students, though, have taken it upon themselves to remedy that situation by searching in their own backyards for garter snakes they have seen with their own eyes. "Nobody's been successful yet," says Mr. Matt, but the summer is young.

Here's an excerpt from SNAKES ON A PLANE By Mr. Matt Barr and his kindergarten class—Jack, Maya, Kayla, Frances, Reece, Trent, Colin, Aidan, Zac, and Henry

You can read the complete story at the above Web site.

MATT'S KIDS SHOW OFF THEIR ARTISTRY IN SNAKES

...The passengers were in the upper part of the plane watching "Harry Potter" on the plane's movie screen and eating delicious airplane food. The storm was loud and made the plane ride very bumpy. A women sitting with two strangers turned to the one on her right and said, "I know we're crowded, but could you please stop rubbing your feet on my leg?" The man said, "I'm not rubbing anything on your leg." "Well, if your not rubbing my leg, then who is?" They both looked down on the ground: SNAKE! It bit the woman's leg hoping for dinner, "AAARRGGGHHH!" she screamed as the snake decided she was too big to eat and slithered away.

"Wow, did you hear that woman scream?" Job asked Agent Neville. "Yup, this Harry Potters' some scary stuff!" answered Agent Neville. Just then a snake slithered down the aisle next to them...

WHEN YOU'RE A KINDERGARTEN TEACHER, YOU CAN'T EVEN WEAR YOUR BEST GORILLA SUIT ALL BY YOURSELF. MR. MATT WENT ALL OUT TO TRY TO WIN A PHOTO CONTEST ON BRIAN FINKELSTEIN'S BLOG, AND WHEN HE TOLD HIS KIDS WHAT HE WAS PLANNING TO DO, THEY BEGGED TO BE IN THE PHOTO.

S.O.A.P. HOCKEY

> > > (http://www.soaphockey.net)
> > > st Louis. Missouri

THE MIGHTY S.O.A.P. BACK ROW (L TO R): CURT PRICE, BILL DAY, J.C. WILSON, JEFF FOSTER, GREG PRICE. FRONT ROW (L TO R): LUKE NAILBORSKI, JEFF PRICE, PAT PETERSON, CHRIS SCHMEIDER. PHOTO BY LAURA PETERSON.

Snakes can be seen on the baseball diamond in the form of the Arizona Diamondbacks. They have been known to congregate on football gridirons and basketball courts (the Florida A&M University Rattlers on both counts). But snakes are not known to be indigenous to the environs of hockey. (For one thing, they don't deal with the ice surface thing too well.) But even that is no longer the case—at least if the hockey is played with wheels instead of blades.

Behold the Snakes on a Plane Roller Hockey Club—S.O.A.P. for short, of course—a group of friends and rink enthusiasts who play in a club league out of St. Louis. Madness, you might say—what could possess a sports team to pick for their mascot a film with a weird title that hasn't even been seen by anyone yet? As it turns out, the decision wasn't just done on a whim. Unlike, say, the naming process of your average celebrity baby, the members of S.O.A.P. put some thought into what they would call themselves. But don't take my word for it—you know, just because I'm writing this book and all. Read the words from the toothy mouths of the players themselves, and marvel at their genius as they wax poetic about teamwork, friendship, Zen and the art of hockey and how fuckin' cool Samuel L. Jackson is.

CURT "THE CAPTAIN" PRICE, #12, FORWARD:

"Earlier this year, Snakes on a Plane goalie Jeff Price (also a fellow coworker of mine) and myself were tossing around names for our team for the upcoming roller hockey session, but we weren't coming up with any winners.

We have been playing hockey for over fifteen years in various leagues in the St. Louis area with pretty much the same good group of guys, and we have had a few different team names, such as 'The Fighting Phone Books,' 'Metro East Moose,' 'Team Fazoli's' and, most recently, 'Team Cobra.' But we wanted something different for the upcoming season—something that was worthy of being associated with the unique personalities on our team.

For a while the popular cult joke on the Internet was the Chuck Norris jokes. But the momentum soon shifted. We had recently discovered a small online phrase that was starting to gain quite a following. That phrase was 'Snakes on a Plane.' After reading up on it and discovering it was actually a movie that was coming out later this year, we were intrigued. We became even more intrigued when we heard Samuel L. Jackson was starring in the film. We became ridiculously intrigued when Mr. Jackson wouldn't do the movie unless it was actually titled Snakes on a Plane. Needless to say, we were hooked instantly.

CURT AND CHRIS, FRIENDS IN HOCKEY, LIFE AND SNAKES.
Photo by Teresa Price.

It was a funny office joke for a week or so. Someone would come in with a complaint or a problem and the typical response from us would be, 'Hey, it's all snakes on a plane to me.' Or 'It ain't nothin' but a snake on a plane,' or something ridiculous (and at the same time hilarious) like that.

And then it hit me—Snakes on a Plane had to be our new team name. It was a great name for a hockey team. It was funny, it was catchy, it was a conversation starter, and it was so ridiculous and stupid that it was cool. And to top it all off, we could create a pretty cool website for a team with the name Snakes on a Plane.

I am proud to say that at the time I am writing this, the Snakes on a Plane Hockey Club is doing quite well this season. After a slow start to the season. we have won three in a row and five of our last six games. (As of 6/20/06, the team is 5-3—DBW.) We are currently in second place in the league and are quickly moving up in the standings. Other teams are starting to fear the Snakes on a Plane.

I'd also like to say that I wouldn't want to go to war each week with any other group of guys than this group. We have all been good friends for quite a long time, and I truly enjoy playing hockey with them every week. A couple years ago, I 'retired' from hockey. After thirteen or fourteen years, I thought I had had enough. But after a while, I really started to miss it. It wasn't so much the sport (that was part of it though), but mostly it was playing this sport with this group of guys and working together towards the single most important goal—having fun (and winning—don't forget winning; it's an important goal too—probably more important than having fun now that I think about it).

In August, when Snakes on a Plane opens in theatres nationwide, the entire team is going to be there opening night, cheering on the movie hyped by the huge Internet phenomenon that also shares our team name.

"I'd have to say that it's an honor to be part of such an Internet phenomenon. Early on I was a little curious when our team captain came up with the name for the team. With our jerseys emblazoned with a cobra's head, it did feel somewhat fitting. I went online at the time and didn't really find too much about the craze. I guess you could say we were the predecessor to many blogs and fan sites. Not to mention that not many hockey teams were rushing down to the rink to change their names from the usual beer-league monikers like 'Chiefs,' 'Puckheads,' or the 'Moose.'

A few sound bytes were posted here and there, which afforded me the opportunity of hearing Mr. Jackson's feelings about the movie and, more importantly, the title. After hearing about his reluctance to take the role if the name were to be changed, I became more open to our team embracing the film's name—and started to eagerly anticipate its release. (Not to mention I enjoy his work.) In an era where romantic comedies and reality TV are king, I think everyone could use this highly touted escape from the norm.

So, here's to *Snakes on a Plane*! I'll be one of 10 guys wearing an unfamiliar hockey jersey waiting in line outside the theatre opening night."

BILL "BILLDO" DAY, #9, DEFENSEMAN

"When I first heard that Samuel L. Jackson was making a movie titled *Snakes on a Plane*, I knew it would be a movie that I would be willing to take the afternoon of opening day off to go see. I am a big fan of campy horror movies. I love it when a studio pours money into a movie that could not possibly gain any critical acclaim.

My favorite thing that I have read on the Internet relating to the movie is the 'I Find Your Lack of Faith Disturbing' blog entry by Josh Freidman in which he uses *Snakes on a Plane* as a Zen koan. That 'Snakes on a Plane' could become someone's mantra à la 'Shit Happens' is awesome. In that vein, the Zen koan could easily apply to our hockey team. Things don't always go well for our hockey team, but we keep on keepin' on. For example, in today's game, I got punched in the face. I was then ejected from the game for pondering aloud the sanity of our officials for having also given me a penalty when I was clearly the victim of retaliation. Everyone knows that in hockey, if you retaliate, you go to the box and feel shame. And I was only doing my job, keeping an opponent from standing in front of our net. I didn't imagine that he would like taking jabs in the kidneys for long. I figured he might give me a two-hand chop across the wrists, as he had done earlier in the game. Instead, he lent me an egregious fist to the head. And in opposition to the unwritten rules of hockey, I was penalized. After I unsuccessfully pled my case and was shown the door, the team went on to block a few shots in the final minute of the game and we won.

Now, while my actions were not Buddhist in nature, nor would they quite follow the 'Snakes on a Plane' koan, overall our team adhered to it, and we were victorious. We can hold our heads high for one more week and our opponents can bemoan that they are no longer ahead of us in the standings. As they go to their jobs where I imagine it smells like tires and/or used motor oil, I don't imagine they will appreciate or even understand the deeper meaning of Snakes On A Motherfucking Plane.

LUKE, ANDY, J.C., PAT AND GREG CONGREGATE BEFORE A CONTEST.
Photo by Teresa Price.

PAT GOES FOR THE THE KILL—LIKE A COBRA!
Photo by Teresa Price.

PAT SHOT, HE SCORED!
Photo by Teresa Price.

GREG PRICE WAITS FOR AN OPENING. PATIENTLY.
Photo by Teresa Price.

GEMMA PETRIE

> > > chicago, illinois
> > > part-time pro bono baker
>   (http://probonobaker.typepad.com/probonobaker/)

GEMMA PETRIE, MASTER OF CHOPSTICKS.

Baking and Snakes on a Plane—they go together like peas and carrots, right? OK, the connection isn't obvious, and that's probably because there is no real connection. Even if snakes wanted to prepare a cake, they have no hands with which to stir the batter. And to use their tails for that—gross. So there's actually no baking involved here. Except for the fact that Chicagoan Gemma Petrie is a would-be lawyer-turned-baker. And when she's not looking for "gainful employment" in her chosen profession, she races shopping carts through the streets of the Windy City.

I know, I know—whither the snakes? Or planes? I'm getting there. Petrie is a woman who's obviously open to new experiences. That's probably why she took news of the existence of *Snakes on a Plane* with much giddiness. "I was immensely pleased to learn that this was a real movie," she says, "and my admiration for Samuel L. Jackson has duly increased." She took in with equal cheer, around the same time, the information about the "Chiditarod," an event that patterned itself as a variation on the Iditarod, the famous Alaskan dogsled races. Only instead of sleds, there'd be shopping carts. And instead of being pulled by by doggies, the carts would be steered by humans. And Chicago isn't exactly Alaska, although it comes pretty damn close in early March, which is when the Chiditarod took place.

Petrie and her group of friends decided pretty quickly to enter the race, which was also a food drive to benefit those in Chicago living with HIV and AIDS. And now this story gets interesting: one of Petrie's friends, Ligaya Beebe, came up with the idea to dub their team of five "Team *Snakes on a Plane*." This was quickly agreed to, and the preparations soon began. A green shopping cart was "borrowed" from a local store to be the main vehicle. "It dressed to the nines in a homemade cardboard plane outfit and covered in hand-braided cloth snakes with googly eyes," says Petrie.

Team "SoaP" pulled out all the stops. The race's route was marked by checkpoints—and, this being Chicago, the checkpoints were bars. When they reached the second bar, "we were informed that we would be expected to perform some

THE NAMEPLATE FOR TEAM "SOAP'S" RIDE.

sort of entertainment at the next stop," says Petrie. So they took a crash course in one of the fan songs in time for their last-minute performance. And in the end, this team of "smokers, drinkers and no-exercisers" finished eighth out of twenty-two entrants. "During our sprint to the final bar, we miraculously overtook the team ahead of us as their cart pitched over on a particularly poor stretch of rocky pavement," Petrie says. "We charged on with the plane and were greeted by an ecstatic crowd at the Hideout Bar. It almost made up for high school gym class."

The day was a success all around. Almost 950 pounds of food was collected for the needy. Petrie and her friends had a blast of an afternoon that ended in a bar. And the baker has yet another reason to love *Snakes on a Plane*—like she needed another one.

"I find the *Snakes on a Plane* hysteria to be heartening," she says. "There is something about a public acknowledgment of absurdity combined with gleeful admiration that makes me quite pleased. And in this particular case, it has also given rise to a large amount of random and creative projects from a wide variety of individuals and I find that to be pretty fun to watch."

Petrie and the rest of Team "SoAP" will take in the show as a group on the night it's released. She doesn't say, though, whether she'll bake anything for the occasion.

To donate to the sponsor of the Chiditarod, Vital Bridges, go to www.vitalbridges.org.

THE GANG'S ALL HERE. THAT'S GEMMA IN THE YELLOW TOP AND LIGAYA MAKING LIKE RALPH MACCHIO. (NOTE THE BEERS—THIS IS OBVIOUSLY AFTER THE RACE.)

MORE CELEBRATING.

FRATERNIZATION AMONG THE TEAMS IS ENCOURAGED.

SNAKES ON (ALMOST) EVERYTHING ELSE 87

CAPTAIN AHAB

> > > Los Angeles, California
> > > Tagworld page (http://tagworld.com/captainahab2)
> > > official site (http://www.captain-ahab.com/)

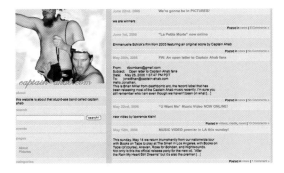

CAPTAIN AHAB'S WEB SITE

In perhaps the best case (so far) of how much New Line got what was going on with Internet fans of *Snakes on a Plane*, the studio teamed up in March with "online ecosystem" TagWorld to stage a unique contest where one musical act would be chosen from a pack of relative unknowns to have their song appear in the film and on its soundtrack CD. Almost 500 entries were submitted for the contest, a response that was so strong than when the time came to choose a winner, the filmmakers actually picked two, giving a spot on the album to the runner-up. Here are the stories about the first and second-place finishers, their songs and how they got here.

A few days after Jonathan Snipes had found out his two-man band, Captain Ahab, had won the New Line/TagWorld *Snakes on a Plane* soundtrack contest, the L.A.-based musician traveled to Virginia for a friend's wedding. For a man who often performs shirtless, who's done a music video that features of content that would make Marilyn Manson blush—and who had reached his possible big break by writing a song about marauding reptiles—it would seem to take a lot to weird Snipes out. But what's weirder than your average American wedding?

"It was the first group of twenty- to twenty-five-year olds that I had been with that hadn't heard of *Snakes on a Plane*," says Snipes, who tried to keep his recent achievement a secret, despite the phone calls and e-mails he was fielding during the marital activities. Making the weekend even odder was the fact that Snipes had had scant time to truly process Captain Ahab's triumph, being that he was sick as a dog when he got the good news. Eventually, word started to leak out among the participants. "The bride's cousin is a fourteen-year-old kid from L.A. who's got a band, and he was following me around. But it was nice to be out there."

Those quiet moments may be few and far between for the next several months thanks to "SoaP" and Captain Ahab's presence not only on the CD, but also in the movie proper. That's the booty that Snipes and bandmate Jim Merson get to take home with them after their song, "Snakes on the Brain," was chosen by the movie's producers to be the best of the twenty-five finalists in the TagWorld contest. That Captain Ahab won is quite appropriate. After all, "Snakes on a Plane" has not been the typical summertime release—and Captain Ahab is not the typical musical act.

For one, there are no instruments, at least in the traditional sense. "It's a laptop band," says Snipes. "It's just a laptop and vocals and dancing right now." Yes, the dancing—that's Merson's primary territory—he's usually even more naked than Snipes, often dressed in nothing more than a Speedo. Snipes, meanwhile, operates the computer and does the brunt of the singing. And then there's the history of Captain Ahab. Snipes has been performing under that name since 1997—but he didn't start performing in public until 2001, didn't put out his first record until the following year.

"It started out when I was writing music on my computer and experimenting with keyboards and things when I was in high school—which was all really bad," explains Snipes. "I see that stuff as musical lessons, almost—[learning] to make music with those tools and not really official output as a band."

By 2003, when Merson joined the group, Captain Ahab had found its singular style—if you can call it singular. While ostensibly an electronic pop-dance band, their description is far more complex. "We shift genres constantly," says Snipes. "I don't think we have a defined sound. It can easily be Gothy industrial music, or it can easily be harsh noise, or it can easily be sort of IDM [intelligent dance music, a form of electronica typified by ornate sequencer programming]. I kind of think that the unifying factor in Captain Ahab's music is that it's all over the map."

Some of their sound can even shift mid-song, but that wasn't quite the case with "Snakes on the Brain," which Snipes co-wrote with Brian Miller, who runs Captain Ahab's record label, Ravesploitative. "Everyone who listens to the radio always says, 'Oh, I could write a better song than this . . . this is easy, boring music,'" Snipes says. "And I was, like, 'Well, here is my chance to put my money where my mouth is and see if I can really just write a pop hit.'" The final product, which he calls "pretty one-note," still combines several different elements—some Nu Metal with a "kind of Modest Mouse vocal" and a dash of "cheap synth saxophone."

"I heard the title of the movie, and I thought, 'Oh, my song is going to be called "Snakes on the Brain,"'" says Snipes. "That was not a big leap. And then once

JIM MERSON (LEFT) AND JONATHAN SNIPES, SUITABLY ATTIRED.
Photo by Eva Aguila.

AHAB'S LATEST ALBUM, AFTER THE RAIN MY HEART STILL DREAMS.
Photo by Shannon Kennedy.

you have the title, writing the hooky chorus for that is not usually a difficult task. Sometimes it is, but in this case I started two or three other versions, and then I was driving to work [Snipes does sound designs for L.A. live theater], I just started humming, and then I went home and wrote it. I actually wrote and recorded the whole thing over twenty-four hours."

Finding out how they did in the TagWorld competition took a little longer. After submitting "Brain," Captain Ahab embarked on a U.S. tour that was as much as campaign swing as concert trek, as the guys implored audiences to vote for their song. Within a week of returning from that, the group found out that they had made the finals. From there, it was totally out of their hands until Snipes got the fateful phone call in late June.

"I've been told it's going to be over the end credits," he says of "Brain's" placement in the movie. "These things have a way of not being exactly what they sound like, so I hesitate to tell people about that, but they've said it's the end credits, and they've told me I can tell people that and that it's official."

Now Snipes and Merson have a reason to see "SoaP." They probably would have watch it anyway. "I miss these kind of movies," says Snipes. "There aren't new B-movies because—because, I guess, they don't make enough money—and now with having straight-to-video movies as a possibility, there's no need for big studios to make theatrical release B-movies. And I'm pretty excited about this film because it's one of the first movies that I can remember, at least in recent times, that seems completely unpretentious, that sort of tells you exactly everything you need to know in the title. All you need to hear about this movie is the title, and you completely understand. And that's kind of refreshing. And, of course, that it's completely fan-driven is pretty exciting too. It's like a new way to make movies—like, now we're telling the studios what we want."

What Captain Ahab wants now is to take advantage of its opening and not just be known as "that *Snakes on a Plane* band," as Snipes puts it. A manager, something the group current is without, may be in the offing. Or maybe even something else: "We might have to throw in some real musicians now," he jokes. But what about some clothes—say, some nice "SoaP" shirts? Well, maybe not. "We're running around so much that we get really sweaty," says Snipes, "and we both have a lot of hair, so it just really practical to not have the clothes hinder us as much." Ahoy.

LOUDEN SWAIN

> > > Los Angeles, Callifornia
> > > http://www.loudenswain.com
> > > http://www.tagworld.com/loudenswain

A few months before *Snakes on a Plane* reared its fang-filled head on the Internet, the pop-rock band Louden Swain (its name is derived from the Matthew Modine character in the coming-of-age drama *Vision Quest*) had a taste of the full force of the World Wide Web. The group's Web site was the main portal when it came to obtaining information about their work or copies of their CDs. One day they received a message from a surprising new fan—Terry Davis, the author of the novel on which *Vision Quest* was based.

DOING THE ROCK STAR: (L TO R) ROB BENEDICT, STEPHEN NORTON AND MIKE BORJA. Photo by Danielle Brancazio.

"He's a professor in Minnesota," says Rob Benedict, the band's guitarist and lead vocalist. "And he was, like, 'I created the name Louden Swain, and I'm thrilled you guys are using it. And without us getting to him first, he bought T-shirts and CD's from us. It was really cool. So I wrote him back, and he ended up sending us these signed posters from *Vision Quest*. It was the power of the Internet. It was really amazing."

It wasn't too long after that that Benedict, an actor best known for his role as a brainy but awkward scientist on the short-lived sci-fi series *Threshold*, found out about *Snakes on a Plane*, and about the unusual contest that New Line Cinema and TagWorld.com was holding to look for budding musicals acts to appear on the film's soundtrack. Curiously, he found about both things at the same time, so his knowledge about the "SoaP"-inspired mania was limited at best.

"A friend of mine told me about this contest and told me what the gist was, so I started asking around about this movie to some of my friends in the business, and found out what the premise of the movie was," says Benedict. His first impressions of the wacky premise? "That it was going to be one of those bubblegum summer movies, and it could do great or it could do horribly. That it's doubtful it was going to be good, just simply from the title and everything."

Still, Benedict's interest was piqued, especially when he found out about the accompanying contest. For he and his band mates and friends—drummer Stephen Norton, guitarist Billy Moran, and the bassist known only as Borja—it was a great chance to break out and cap off what had been a positive year for Louden Swain, which has been together since 1998 and had just recently self-released a new album, *Suit and Tie*. There

WAITING FOR THEIR FLOOR: (L TO R)
MIKE BORJA, ROB BENEDICT AND
STEPHEN NORTON.
Photo by Danielle Brancazio.

LOUDEN SWAIN'S LATEST
RELEASE, SUIT AND TIE.
ARTWORK BY DANIELLE
BRANCAZIO.

was only one slight complication: There was only one week to go before the submissions process ended. Not exactly facing off against a cobra at 30,000 feet, but still a challenge.

Benedict took that challenge: "I literally went, 'Let's see if I can do this.'" In a way, the pressure and the lack of time to really study up on the "Snakes" wildness may have served him well. Even though he describes Louden Swain as an act that likes to add a bit of humor to its songs, Benedict played things relatively straight this time. "I set out to write something that was not a send-up so much as it was an honest soundtrack song," he says. "I didn't so much go for the joke as much as I honestly write a song that could fit the movie, but that also could be a song about taking control or that sort of thing."

The resulting tune, "Here Comes the Snakes," manages to capture the essence of the movie's plot in non-ironic terms, surrounded by some jamming guitar riffs. "I felt like I had a grasp that, 'OK, there are snakes on a plane, and Samuel Jackson is going to kick some ass,'" says Benedict. "So I sort of wrote from that vibe. I never really even sat down and saw the whole preview. I heard sort of soundbites from it. Certainly if I would have watched the movie and known more about it, I probably would have probably written a different song, so maybe in that regard it did help me keep the song a little more general and less specific. So the quotes in the song are about being on a plane and discovering something really bad, something's wrong. And the chorus is about taking control and 'here we go.'"

Benedict wrote the song in one day, and the group recorded the tune soon after that. And now that Louden Swain's efforts have landed them the runner-up position in the TagWorld contest onto the "SoaP" album, the team is ready to reap the benefits, including a possible mini-tour. Meanwhile, Benedict has to explain the situation to his mother. "I told my mom, and she was, like, 'Oh my God, I have to go watch the movie to hear the song.' And I was, like, 'You know, we're not in the movie. We're just on the soundtrack.' And she didn't understand the whole concept of, 'You mean there are songs on the soundtrack that's are not in the movie?'"

Even though "Here Come the Snakes" won't be heard in the movie proper, Benedict, for one, is now looking forward to seeing *Snakes on a Plane* in all of its glory, and is preparing to undergo a crash course on "SoaP"-ology. "I'm totally into it. The movie's has such an effect on me now, with such little knowledge of it—that's what's so crazy," he says. "I don't know much other than that there are snakes on a plane, and there's Sam Jackson. I just found out that Julianna Margulies is in it. I had no idea of that."

ONE MORE THING . . .

In the end, of course, it's all about snakes on a plane, but, seriously, how realistic is *Snakes on a Plane*? What would happen if a bunch of forked-tonged beasties ended up on a passenger flight? Would they cause havoc? Would they mind their own business? Would they like the food? Could they afford the food?

A blogger with the screen name of "nootropic" (he prefers to remain anonymous) wondered not so much how the snakes would behave in coach, but rather something even more basic: could snakes even end up flying the friendly skies. And, in keeping with the tradition of American ingenuity—or at least of Americans having time to kill—he took it upon himself to launch a personal project. He called several major airline carriers to ask them about their snake policy. The results were, not unlike the "SoaP" community in general, both uniform and diverse. The bottom line is that pretty much all of the airlines nootropic contacted frowned upon their customers carrying snakes in their luggage alongside their unmentionables. But they took the inquires in different ways. "Their responses varied from humorless [and] clueless, to downright funny," wrote nootropic in his blog chronicling his research. See if you can guess which company was "humorous" and which one got the joke.

NORTHWEST AIRLINES PETS (SNAKES) POLICY: "Carry-on pets are limited to small dogs, cats, and household birds (birds are allowed only within the 48 contiguous U.S. and Alaska). All other pets, including ferrets and reptiles, must travel as cargo."

nootropic: "Service representative Mark seemed annoyed at my inquiry. I could almost hear his eyes rolling over the phone line."

noo: I have a question about your policies about bringing pets on board.
NWA: OK . . .
noo: Can I bring a snake?
NWA: A what?
noo: A snake.
NWA: No, only household pets . . .
noo: It is a household pet.
NWA: You can only bring dogs cats or birds. Reptiles have to be checked in air cargo.

noo: Air cargo, huh. No snakes in the cabin.

NWA: No. Most carriers [inaudible] they don't take snakes or anything.

noo: OK, thanks.

SOUTHWEST AIRLINES PETS POLICY: "Southwest Airlines does not accept live animals in the aircraft cabin or cargo compartment other than fully trained service animals accompanying a person with a disability or being delivered to a person with a disability."

noo: I have a question about your policies about bringing pets on board. Can I bring a snake?

SWA: Actually no, Southwest doesn't allow any animals on our flights at all.

noo: None at all?

SWA: No.

noo: Can I check my snake as baggage?

SWA: [pause]

noo: As cargo?

SWA: No, Southwest doesn't allow any animals on our flights at all.

noo: Oh, none at all.

SWA: No, none at all.

noo: OK, thanks.

JETBLUE PETS POLICY: JetBlue accepts a combined total of three small cats and dogs in the passenger cabin of the aircraft. The fee for a pet is $50 USD each way. Only one pet is allowed per customer unless you are bringing a certified service animal or documented emotional support animal.

nootropic: "Debra was very pleasant and had a great sense of humor. Kudos to JetBlue!"

noo: Hi, I have a question about pets. What kind of pets can I bring on board the aircraft in the cabin?

JetBlue: No, only small dogs and cats.

noo: Ooooh, that's gonna be a problem. [long pause] I have a snake.

JetBlue: Nope, no snakes. Unless you can put tail and ears on it.

noo: That's a great idea!

JetBlue: You can call it a wiener dog, then.

noo: That's the most innovative idea I've heard all day.

JetBlue: [laughs]

noo: Thanks!

CONTINENTAL AIRLINES PETS POLICY: "Continental allows domesticated cats, dogs, pet rabbits, and household birds to be carried in the aircraft cabin on all US domestic flights (except to/from Hawaii). An in-cabin pet may be carried in lieu of a carry-on bag and is subject to an $80.00 service charge each way ($160.00 for round trip travel)."

noo: Hi, I have a pet snake that I need to take on a flight.

Continental: I'm sorry what is that? You have a what?

noo: A pet snake.

Continental: Oh, a pet snake. No, we only allow dogs, cats, birds and pet rabbits.

noo: You allow pet rabbits, but not pet snakes.

Continental: Yes. You'd have to check with our Animal Desk to see if they will take it as cargo.

noo: Oh, you have an Animal Desk?

Continental: Yes, would you like their number?

noo: Sure.

Continental: 1.800.xxx.xxxx

noo: OK, thanks. [He did not call the animal "Animal Desk."]

Well, there you have it—no snakes on planes, or at least in the passenger section. But what would the airlines have said if Samuel L. Jackson had been doing the calling? We probably won't know—unless nootropic *is* Samuel L. Jackson. Hmmm . . .

ACKNOWLEDGMENTS

I owe tons of gratitude to a plethora of people, so if you know me and you're not mentioned here, don't chalk it up to a snub but rather to my spotty memory. For their unconditional support and love, thanks to my immediate family, including my father Gene; my stepmother Elizabeth; my brother Ryan; my sister-in-law Johnna; my stepsisters Julie, Ellen and Lynn, and all others who share my name, my blood or other forms of identification.

For their professional guidance, cogent advice and deep friendship, thanks to the best editors and friends a writer could have: Jennifer Bulat, Beth Kujawski, Jennifer Brummett-Martin, Jessica Solomon and Debbie Calhoun. A special thanks to Milton M. Reigelman for getting the ball rolling, and to Paul Camp and Mary Connors for facilitating my rise from amateur to professional.

For just being best buds who help to keep me sane—now, in the past and (hopefully) in the future—thanks to Anne Bannon and Michel Holland, Kay Chubbuck, Brent Furdyk, Anna Goodman, Rhonda Headley, Sue Hiering, Sarah Jolie, Nicole Justice, Sharon Kahn, Susan Skibell, Lisa Mayer, Stephanie Pearson, Rachael Scalf, Judy Sloane and especially Karen Heyman.

A thank-you also goes to my agent, Steve Harris, for his trust; and to the entire staff at Avalon Publishing Group, including John Oakes. And thanks to Mary at Getty Images for her help.

Finally, much thanks to the liver transplant team at the University of Nebraska Medical Center, because without them, *none* of this would be possible—and I mean that. Keep up the good work, guys.

Eamus Catuli!